NEW DIRECTIONS IN PICTUREBOOK RESEARCH

Children's Literature and Culture
Jack Zipes, *Series Editor*

Reimagining Shakespeare for Children and Young Adults
edited by Naomi J. Miller

Representing the Holocaust in Youth Literature
Lydia Kokkola

Translating for Children
Riitta Oittinen

Beatrix Potter
Writing in Code
M. Daphne Kutzer

Children's Films
History, Ideology, Pedagogy, Theory
Ian Wojcik-Andrews

Utopian and Dystopian Writing for Children and Young Adults
edited by Carrie Hintz and Elaine Ostry

Transcending Boundaries
Writing for a Dual Audience of Children and Adults
edited by Sandra L. Beckett

The Making of the Modern Child
Children's Literature and Childhood in the Late Eighteenth Century
Andrew O'Malley

How Picturebooks Work
Maria Nikolajeva and Carole Scott

Brown Gold
Milestones of African American Children's Picture Books, 1845-2002
Michelle H. Martin

Russell Hoban/Forty Years
Essays on His Writing for Children
Alida Allison

Apartheid and Racism in South African Children's Literature
by Donnarae MacCann and Amadu Maddy

Empire's Children
Empire and Imperialism in Classic British Children's Books
M. Daphne Kutzer

Constructing the Canon of Children's Literature
Beyond Library Walls and Ivory Towers
Anne Lundin

Youth of Darkest England
Working Class Children at the Heart of Victorian Empire
Troy Boone

Ursula K. Le Guin Beyond Genre
Literature for Children and Adults
Mike Cadden

Twice-Told Children's Tales
edited by Betty Greenway

Diana Wynne Jones
The Fantastic Tradition and Children's Literature
Farah Mendlesohn

Childhood and Children's Books in Early Modern Europe, 1550-1800
edited by Andrea Immel and Michael Witmore

Voracious Children
Who Eats Whom in Children's Literature
Carolyn Daniel

National Character in South African Children's Literature
Elwyn Jenkins

Myth, Symbol, and Meaning in *Mary Poppins*
The Governess as Provocateur
Georgia Grilli

A Critical History of French Children's Literature, Vol. 1 & 2
Penny Brown

Once Upon a Time in a Different World
Issues and Ideas in African American Children's Literature
Neal A. Lester

The Gothic in Children's Literature
Haunting the Borders
edited by Anna Jackson, Karen Coats, and Roderick McGillis

Reading Victorian Schoolrooms
Childhood and Education in Nineteenth-Century Fiction
Elizabeth Gargano

Soon Come Home to This Island
West Indians in British Children's Literature
Karen Sands-O'Connor

Boys in Children's Literature and
Popular Culture
*Masculinity, Abjection, and the
Fictional Child*
Annette Wannamaker

Into the Closet
*Cross-Dressing and the Gendered Body
in Children's Literature*
Victoria Flanagan

Russian Children's Literature and Culture
edited by Marina Balina and
Larissa Rudova

The Outside Child In and Out of the Book
Christine Wilkie-Stibbs

Representing Africa in Children's Literature
Old and New Ways of Seeing
Vivian Yenika-Agbaw

The Fantasy of Family
*Nineteenth-Century Children's Literature
and the Myth of the Domestic Ideal*
Liz Thiel

From Nursery Rhymes to Nationhood
*Children's Literature and the Construction
of Canadian Identity*
Elizabeth A. Galway

The Family in English Children's Literature
Ann Alston

Enterprising Youth
*Social Values and Acculturation in
Nineteenth-Century American
Children's Literature*
Monika Elbert

Constructing Adolescence in
Fantastic Realism
Alison Waller

Crossover Fiction
Global and Historical Perspectives
Sandra L. Beckett

The Crossover Novel
*Contemporary Children's Fiction and Its
Adult Readership*
Rachel Falconer

Shakespeare in Children's Literature
Gender and Cultural Capital
Erica Hateley

Critical Approaches to Food in
Children's Literature
edited by Kara K. Keeling and
Scott T. Pollard

Neo-Imperialism in Children's Literature
About Africa
A Study of Contemporary Fiction
Yulisa Amadu Maddy and Donnarae
MacCann

Death, Gender and Sexuality in
Contemporary Adolescent Literature
Kathryn James

Fundamental Concepts of Children's
Literature Research
Literary and Sociological Approaches
Hans-Heino Ewers

Translation under State Control
*Books for Young People in the German
Democratic Republic*
Gaby Thomson-Wohlgemuth

Representations of Technology in Science
Fiction for Young People
Noga Applebaum

Children's Fiction about 9/11
Ethnic, Heroic and National Identities
Jo Lampert

The Place of Lewis Carroll in Children's
Literature
Jan Susina

Power, Voice and Subjectivity in Literature
for Young Readers
Maria Nikolajeva

"Juvenile" Literature and British Society,
1850–1950
The Age of Adolescence
Charles Ferrall and Anna Jackson

Picturing the Wolf in Children's Literature
Debra Mitts-Smith

New Directions in Picturebook Research
edited by Teresa Colomer, Bettina
Kümmerling-Meibauer, and Cecilia
Silva-Díaz

NEW DIRECTIONS IN PICTUREBOOK RESEARCH

EDITED BY TERESA COLOMER,
BETTINA KÜMMERLING-MEIBAUER,
AND CECILIA SILVA-DÍAZ

Routledge
Taylor & Francis Group
NEW YORK AND LONDON

First published 2010
by Routledge
270 Madison Avenue, New York, NY 10016

Simultaneously published in the UK
by Routledge
2 Park Square, Milton Park, Abingdon, Oxon OX14 4RN

Routledge is an imprint of the Taylor & Francis Group, an informa business

© 2010 Taylor & Francis

The right of Teresa Colomer, Bettina Kümmerling-Meibauer, and Cecilia Silva-Díaz to be identified as authors of this work has been asserted by them in accordance with sections 77 and 78 of the Copyright, Designs and Patents Act 1988.

Typeset in by Minion by IBT Global.
Printed and bound in the United States of America on acid-free paper by IBT Global.

All rights reserved. No part of this book may be reprinted or reproduced or utilised in any form or by any electronic, mechanical, or other means, now known or hereafter invented, including photocopying and recording, or in any information storage or retrieval system, without permission in writing from the publishers.

Trademark Notice: Product or corporate names may be trademarks or registered trademarks, and are used only for identification and explanation without intent to infringe.

Library of Congress Cataloging-in-Publication Data
New directions in picturebook research / edited by Teresa Colomer, Bettina Kümmerling-Meibauer, Cecilia Silva-Díaz.
    p. cm.
    Includes bibliographical references and index.
    1. Picture books for children—Social aspects. 2. Children's literature—History and criticism. 3. Picture books for children—Authorship. 4. Picture books for children—Technique. I. Colomer, Teresa. II. Kümmerling-Meibauer, Bettina. III. Silva-Díaz, Cecilia.
    PN1009.A1N39 2010
    002—dc22

ISBN13: 978-0-415-87690-2 (hbk)
ISBN13: 978-0-203-83917-1 (ebk)

Contents

List of Figures	xi
List of Tables	xiii
Series Editor's Foreword	xv
Permissions	xvii
Introduction: Current Trends in Picturebook Research TERESA COLOMER, BETTINA KÜMMERLING-MEIBAUER, CECILIA SILVA-DÍAZ	1

PART I
Picturebooks, Literacy, and Cultural Context

Chapter 1	Words Claimed: Picturebook Narratives and the Project of Children's Literature PERRY NODELMAN	11
Chapter 2	Interpretative Codes and Implied Readers of Children's Picturebooks MARIA NIKOLAJEVA	27
Chapter 3	Picturebooks and Changing Values at the Turn of the Century TERESA COLOMER	41
Chapter 4	How to Make Sense: Reflections on the Influence of Eighteenth Century Picturebooks on Picturebooks of Today NINA CHRISTENSEN	55

Chapter 5	"All this book is about books": Picturebooks, Culture, and Metaliterary Awareness EVELYN ARIZPE	69
Chapter 6	Artistic Allusions in Picturebooks SANDRA L. BECKETT	83

PART II
Picturebooks and Storytelling

Chapter 7	Frame-making and Frame-breaking in Picturebooks CAROLE SCOTT	101
Chapter 8	Surprised Readers: Twist Endings in Narrative Picturebooks BRENDA BELLORÍN AND CECILIA SILVA-DÍAZ	113
Chapter 9	The Narrative Power of Pictures: *L'Orage* (The Thunderstorm) by Anne Brouillard ISABELLE NIÈRES-CHEVREL	129
Chapter 10	Picturebooks and Trojan Horses: The Nordic Picturebook as a Site for Artistic Experiment during the 1950s ELINA DRUKER	139
Chapter 11	A Strawberry? Or the Planet? Children's Aesthetic Response to the Picturebook *Strawberries* by Susumi Shingu, Moving Art Sculptor TOMOKO MASAKI	151
Chapter 12	Off-Screen: The Importance of Blank Space FERNANDO ZAPARAÍN	165

PART III
Making Sense Out of Picturebooks

Chapter 13	Being a Guide into Picturebook Literacy: Challenges of Cognition and Connotation INGEBORG MJØR	179

| Chapter 14 | First-Person Narratives in Picturebooks: An Inquiry into the Acquisition of Picturebook Competence
EVA GRESSNICH AND JÖRG MEIBAUER | 191 |

| Chapter 15 | Remembering the Past in Words and Pictures: How Autobiographical Stories Become Picturebooks
BETTINA KÜMMERLING-MEIBAUER | 205 |

| Chapter 16 | Do Sons Inherit the Sins of Their Fathers? An Analysis of the Picturebook *Angry Man*
AGNES-MARGRETHE BJORVAND | 217 |

| Chapter 17 | Imagination or Reality? Mindscapes and Characterization in a Finnish and a Swedish Picturebook
ANNA-MAIJA KOSKIMIES-HELLMAN | 233 |

Contributors   243

Selected Bibliography   249

Index   253

Figures

Cover Image from *I Like Books* by Anthony Browne. London: Walker, 2003.

3.1	Illustration from Joi Carlin and Morella Fuenmayor. *La cama de mamá*. Caracas, California: Ediciones Ekaré; Volcano Press, 1994.	44
3.2	Illustration from Shaun Tan: *The Red Tree*. Port Melbourne: Thomas C. Lothian, 2005.	47
4.1	Page from *CCLII Udvalde og med 800 Billeder udlagde Bibelske Hoved-Sprog*. [52 Selected Biblical Proverbs Interpreted with 800 Pictures]. Copenhagen: Nicolaus Møller, 1775, p. 176.	57
4.2	Illustration from Dorte Karrebæk: *Den sorte bog. Om de syv dødssynder*. Copenhagen: Alma, 2007.	63
6.1	Illustration from Yvan Pommaux. *John Chatterton détective*. Paris: L'École des loisirs, 1993.	92
6.2	Illustration from Fam Ekman. Kattens Skrekk. Oslo: Cappelen, 1992.	93
7.1	Illustration from Dorte Karrebæk: *Pigen Der Var Go' Til Mange Ting* [The Girl Who Could Do Many Things]. Copenhagen: Forum, 1997.	106
8.1	Illustration from Jeanne Willis and Tony Ross: *Susan Laughs*. London: Andersen Press, 1999.	120
8.2	Illustration from Jeanne Willis and Tony Ross: *Susan Laughs*. London: Andersen Press, 1999.	121
9.1	Illustration from Anne Brouillard: *L'Orage*. Nîmes: Editions Grandir, 1998.	133

10.1	Illustration from Åke Löfgren and Egon Møller-Nielsen: *Historien om någon*. Stockholm: Kooperativa Förbundets förlag, 1951.	140
10.2	Sculpture "Tufsen" (1948) by Egon Møller-Nielsen at Park Humlegården, Stockholm.	145
11.1	Book cover from Susumi Shingu: *Strawberries*. Tokyo: Bunka Publishing Bureau, 1975.	152
11.2	Illustration from Susumi Shingu: *Strawberries*. Tokyo: Bunka Publishing Bureau, 1975.	156
12.1	Table "General Perceptic Diagram" by Fernando Zaparaín.	170
13.1	Illustration from Anna-Clara Tidholm: *Apan fin*. Stockholm: Alfabeta, 1999.	183
13.2	Illustration from Anna-Clara Tidholm: *Apan fin*. Stockholm: Alfabeta, 1999.	184
15.1	Illustration from Peter Sís: *Tibet Through the Red Box*. New York: Farrar, Straus & Giroux, 1998.	209
15.2	Book Cover from Trina Schart Hyman: *Self-Portrait. Trina Schart Hyman*. New York: Harper & Row, 1981.	213
16.1	Illustration from Gro Dahle and Svein Nyhus: *Sinna Mann*. Oslo: Cappelen, 2003.	224
16.2	Illustration from Gro Dahle and Svein Nyhus: *Sinna Mann*. Oslo: Cappelen, 2003.	227
17.1	Illustration from Mervi Lindman: *Urhea pikku Memmuli*. Helsinki: Tammi, 2005.	235
17.2	Illustration from Anna-Clara Tidholm: *Hanna huset hunden*. Stockholm: Alfabeta, 2004.	238

Tables

3.1	Social Representations and Values in the Late 20th Century Children's Literature	45
3.2	Social Representations and Values in Contemporary Children's Literature	51

Series Editor's Foreword

Dedicated to furthering original research in children's literature and culture, the Children's Literature and Culture series includes monographs on individual authors and illustrators, historical examinations of different periods, literary analyses of genres, and comparative studies on literature and the mass media. The series is international in scope and is intended to encourage innovative research in children's literature with a focus on interdisciplinary methodology.

Children's literature and culture are understood in the broadest sense of the term children to encompass the period of childhood up through adolescence. Owing to the fact that the notion of childhood has changed so much since the origination of children's literature, this Routledge series is particularly concerned with transformations in children's culture and how they have affected the representation and socialization of children. While the emphasis of the series is on children's literature, all types of studies that deal with children's radio, film, television, and art are included in an endeavor to grasp the aesthetics and values of children's culture. Not only have there been momentous changes in children's culture in the last fifty years, but there have also been radical shifts in the scholarship that deals with these changes. In this regard, the goal of the Children's Literature and Culture series is to enhance research in this field and, at the same time, point to new directions that bring together the best scholarly work throughout the world.

Jack Zipes

Permissions

Book Cover: Image from *I Like Books* by Anthony Browne. London: Walker, 2003. First edition: London: Julia MacRae, 1988. © 1988 Anthony Browne. Reprinted by permission of, and with thanks to, Anthony Browne.

Chapter 3: Image from *La cama de mamá* by Joi Carlín and Morella Fuenmayor. Caracas; Volcano, California: Ediciones Ekaré; Volcano Press, 1994. Reprinted by kind permission of Ediciones Ekaré.

Image from *The Red Tree* by Shaun Tan. Sydney: Lothian Children's Books, an imprint of Hachette Australia, 2001. Reprinted by permission of Hachette Australia.

Chapter 4: Image from *CCLII Udvalde og med 800 Billeder Udlagde Bibelske Hoved-Sprog*. Copenhagen: Nicolaus Møller, 1775. Private collection. Reprinted by kind permission of the owner.

Image from *Den sorte bog. Om de syv dødssynder* by Dorte Karrebæk. Copenhagen: Alma, 2007. Reprinted by kind permission of Dorte Karrebæk.

Chapter 6: Image from *Kattens Skrekk* by Fam Ekman. Oslo: Cappelen, 1992. Reprinted by kind permission of Fam Ekman.

Image from *John Chatterton detective* by Yvan Pommaux. Paris: L'Ecole des loisirs, 1993. Reprinted by kind permission of Yvan Pommaux.

Chapter 7: Image from *Pigen der var go' til mange ting* from Dorte Karrebæk. Copenhagen: Forum, 1992. Reprinted by permission of Dorte Karrebæk.

Chapter 8: Two images from *Susan Laughs* by Jeanne Willis and Tony Ross. London: Andersen Press, 1999. Reprinted by permission of Andersen Press.

Chapter 9: Image from *L'Orage* de Anne Brouillard. Nîmes: Éditions Grandir, 1998. Reprinted by permission of Éditions Grandir.

Chapter 10: Image from *Historien om någon* by Åke Löfgren and Egon Møller-Nielsen. Stockholm: Kooperativa Förbundets förlag, 1959. Reprinted with permission of Kerstin Møller-Nielsen.

Photographic Image of "Tufsen" by Egon Møller-Nielsen. Reprinted with kind permission of Kerstin Møller-Nielsen.

Chapter 11: Cover and doublespread from *Strawberries* by Susumi Shingu. Tokyo: Bunka Publishing Bureau, 1975. Reprinted by kind permission of Susumi Shingu.

Chapter 12: Schema by Fernando Zaparaín. Reproduced by permission of Fernando Zaparaín.

Chapter 13: Two images from *Apan fin* by Anna-Clara Tidholm. Stockholm: Alfabeta, 1999. © 1999 Anna-Clara Tidholm. Reprinted by permission of Alfabeta Bokförlag AB, Sweden.

Chapter 15: Image from *Tibet through the Red Box* by Peter Sís. New York: Farrar, Straus & Giroux, 1998. © by Peter Sís. Reprinted by permission of Farrar, Straus and Giroux, LLC.

Cover from *Self-Portrait: Trina Schart Hyman* by Trina Schart Hyman. New York: Harper & Row, 1981. Reprinted by kind permission of Katrin Tchana.

Chapter 16: Two images from *Sinna Mann* by Gro Dahle and Svein Nyhus. Oslo: Cappelen, 2003. Reprinted by permission of Svein Nyhus.

Chapter 17: Doublespread from *Urhea pikku Memmuli* by Mervi Lindman. Helsinki: Tammi, 2005. Reprinted by permission of Tammi Publishers, Helsinki.

Doublespread from *Hanna huset hunden* by Anna-Clara Tidholm. Stockholm: Alfabeta, 2004. ©Bokförlag/Publishers. Reprinted by permission of Alfabeta Bokförlag AB, Sweden.

Introduction
Current Trends in Picturebook Research

Teresa Colomer, Bettina Kümmerling-Meibauer,
Cecilia Silva-Díaz

Picturebook research underwent considerable changes by the end of the twentieth century. Initially, historical perspective dominated the field: most surveys focused on the emergence and development of picturebooks. In the 1980s they began to be regarded by scholars as either an art form or as educational tools for language acquisition, introduction to literature and visual literacy. However, picturebooks have never received such enthusiastic critical attention as they have in recent years. The number of studies has increased as the artistic effects of picturebooks have developed considerably due to intensive experimentation with the interplay of text and image. Research confirms that, at its best, picturebook illustration is a subtle and complex art form that can communicate on many levels and leave a deep imprint on a child's consciousness.

The unique character of picturebooks as an art form has been amply described by scholars like Perry Nodelman in *Words About Pictures* (1988) and Maria Nikolajeva and Carole Scott in *How Picturebooks Work* (2001). They have provided students and scholars who have an interest in narrative, design, and communication with a growing awareness of the opportunities that picturebooks offer. The innovation of modern picturebooks underlines their potential for the development of linguistic, written and visual literacy. These features were already recognized by critics in the 1980s, and new ones have been examined, such as the understanding that reading picturebooks involves complex aesthetic and cognitive processes. For example, some poetic and visual effects tend to interfere with, or, at the very least, delay the process of interpretation, hence affecting the regular course of cognitive processes.

Therefore, our book is mainly aimed at discussing the general aesthetic and cognitive constraints on which the understanding of picturebooks depends.

This collection seeks to contribute to the ongoing debate on the importance of picturebook research, focusing on aesthetic and cognitive aspects of picturebooks. The thirteen articles are revised versions of papers given at the international conference on "New Impulses in Picturebook Research," held at the Universidad Autónoma de Barcelona, Spain, in September 2007, and organized by Teresa Colomer and Cecilia Silva-Díaz in cooperation with Bettina Kümmerling-Meibauer. Four additional chapters complement these contributions in order to demonstrate the wide spectrum of the field. Written by scholars from twelve countries (Canada, Denmark, Finland, France, Germany, Japan, Norway, Spain, Sweden, United Kingdom, United States, and Venezuela), the articles clearly suggest that the study of the intersection of cognitive and aesthetic aspects in picturebook research is a major, widespread trend. Moreover, they all focus on interdisciplinary approaches that integrate different disciplines such as literary studies, art history, linguistics, narratology, cognitive psychology, sociology, memory studies, and picture theory.

Picturebooks, Literacy, and Cultural Context

The first five chapters focus on the relationship between children's response, literacy, metaliterary awareness, the values of contemporary societies, the artistic constructiveness of visual and written text and its implication in cognitive development, thus presenting picturebooks from a multidimensional perspective. Based on his recently published study, *The Hidden Adult: Characteristics of Children's Literature* (2008), Perry Nodelman argues that the picturebook may help scholars to have a better understanding of children's literature. In order to build his case, a typical picturebook, Nan Gregory's *Amber Waiting* (2002), is thoroughly analysed, thus revealing a paradoxical dynamic between the somewhat simple texts and the relatively more complex visual information of the pictures. This article reveals that texts in picturebooks usually purport to be childlike, to represent how adults like to believe children see and understand the world, while the pictures tend to undercut that childlike simplicity with a more sophisticated adult view of things. By considering the implications of the ways in which picturebooks characteristically create childhood and at the same time undermine it, Nodelman demonstrates that they give children the adult knowledge they purportedly suppress while constructing profound paradoxical childhood subjectivity.

The juxtaposition of the concept of the implied reader and the child's developing sense of visual literacy and literary competence is the starting point in Maria Nikolajeva's thought-provoking article. Based on Roland Barthes' seminal work on reader-oriented semiotics, *S/Z*, she argues that readers need to have access to a number of codes (i.e., proairetic, hermeneutic, semic, symbolic, and referential code) and how these codes become specific in multimodal texts. By emphasizing the impact of these codes for the decoding of the plot, meaning making, the understanding of fictionality, symbolic representation and intervisual/intertextual references, Nikolajeva thoroughly demonstrates that visual and literary decoding must be gradually acquired by children in order to enable the interpretation and appreciation of complex picturebooks. In a last step Nikolajeva draws upon Barthes' distinction between readerly and writerly texts, applying these categories to picturebooks. She claims that picturebooks belonging to the category of writerly texts stimulate a creative dialogue between text/image and reader/viewer, thus encouraging visual and literary competence.

Teresa Colomer's article shows that the establishment of new values promoted by children's books during the 1960s and 1970s became significantly modified by the beginning of the twenty-first century, reflecting a shift towards the social representation of childhood. The comparison between the two periods reveals that, as a consequence of changes in the social context, picturebooks show a particular emphasis on topics that deal with sentimental education, especially in reference to the building-up of personality, as well as complex values of multicultural and social coexistence. In addition, the chapter shows that, ever since modern picturebooks started to develop, they have introduced innovative aspects such as metafiction, irony or the blurring of fictional borders, which raise questions about the understanding children may have of these artistic post-modern forms. These new picturebooks are regarded as the ideal means to explore sentimental questions through the emotive use of illustrations, the text's proximity to connotative and metaphoric poetic functions, or the possibility of combining codes in order to articulate different levels of comprehension. This new production poses a number of new questions for critics to tackle.

Nina Christensen deals with the differences and similarities between eighteenth-century picturebooks and today's modern picturebooks with regard to two aspects: One is how the books introduce the child to the process of semiosis—how children are implicitly expected to be able to deduce meaning from language and image. The second aspect is related to the content of the books and is a discussion of how human behavior is discussed in relation to descriptions of vices and virtues. Christensen compares Dorte Karrebaek's mock-scientific image of creatures representing the seven deadly sins, *The Black Book. On the seven Deadly Sins* (Den sorte bog. Om de syv dødssynder, 2007), with two books from the eighteenth century: *CCLII Udvalde og med 800 Billeder udlagde Bibelske Hoved-Sprog*, (252 selected Biblical Proverbs with 800 images. Published anonymously in 1775), Karl Philipp Moritz's *Neues ABC Buch welches zugleich eine Anleitung zum Denken für Kinder* (New ABC including an encouragement for children to think, 1790) stresses the changes in the process of meaning-making and in the child's education.

Based on the findings of a research project, Evelyn Arizpe stresses the importance of picturebooks for primary school children from ethnic minority backgrounds. She investigates how these children responded to two picturebooks set within their new culture: *Traction Man Is Here* (2005) by Mini Grey and *The Incredible Book Eating Boy* (2006) by Oliver Jeffers. Her analysis concentrates on the response-inviting structures of the picturebooks selected, which involve some of the "post-modern" aspects of this genre, such as metafiction, fragmentation, intertextuality and non-traditional textual, and spatial arrangements. The implications reveal how the interplay between different literacies and cultures affects and creates metaliterary awareness of verbal and visual texts such as in metafictive picturebooks, thus offering a new perspective for future research in this field.

Sandra L. Beckett stresses that visual allusions to art works are an important trend in contemporary picturebooks. She differentiates between three categories of artistic allusions: a) allusions to the stylistic conventions of an entire genre; b) allusions to the style of a period or movement; and c) reference to the characteristic manner of a particular artist. Since children are more apt to decode allusions to specific works of art than general allusions to an artistic movement, the former are more common in picturebooks. In addition, this article shows that allusions to individual works of art tend quite often to be parodic, thus revealing sophisticated, multi-level parodies. By means of a thorough description of picturebooks by renowned artists from five countries, the influence of artistic allusions on the multi-layered meanings of the respective works is clearly demonstrated. In the final section Beckett discusses under what conditions children might recognize the complex visual allusions and whether the illustrators help them by providing them with some clues to decipher the hidden references to art works.

Picturebooks and Storytelling

The next section comprises six articles that focus on the relationship between picturebook research and narratology by investigating such topics as the role of frame-making and frame-breaking, twist endings in picturebooks, narrative constraints of wordless picturebooks, the influence of modernism on the development of new narrative strategies, the mutual relationship between narrative perspectives used in different art forms, and ellipsis and off-screen as narrative devices.

Carole Scott's article explores the purposes and effects of framing in picturebooks. Besides the aesthetic aspects of graphic design, it considers graphic-narrative metafictive devices as literary constructs; the expressions of social and psychological boundaries and distinctions; psychological states of mind; and the communication of social commentary. Scott alludes to theory about architecture whose structures order our three-dimensional world as picturebooks reflect it in two dimensions, particularly James Steele's *Architecture Today* (1997). In this regard, frames in picturebooks are not only aesthetic devices that influence the viewer's sense of involvement in the action of the work, but also must be considered as the ordered application of a certain belief system. Of particular interest is the consideration of how children's developing perception might be influenced by their understanding of boundaries and how they may be broken, together with their increasing realization of fictionality—the relationship between creative invention and real-life experience.

The chapter written by Brenda Bellorín and Cecilia Silva-Díaz deals with surprise endings in picturebooks. By means of a thorough study of the forms, effects, and implications of these unexpected endings, the authors show how they create patterns of concealment and revelation, both in their narrative and physical dimensions, and through the interplay of text and image. Considering that twist endings usually surprise readers by concealing an important part of the narrative, Bellorin and Silva-Díaz have analysed and organized some picturebooks according to the type of concealment. Their twist ending classification includes stories with disturbing epilogues, concealed intentions, hidden characters, sneaky narrators, non-explicit turning points, and stories within stories. As a preliminary approach to future research on the subject, the authors have also shared the reading of the books with individual readers and have presented a short report on their reactions.

Isabelle Nières-Chevrel's chapter focuses on the complexity of the French wordless picturebook *L'Orage* (The Thunderstorm, 1998) by Anne Brouillard. Through a meticulous analysis of the sequence of illustrations, she demonstrates the narrative power of pictures as well as the commitment required by the reader to understand the book. By linking together description and narration in pictures, the artist realizes a visual translation of the different experiences involved by the depicted event. Whereas time is fairly readable because the narrative follows the chronological order of the storm, space is utterly bewildering—half a maze and half a jigsaw. The book requires an active reader: he/she must look for clues, put forward hypotheses about the laying out and the linking of the pictures and elude the traps set by reflections in mirrors. In the final discussion, a genuine investigation of the powers and limits of pictures when used as the only narrative medium is undertaken in order to consider the readability of the mismatch of time, space, and actions in this wordless picturebook.

Elina Druker discusses the conceptual and spatial innovations of the Nordic picturebook during the 1950s, which is deeply influenced by avant-garde and modernist movements. Concentrating on picturebooks by Egon Møller-Nielsen as well as his monumental play ground sculptures, it shows that the artists refer to both these artistic movements and attempt to activate the reader's role by using new spatial concepts, such as holes in the pages, pop-up elements, and a continuous red thread as page turner. This observation refers to the meta-artistic structure that is either stressed by the Chinese box-principle or by the analogy between book form and architectural design. Through these artistic devices the picturebooks discussed introduce modernist aesthetics into children's literature, thus anticipating post-modern features.

Tomoko Masaki's article is a detailed analysis of Susumi Shingu's first picturebook, *Strawberries* (1975), which stands out for its extraordinary illustrations and plot. This is due to the impact of Shingu's previous sculptural work on the unusual proportions and dimensions of the illustrations. Moreover, Shingu wishes to involve the viewer/reader in the perception and re-creation of the picturebook's meaning by referring to different aspects of movement (a main trait in Shingu's sculptures). Masaki also reports about her reading sessions with Japanese and British children (fourth and sixth grade), which reveal astonishing differences in the way this picturebook is received. These differences are rooted in the diverse cultural assumptions about the role of illustrations and stories, and the children's varied access to picturebooks.

Dealing with the off-screen, i.e., a spatial ellipsis that omits a scenic portion that is significant for the story, Fernando Zaparaín claims that off-screen is a fundamental instrument which an author-illustrator can use in order to introduce gaps into his work. Several types of off-screen are discussed: objective off-screen as representations of those areas that have not entered into the frame but are nevertheless recognized by the viewer; internal off-screen that is represented by different frames, such as windows, doors, books or mirrors; subjective off-screen, produced by the viewpoint of the observer; and *mise en abyme* that occurs when the viewer is placed behind the observer. This special type of off-screen is typical for picturebooks that present the artist in his study creating the work in question, or when the endpapers and back covers give details about the making of the book.

Making Sense Out of Picturebooks

The last five articles deal with the impact of linguistics and psychology on the making and research of modern picturebooks by showing that the inclusion of child psychology, cognitive linguistics, cognitive psychology, and memory research shed new light on both pictorial and linguistic aspects of picturebooks.

Ingeborg Mjør's chapter is based on empirical studies showing how reading aloud of picturebooks can make a contribution to children's ability to be involved in meaning making processes, and on the development of literacy, especially *visual* literacy. Based on semiotics and cognitive psychology this article analyses the challenges parents face when reading a specific picturebook to their toddlers. During reading aloud, parents might analyse the relationship between the real and implied reader to be out of balance. Therefore, they try to compensate this imbalance through different strategies: adding redundancy, creating a different verbal text, stressing the role of body and gestures, and replacing telling by showing.

Eva Gressnich and Jörg Meibauer attempt to link relevant categories of narrative analysis to deictic categories by pointing out the abilities a child must have in order to understand the deictic references within the text as well as the text-picture relationship, drawing largely on recent research on the acquisition of deixis and discourse strategies. Thus, they show that the interaction between language acquisition and the acquisition of literary competence is a demanding and complex process. In this analysis, the authors concentrate on the use of deictic expressions in picturebooks with a first-person narrator. In this way they show the difficulties children may have when confronted with this specific point of view and how deictic expressions influence the text-picture relationship. Moreover, they establish a typology of different combinations of verbal and visual point of views suggesting varying degrees of complexity as well as a possible order of acquisition.

The article by Bettina Kümmerling-Meibauer focuses on picturebooks with first-person narrators that consist of autobiographical stories written and illustrated by the authors. Since the storyteller is also the key figure in the story, the artists have to tackle the representation of their point of view in the pictures. In this regard, a shift between telling and focalization is obvious. The story is told in the first person whereas the pictures are presented in the third person. Confronted by these different points of view, the reader is encouraged to empathize with the narrator on the one hand, and to have a more objective position of distance on the other, thus calling his attention to the different time levels presented in these picturebooks: reminiscences of the past, most often childhood memories, and the present situation of the narrator.

Agnes-Margrethe Bjorvand demonstrates that the presentation of dysfunctional families and complex relationships between adults and children is new for Scandinavian picturebooks. Her article deals with the Norwegian picturebook *Sinna Mann* (Angry Man, 2003) by Gro Dahle and Svein Nyhus, which depicts a disturbing story about a violent father who threatens both his wife and his son. The analysis of the picturebook is based on recent research in child psychology and the concept of multimodal literacy. The juxtaposition of both fields serves as an interdisciplinary approach to investigate the multi-layered structure of *Sinna Mann*. Bjorvand shows that the color scheme, the surrealist surroundings, and the distorted proportions largely contribute to the menacing, even nightmarish atmosphere, whereas the lyrical text builds a contrast to the illustrations. The gaps in text and pictures and the open ending of the narrative leave the final decision about the meaning of the whole story to the reader.

Finally, Anna-Maija Koskimies-Hellman reflects on the motif of mindscapes (as a newly-established term for psychological landscapes) by analysing two picturebooks from Finland and Sweden: *Urhea pikku Memmuli* (Brave little Memmuli, 2005) by Mervi Lindman and *Hanna huset hunden* (Hanna, the house, the dog, 2004) by Anna-Clara Tidholm. Both books are ambivalent on several levels. Visually they are on the border between imagination or dream and reality. Yet the verbal narrator in both books presents the mindscapes as real, without a didactic comment indicating that the events are dream or fantasy. Therefore the mindscapes also support the characterization of the main protagonists, because the reader is given access to the characters' inner lives. In addition, the books are ambivalent with regard to the implied reader; both picturebooks address adults and children at the same time on different levels.

In conclusion, the variety of aspects that are analysed and the multiplicity of critical approaches illustrate the complex issues raised when modern picturebooks are approached through different perspectives that come together and tend to interact with each other. These issues link picturebook studies with some of the main trends in social sciences, cognitive studies and literacy such as the reflection on contemporary society, literacy in contemporary cultures, childhood, learning, multimodal communication or artistic interpretation. This anthology by specialists from different countries is also a testimony to the general academic interest in picturebooks as a new artistic form and is therefore representative of the different trends and opportunities for research in this emerging field.

Part I
Picturebooks, Literacy, and Cultural Context

Chapter One
Words Claimed
Picturebook Narratives and the Project of Children's Literature

Perry Nodelman

There are many kinds of children's literature. There are novels, stories, poems, and plays. There are texts of science fiction, fantasy, mystery, and adventure. There are domestic stories and stories about animals and stories of life in the wilds. And so on and so on. But as the adaptation theories popular with German and Scandinavian children's literature theorists suggest, the children's texts of these sorts have clear connections with the adult ones that, usually, pre-existed them. As Torben Weinreich says, "Writers do not primarily adapt because children have *other* experiences and *other* knowledge, but because they lack experience and knowledge" (49)—and so, many conclude, children's literature can best be understood as consisting of adapted—i.e., usually, simplified—versions of adult literary forms.

But if that is true, then what about picturebooks? The mere fact that they exist makes adaptation theories problematic, simply because there is no equivalent adult form of literature to understand them as adaptations of. Picturebooks either predated or began to be produced around the same time as related forms of literature for adults that combine visual and verbal texts: comic books, graphic novels, newspapers and magazines with lots of photos and drawings in them, coffee-table texts of non-fiction. The picturebook is, I believe, the one form of literature invented specifically for audiences of children—and despite recent claims for a growing adult audience for more sophisticated books,[1] the picturebook remains firmly connected to the idea of an implied child-reader/viewer.

It strikes me, then, that the mere existence of the picturebook and its continuing popularity as the main form of literature produced for young people before they begin to read and in their early experiences of reading on their own might help us to understand a lot about children's literature generally: what it is, why it exists, why it takes the forms it does. Rather than being an exception to adaptation theory, in fact, it might throw it into question altogether.

I have to be honest and say I hope it does. I spent some years working on a book on the distinguishing characteristics of children literature—published as *The Hidden Adult: Defining Children's Literature* in 2008. A key assumption of my book is that texts written for children and young adults—indeed, any texts written for an audience understood as being younger than their writers in a central and important way—tend to share characteristic structural and narrative features that make them less adaptive than distinct. Like Weinreich, "I prefer to see children's literature as a *genre* and by 'genre' I mean here a notion of a group of texts characterised by recurrent features" (34). As it happens, furthermore, I believe those recurrent features are most clearly visible in picturebooks. The one kind of narrative invented specifically for children might then represent the formal characteristics of children's literature in their most essential and characteristic form, and thus reveal its underpinnings and implications in a particularly explicit way. In what follows, I consider how the form and structure conventional to the picturebook narrative represent what the project of children's literature essentially is, in order to open some questions about the validity of that project.

So let's begin with the most obvious question: why picturebooks? What is it about the way adults have conventionally thought about children in the last century or so that has made the production of picturebooks so central to the children's literature industry world-wide?

Well, what distinguishes picturebooks from other texts is exactly what their name suggests: the presence of pictures. They have pictures because children, people believe, need or are at least greatly benefited by their presence. Without pictures, people think, children cannot make much sense of words.

But perhaps that is just because the words are so simple that they do not make much sense on their own anyway. Consider the pictures in books for the youngest children—the kind of books that offer images accompanied by one-word labels—"apple," "ball," "tree," etc. On its own, the word "tree" says little. It names an object—but why? Why is the word being said, or written down? Or even more problematic, for those not yet familiar with the language, for foreigners or very young children—what does "tree" mean anyway? We need to know what object this particular conformation of sounds represents before we can even begin to think about why it has been named.

Once a picture is present, however, the answer becomes clearer: the word is there in order to be associated with the object it represents. This word—"tree"—represents this thing you see here. And once that is clear, the reason for "tree" being uttered is also clear—it is being defined. This is a situation a lot like a dictionary, except that the many words that account for and explain one word in the definitions there are replaced by a picture.

The picture would not be necessary if a lot of other words—the kind of words we find in dictionary definitions—were there.[2] But they are not there. They cannot be there because we believe they are too complicated for the young readers implied as the audience for this sort of book. So they have been replaced by an image.

If we stop just taking this for granted as an obvious thing to do, we can see that it is really pretty strange. There are a number of paradoxes here.

First: simple words, it turns out, are complicated—too complicated, it seems, too mysterious and uncertain, to stand on their own without the support of the picture. Their simplicity makes them difficult. There are two reasons for that. First, written words are what are known as arbitrary signs: they look nothing like the things they represent.[3] Just as someone unfamiliar with, say, Chinese, could not figure out what object a Chinese word might represent merely by looking at the word 橄树, English speakers who cannot read English cannot figure out that the letters T R E E represent the sound "tree," which represents a certain kind of large plant. So—ironically, perhaps—they cannot figure out a presumably very simple verbal text.

The second reason simple words are difficult is that words always exist and take their meaning within a complex network of other words. The sound "tree" on its own means nothing in particular. "Tree" in relation to a lot of other words—not just its dictionary definition, but also words like "nature," "seed," "flower," "people," "soil," "sky," "growth," "spring," "branch," and so on—has a quite specific meaning. Its meaning emerges from its relationships with the meanings of all those other words.[4]

But only for someone who knows those other words—or if, as in a dictionary, some of those other words are there to explain the first word. In a simple book for young children, those other words are not there—are not there, ironically, because adults assume young readers will not be able to read them or, if adults speak the words, child listeners will not understand them. This is, in fact, exactly why children's literature exists in the first place: because adults assume children are capable of understanding less than adults—or perhaps because adults *want* children to understand less, want them not to know certain aspects of the world—children need a literature that says less.

Paradoxically, however, the absence of complicated words makes the simpler words left behind incomplete, mysterious—complicated. At which point, enter pictures. As I have suggested, the picture of the tree is there in place of all the more complex words that might help communicate what the word "tree" signifies. Adults tend to assume that a young person who could not make sense of all those complex words could in fact make sense of a picture. As a system of representation, pictures are, clearly, less arbitrary than words are. They are the kind of sign known as "iconic"—i.e., they do in some ways resemble the objects they represent. The letters T R E E do not look like a tree. A picture of a tree does.

Or rather, sort of does. Unlike the trees seen even in what most people might consider a very realistic photograph, real trees are significantly larger; have a third dimension, not just two; move and make sounds in the wind rather than being fixed in one place and eternally silent. The trees shown in the simplified outline drawings found in many books for very young children are even more unlike real ones—they tend to have fewer colors and textures, and often exist in a void, not even attached to any depiction of the ground. Even so, people tend to assume that even the very youngest of children can derive the idea of a tree from exactly these kinds of pictures of one. The images that appear in books for the youngest and least experienced readers are either ones that have been simplified to provide a minimal amount of information of how an object looks—simple outline drawings, for instance—or else, they are complexly detailed color photographs that provide enough of that sort of information to seem to be as accurately "realistic" as possible.

The first of these possibilities is interesting because it duplicates the original problem with simple words that it is meant to solve. It provides more information to make up for the absence of more words, but offers very little of that information, and assumes an ability to read more into it—to see the complex tree in the simple outline.

Even so, there is logic to support this—research in picture perception suggests that outline drawings seem to be comprehensible by all sorts of untrained people, including very young children previously unfamiliar with pictures.[5] And in any case, even a simple outline picture tends to imply more information that just the word itself. It is not just a tree, but, perhaps, a green tree, a fir tree—always a particular sort and size and shape of tree. There is more information than necessary. The word "tree" can refer to any and all trees. But any picture of a tree, no matter how representative of all trees it is meant to be, can depict nothing more than just one particular tree—never just the idea of "tree," always just one specific example to represent that idea.

And it always does so more exactly, in a more specific way than just the word itself. Because pictures are, in fact, less arbitrary, easier to understand than words, it seems safe to assume that that extra information will not confuse or upset young viewers. Certainly, the pictures in books for young people do tend to provide a lot more information than a simple text might seem to require. Consider this text:

> *Here's something good about kindergarten. Getting a turn on the swing. Amber swings high. Her toes reach for the roof of the school. She's almost flying.*

The picture accompanying that text, Canadian illustrator Kady Macdonald Denton's illustration for Canadian author Nan Gregory's *Amber Waiting*, is drawn in a very simple style, and has little in the way of background detail.

Nevertheless, its excess information includes what Amber looks like, what color her hair is, approximately how old she is, what she is wearing and how that signifies her class and country and lifestyle, the cultural and genetic background of her classmates and herself, the fact that Amber is not alone but with and interacting with others, the existence of other objects in the schoolyard beside the swing, the fact that she is really not reaching the roof or flying as the text claims, the time of year (there is snow on the ground, but no heavy coats, so in Canada that means it's likely to be late fall or early spring). And so on. The picture tells viewers a lot more than the text manages to say, or that adults would allow it to say in the context of a children's picturebook.

There is a paradox here. The more detailed words get—the closer they get to being an accurate and complete description of an event or an object—the less child-appropriate adults tend to assume they are. But the more complete and detailed a picture is—the closer it comes to what we conventionally call realistic—then the more appropriate we tend to assume it is for children. A clear, detailed photograph is likely to seem ideal in these circumstances, and I suspect fewer people would imagine young children having trouble with, say a detailed color photograph of a landscape than an impressionistic painting of one. The former seems "real," while the latter, despite its more simplified shapes and colors, exists within a complex web of assumptions about art that make it seem too sophisticated for the young. When I have asked parents or students in children's literature classes which kinds of pictures they think young, untrained children have the least trouble understanding, these adults tend to name either simple line drawings or realistic photographs, both of which seem somehow appropriately childlike—like what we tend to believe children themselves see. And they are certain anything more abstract or impressionistic—what, paradoxically, reviewers of adult art call childlike or primitive—simply will not do.[6]

In any case, the presence of any kind of picture—perhaps the realistic ones more than the outline drawings—signals another key paradox about literature for children. It exists because adults think children can understand less and/or should be prevented from understanding more. But at the same time, we adults we produce books for children seem to harbor a wish, a need to say more anyway—or at least, we are rarely content with saying less. We want to provide simple texts but do so with the understanding that simple texts on their own are never enough—never quite adequate.

In a sense, we cannot avoid doing that—for as I said earlier, simple words can communicate only in terms of their connections to an unspoken network of more complex words that they inevitably imply. But our awareness of that as a problem with simple texts leads us—or perhaps, allows us—to solve the problem by providing a richer source of information in pictures. We can do that in part, I think, because we tend to be unaware of how rich the content is—especially in pictures we consider to be realistic. We tend to see even a picture as simplified as the one of Amber swinging I referred to earlier as a transparent representation of what is, and do not then notice all the complex information, pictures offer about the things they depict—especially ideological information about the culture illustrators are located in that illustrators tend to take for granted simply as the ways things are.

A picture can convey all this *as* specific information viewers might learn to be aware of simply because it *is* a picture—and therefore, the experience of connecting words to it is different from just saying a word like "tree" while pointing to an actual tree. The real tree simply is what it is. It means nothing but itself. But in a picture in a book accompanied by a text, it enters into a complex system of representation with complex meanings and implications. The specific tree depicted represents, not just tree-hood, but also, the tree's relationship to other objects in the picture and outside it, and to a whole set of values implied by those relationships. A tree in a forest is not there to say, for instance, I am beautiful, or, I represent the bounty of nature or the cycle of ecology or the meaning of life; a tree in a picture often is.

Furthermore, a picture works to claim the world it purports to depict—to be realistic. To say a picture looks like the objects it depicts is to accept the idea that the real things do look like that—do mean that. E.H. Gombrich reports how artists trained in a Chinese style drew English landscapes in a way that might seem curiously alien to viewers who believe a painter like Constable shows things the way they are, but that surely seemed as "realistic" to the artist as Constable seems to those familiar with Constable.[7] Each style claims the landscape in the name of its own truths. A picture of a specific tree accompanied by the word "tree" suggests that the essence of tree-hood—the most representative way of being a tree—is one like the one in the picture. And that representative tree is rarely, for instance, a fallen one, or a dead one—that would significantly change what we usually mean most centrally in using the word "tree."

That all happens, I think, because, once they are present, pictures tend to *claim* words. According to Michel Foucault, "Without saying anything, a mute and adequately recognizable figure displays the object in its essence; from the image, a name written below receives its 'meaning' or rule for usage" (23). The tree depicted along with the word "tree" *is* what trees are. The combination does not just say, a tree looks sort of like this thing here does—is somehow more or less similar to this; it says, a tree *is* this. "Let a figure resemble an object . . . , " says Foucault, "and that alone is enough for there to slip into the pure play of the painting a statement—obvious, banal, repeated a thousand times yet almost always silent. (It is like an infinite murmur—haunting, enclosing the silence of figures, investing it, mastering it, extricating the silence from itself, and finally reversing it within the domain of things that can be named.) 'What you see is that'" (34).

Consider, for a different example, the word "pipe." Place it near an image, and that image becomes what a pipe essentially is—a process the artist René Magritte reveals by denying it in his well-known image of one that includes the words "Ceci n'est pas un pipe." Magritte is literally correct here—this is not a pipe, just an image of one—and not any pipe, but just a picture of one pipe that purports to stand for all pipes, to be representative, and thus, to attach all its specific properties, and what they mean, and how they connect to culture, values, ideology, and so on, to the idea of pipes generally. Magritte's painting points out how fictional are the ways in which pictures represent texts—*and* how, until something like Magritte's picture makes us aware of it, reader/viewers tend to accept those fictions as the ways things actually are. The pictures claim the words, and claim them in the name of specific and surprisingly complex views not just of what the words mean, but of what reality is and means in general.

As with pipes, so are the things depicted in the pictures in picturebooks. They work to place child-readers within the complex relationships of the ideologies that adult illustrators and the editors and publishers, librarians, teachers, and parents who make them available to children occupy themselves—and thus, represent in their pictures. They do so in a number of ways.

First, for the reasons I explored earlier, the pictures in picturebooks are almost always more complex, more detailed, more sophisticated than the texts are. Conventions of publishing and assumptions about what is possible that are merely taken for granted by the producers and purchasers of picturebooks allows illustrators a much wider range of sophistication than that available to the writers of texts. And the more sophisticated and the more "real" a picture looks, the more it imposes a cultural order of reality, i.e., the adult world. Texts in picturebooks most usually purport to be childlike—to represent something like how adults like to believe children see and understand the world—or ought to see and understand the world. But the pictures tend characteristically to undercut that childlike simplicity with a more sophisticated adult view of things—a view that place the childlike text firmly in adult culture.

Second, they accomplish that in part by quite literally doing it. Whereas the texts of picturebooks tend conventionally to focalize events through their child protagonist, the pictures usually show that same child as seen from a distance and therefore, presumably, by someone else—someone whom, it seems, has the ability to record all the visual surrounding details the child is not necessarily conscious of (as Amber, swinging, is not conscious of the bare trees behind her). In effect, then, the picture places the child protagonist—and the child-focalized text—in the context of another point of view: the view of a hidden but clearly implied observer who tends to see more details, to be, that is, more adult.

But while the observer seems to be adult, the view offered is there primarily for the pleasure of an implied child viewer. The child viewer is being invited to adopt an adult perspective on the child protagonist he or she reads or hears about and, presumably (since this is how most adults assume child-readers do and should interact with texts), is being invited to identify with. The child viewer is being invited to understand him or herself as adults see and understand him or her.

At the same time, however, the text is inviting an identification with a childlike protagonist who seems unaware of the exterior adult viewpoint on him or herself. Some texts are in the first person: "I went to bed with gum in my mouth," reads the text of Judith Viorst's *Alexander and the Terrible, Horrible, No-Good Very Bad Day*, "and now I have gum in my hair. . . . and I could tell it was going to be a terrible, horrible, no good, very bad day." The simple language of a text in the third person—"Amber swings high. Her toes reach for the roof of the school"—might imply an adult narrator, but it is one who always at least pretends to adopt a childlike way of seeing, in simple childlike language. Pictures in picturebooks also do sometimes seem to be trying to be childlike—to be in simple cartoon styles like the ones in *Amber Waiting*, for instance; but they always imply an exterior view of their child or childlike characters—a view, I believe that is both adult and meant to be adopted by child-readers at the same time as they relate to, identify with, or in fact adopt the text's childlike view of the child protagonist.

The central dynamic of the most conventional picturebooks is, then, the relationship between a relatively simple text with a supposedly childlike point of view and a relatively more complex picture offering an adult perspective on the children being depicted—a perspective children are meant to acknowledge and accept. But what they are being asked to accept is an adult view of themselves as being childlike—an understanding of being childlike firmly enmeshed in adult cultural assumptions—and, I think, especially, adult desires—about how to be a child. As a result, the swerve the pictures take through adult perceptions seems to be meant to be forgotten, or simply not acknowledged. It is a hidden adult content. The childlike text is what is acknowledgeably childlike, and an implied reader/viewer learns or already knows how to hide the adult knowledge that allowed an understanding of what being a limited child is—that it *is* a matter of being limited, being or pretending to be less than you actually are, and that you have to be limited in that way to please adults.

And in this way, I think, picturebooks represent the normal and constant situation of all books produced by adults for people younger than themselves. Indeed, they do so in a number of significant ways:

First, they are inherently and unchangingly double—as, I believe, in its primal scene of an adult choosing to write for a reader conceived as being different from and even, often, opposite to the adult writer, children's literature generally is. There are two different means of communication: words and pictures. There are two differing focalizations, with two different levels of sophistication.

While none of these qualities is literally true of texts for children without pictures, those texts do represent similar tendencies to doubleness in other, less obvious ways. The always relatively simple texts imply a more complex unwritten repertoire—it is intriguing that as implied readers of texts for children grow older, the number of pictures accompanying them lessens, replaced by more and more complex language. Picturebooks for the youngest readers are replaced by novels with pictures here and there for slightly older ones, and finally by ones with no pictures except the ones on the cover for yet older children and young adults. There also tends to be, in the most conventional texts, a focalization through a child character, reported by a narrator who is, by implication and conventional understanding, adult. Indeed, adults tend to make a point of that for children—teaching them that the books they read are by adults, including photos of authors on books covers, asking students to do author studies or write letters to writers. It is important for adults that children realize, not just that a book describes childhood, but that it is an adult—i.e., an authorized, culturally sanctioned, desirable—depiction of childhood.

So texts of children's literature are inherently binary, inherently offering adult views of childhood and inherently inscribing the division between adult and child in doing so, inherently insisting on the division between the two and the importance of one being different from and understanding itself in its difference as that difference is understood by the other. And most conventionally, they do so by offering children access to adult knowledge that implied child-readers are meant to experience and then ignore—keep hidden. These readers are meant to stop being whatever kind of children they already are, learn an adult perspective on what is desirably childlike, accept that adult wisdom and become or more accurately pretend to become childlike, and then hide or perhaps ideally lose their awareness of how this is an adult perception of themselves they have accepted as their own. They are to become appropriately childlike by accepting and then closeting their knowledge of the degree to which this form of childlikeness is imposed upon them from outside by adults—less what they actually are than what adults would like them to be, or at least pretend to be for adults.

I am not saying that some texts do not diverge from these qualities. But they can do so only by fighting against the constrictions and tendencies of the genre. Children's literature most centrally teaches children how to be childlike, in terms of adult-authorized ideas of childlike-ness. The picturebook's dynamic is merely the most obvious representation of this central quality of the genre.

As inherently binary, children's literature exults in two-ness. There is almost always a black and a white, a good and a bad, a true and a false. There is almost always a home and an away, a safe place made secure but constraining by adults and a dangerous but exciting place where children free from adult constraint can have adventures. There is almost always a childlike way of thinking and doing and a more mature one. There is almost always an awareness of the child as significantly less—less wise, less experienced, less mature, and less damaged. In some texts that is cause for celebration, in others, something to be rooted out. In some texts, happy endings emerge from child characters coming to appreciate adult containment (we tend to identify those as the didactic ones). In others, the happy ending is freedom from oppressive adult unimaginativeness (we tend to see these as the trashy ones designed merely to entertain children). In the most characteristic texts, there is ambivalence, a balance between the two.

In terms of the swerve through adult content, however, texts of children's literature characteristically work by teaching a child-reader more in order to understand the value of knowing less—accessing adult sophistication in order to understand the appropriate way of being childlike as understood in adult thinking about children. It is, therefore, both conservative of childhood and undercutting of its own conservatism—or, alternately, in conserving the childlike, it is radical, and in hiding but nevertheless reinforcing the adult, it undercuts its own radicalism. It is not so much ambivalent about these matters as it is paradoxical.

As a fairly typical text for children, *Amber Waiting* can stand as an example. It is an enjoyable book, I think, and an ingenious one; in a review I wrote some years ago of almost eighty Canadian picturebooks, I singled it out as the one I appreciated the most: "*Amber Waiting* reveals in awareness of a long and noble history of previous picturebooks showing what goes on in children's minds . . . but offers a subtle and interesting variation on them. It is, quite simply, an excellent picturebook" (123). In other words, my pleasure in it derived less from its uniqueness than from the ways in which it represents, and also, acts as an interesting variation, not just on a certain kind of picturebook—consider Potter's *Tale of Peter Rabbit,* Sendak's *Where the Wild Things Are,* and many other voyages into imaginary dangerous but exciting places—but also of the characteristics of children's literature generally.

Like *Peter Rabbit* and *Where the Wild Things Are, Amber Waiting* is centrally about the dispute between a young child and her parent, and its story arc takes the child away from a place set up by adults as a safe place for children into a more exotic one adults would not allow the child to go to but where the child solves its problems on its own. Having proven to be mature enough to be more capable than a parent imagined, the child is, paradoxically, rewarded with a return to the safe place and the comforting restrictions of childhood—a safe roof, a soft bed, a hot meal.

Amber Waiting tells that familiar story this way: As Amber sadly waits alone in the school hallway for her tardy father to finally show up and take her home from kindergarten, she imagines herself dropping her dad off to be alone and unhappy on the moon, and then taking herself on a voyage around the world, doing amazing things that impress fathers everywhere. Then she imagines that she returns to her own lonely, deserted father, who now has learned about waiting and will always be there on time ever after—along with all the other late dad and moms in the world. When Amber's dad does finally really arrive in real life at the end of the book, she is able to communicate enough of what she has imagined to make him understand how unhappy she has been, and she is rewarded by the love and attention she felt lacking before—with a kiss and a ride home on his shoulders.

How, then, does Amber waiting represent the conventions of children's literature? In *The Hidden Adult*, I develop a definition of children's literature as a genre that lists a number of its common characteristics. I would like to repeat that definition here, along with some comments on how *Amber Waiting* represents those characteristics.

Children's literature—the literature published specifically for audiences of children and therefore produced in terms of adult ideas about children, is a distinct and definable genre of literature, with characteristics that emerge from enduring adult ideas about childhood and that have consequently remained stable over the stretch of time in which this literature has been produced. Those ideas are inherently ambivalent, and therefore the literature is ambivalent.	The ambivalence of *Amber Waiting* resides in the paradox of the situation. Amber imagines herself in control in order to show her father he should be more in control; she is independent in order to achieve a comforting dependency.
It offers children both what adults think children will like and what adults want them to need, but does so always in order to satisfy adults' needs in regard to children. It offers what children presumably like by describing characters and telling stories that fulfill theoretically childlike wishes for power and independence. It fulfills real adult needs and children's presumed needs by working to colonize children—imagining a fictional child-reader as a model for actual child-readers to adopt.	*Amber Waiting* offers children a fantasy of empowerment, adults a child who wants and needs adult love and protection
But its imagined child-reader is divided, both teachable and incorrigible, savage and innocent--eternally ambivalent. It possesses a double vision of childhood, simultaneously both celebrating and denigrating both childhood desire and adult knowledge, and therefore, simultaneously protecting children from adult knowledge and working to teach it to them.	Amber is always both independent and dependent, always more knowing than her father about love and more innocent than he in her unquestioning acceptance that this man who seems to slide his way thoughtlessly through life by, as the text says, smiling "his famous smile" has actually learned something and changed at the end.
It is both conservative and subversive, and subverts both its conservatism and its own subversiveness.	*Amber Waiting* allows Amber to imagine her subversion of her father's authority, but only in the course of establishing her need for his care and attention.
It finds its models in literary forms of earlier times, especially the fairy tale and the pastoral idyll—sophisticated versions of less sophisticated forms.	As a pastoral idyll makes rural poverty utopian, *Amber Waiting* offers adult readers the charmingly nostalgic innocence of Amber's understanding of ideal parenting as established in her fantasy. It presents childhood as a place whose troubles are relatively small ones, relatively easily solved.

It central characters are children or childlike beings, and its main concern is the meaning and value of being childlike as understood by adults.	Both Amber and her father are childlike—he in a bad but charming way, she in a good and charming way.
It implies (or hides) a relationship between an adult narrator and a child narratee. It describes events from what purports to be a childlike point of view in order to teach children to occupy or enact that childlike point of view.	The narrator appears to be an adult telling Amber's story to child-reader/viewers in terms of how Amber herself might understand it. It offer Amber's point of view, but describes it in language somewhat more organized and sophisticated than we might expect of a kindergartener. The purpose of the story is, clearly, for readers to develop empathy with Amber and thus learn from her imaginative solution to her feeling of being deserted.
It is an apparently simple literature in which adults leave things out—tell children less than the adults know themselves, especially about sexuality.	For an adult reader, the father's "famous smile" speaks volumes about his confidence in his own sexuality, and implies a whole subplot about the father's untrustworthiness and way of handling people generally that Amber herself seems relatively oblivious to.
It is a plot-oriented literature that shows rather than tells.	As I have argued here, this is particularly true of most picturebooks, with relatively simple texts and relatively complex pictures. Furthermore, *Amber Waiting* moves forward by means of descriptions of Amber's real and imagined actions rather than saying much specifically about her feelings.
But it implies more than it says—sublimates deeper and subtler adult knowledge in an unspoken but clearly present shadow text necessarily available to all its readers, both adults and children.	Amber's feelings as expressed by the events she experiences and imagines seem fairly obvious to me (there is little subtlety in the image of Amber's father sitting in the dark of the moon as he observes the warm light of the sun from an isolating distance). It also seems obvious that the author and illustrator believe Amber's feelings must be clear to child-readers, who could make little sense of the book and its messages for them without being able to interpret the fantasy and the pictures in this way.
It tends to be utopian in that it imagines childhood innocence as utopian, but its plots tend to place child characters in un-childlike situations that deprive them of their innocence.	In order to get back the security and comfort of her father's attention, Amber must undergo separation and isolation and imagine an un-childlike circumnavigation of the globe.

It is nevertheless hopeful and optimistic in tone, and tells stories with what purport to be happy endings, as child or childlike characters purportedly achieve maturity by retreating from adult experience and accepting adult protection and limiting adult ideas about their own childlikeness. It characters achieve innocence after having experience. It tends to represent visions of childhood pleasing to adults in terms of images and ideas of home, and its happy endings often involves returning to or arriving at what is presented as home.	These are obvious qualities of *Amber Waiting*. Amber's desolation is expressed by means of a joyful adventure, and she is merely mature enough to guarantee that her father thinks of her and acts towards her as if she was an innocent child, and to embrace her in his comforting support and carry her back to what readers have to assume is a safely loving home.
It is binary oppositional in structure and in theme. Its stories tend to have two main settings, each of which represents one of a pair of central opposites. Its protagonists tend to represent combinations of pairs of characteristics that tend more usually in the world of discourse outside these texts to function separately and in opposition to each other.	*Amber Waiting* takes place at school (theoretically safe and familiar but currently devoid of the comforts of parenting) and in the world of Amber's imagination (theoretically isolating and away from loved ones but allowing control and mastery). Amber is a child wise beyond her years, her father a childish adult—but also, Amber is a needy innocent in search of a safe childhood, and her father a loving parent after all.
It is ambivalently unable to dismiss either half of each of its pair of binaries. Its texts are internally repetitive and/or variational in form and content, and tend to operate as repetitions and/or variations of other texts in the genre.	I have described how *Amber Waiting* represents a variation on the plots, characters and themes of central books like *Peter Rabbit* and *Where the Wild Things Are*. Its fantasy section, in which deserted Amber deserts her dad, clearly operates as a variation, an inversion of the situation in the real world outside it.

For all its clever inventiveness, its imaginative evocation of strong emotions and its pleasing good spirits, *Amber Waiting* is nevertheless representative of the most typical characteristics of children's literature as a genre. And it is so most essentially because it is a picturebook, telling a story built on binaries by means of two differing media of communication.

What, then, might be learned from that? This, I think: in a sense, children's literature is a doomed project. It exists in confirmation of the adult view that children are different from and less than adults, in need of childlike texts that show them less than adult readers know. But as picturebooks most clearly reveal, and as I believe *Amber Waiting* makes obvious, it can never be adult. It can invite from child-readers a lack of awareness of its adult content, but, as a product of adult minds and dependent on the language children share with adults, it cannot actually eliminate that content. The simplest text, the simplest picture can be meaningful only in terms of its relationship to the entire body of the language it is written in, the entire complex network of meanings and values of the culture it exists in, the entire body of adult knowledge that understands and defines children as lesser and different. For these reasons, children's literature both creates childhood—works to make children the children adults want and need—and at the same time undermines it—gives children the adult knowledge it purportedly suppresses, in the act of constructing a deeply paradoxical childhood subjectivity.

And I have to say finally that I think that is a good thing. It means that even texts that offer the most radical support of the joys of childlike anarchy are nevertheless enmeshed in adults systems of culture, and even the texts that work hardest to suppress children are nevertheless offering them ways of moving beyond the intended suppression. It means that Amber can be adult enough to teach her childishly irresponsible father to be suitably responsible—and that she can do so, ironically, in support of her need to be child enough to be able to depend on the security and protection he as an adult is supposed to offer. Like, I believe, all the most interesting and involving texts of children's literature, *Amber Waiting* is enough at war with itself to offer its implied reader/viewers an entertainingly unsettling opportunity both to enter into and to question the values of their elders.

Notes

1. See, for instance, Maria Nikolajeva (1998).
2. For instance, for "tree," the *Oxford English Dictionary* offers these words: "1. a. A perennial plant having a self-supporting woody main stem or trunk (which usually develops woody branches at some distance from the ground), and growing to a considerable height and size. (Usually distinguished from a bush or shrub by size and manner of growth; but cf. b.) c825, c890, c897 [see A. 2]. c1000 ÆLFRIC Gen. iii. 6 <Th>æt treow wæs god to etanne. c1175 Lamb. Hom. 109 Iliche <th>an treo <th>e bere<edh> lef and blosman. c1290 St. Brendan 41 in S. Eng. Leg. I. 221 Of treon and herbes, <th>ikke i-nov<ygh>. 1377 LANGL. P. Pl. B. xv. 327 A forest. .ful of faire trees. 1398 TREVISA Barth. De P.R. XVII. i. (Tollem. MS.), A tre ha<th>. .<th>e rynde, bowes, twigges, leues, blosmes, floures and frute. c1400 Destr. Troy 12467 Trees thurgh tempestes tynde hade <th>ere leues. 1481 CAXTON Reynard xii. (Arb.) 28 He brake a rodde of a tree. c1530 R. HILLES Common-Pl. Bk. (1858) 140 Hyt ys a febyll tre thet fallyth at the fyrst strok. 1600 FAIRFAX Tasso VII. i, Through forrests thicke among the shadie treene. 1635 LAUD Diary 1 Dec., Many elm leaves yet upon the trees. 1771 Junius Lett. lvii. (1820) 298 He or his deputy were authorised to cut down. .trees.

1861 BENTLEY Man. Bot. 540 Cunoniaceæ... Nearly allied to Saxifragaceæ, but differing from them in being trees or shrubs. b. Extended to include bushes or shrubs of erect growth and having a single stem; and even some perennial herbaceous plants which grow to a great height, as the banana and plantain.c1340- [see ROSE-TREE]. c1532 [see GOOSEBERRY 7]. 1640 [see PLANTAIN3 4]. 1649 [see CURRANT 4]. 1697 [see BANANA 1]. 1765 [see RASPBERRY 6]. 1855 BROWNING Women & Roses i, I dream of a red-rose tree. 1858 HOGG Veg. Kingd. 790 As a food, the Plantain is wholesome and agreeable. A tree generally contains three or four clusters."

3. See Chandler "Semiotics for Beginners," for an explanation of the difference between "symbols"—arbitrary signs like written language—and "iconic" representations, like pictures, which resemble the objects they refer to.
4. The ways in which words depend on each other for their meanings is a basic principle of the linguistics of de Saussure, which understands language as a system of relationships.
5. See, for instance, Kennedy (1974).
6. For complex art as childlike see Ruskin's famous comments on the "innocent eye": "The whole technical power of painting depends on our recovery of what may be called the *innocence of the eye;* that is to say, of a sort of childish perception of these flat stains of colour, merely as such, without consciousness of what they signify,—as a blind man would see them if suddenly gifted with sight" (2).
7. For a Chinese view of an English landscape, see Chiang Yee's "Cows in Derwentwater," reproduced in Gombrich (1961, 84).

Bibliography

Primary Sources

Gregory, Nan and Kady MacDonald Denton. *Amber Waiting.* Calgary: Red Deer Press, 2002.
Viorst, Judith and Ray Cruz. *Alexander and the Terrible, Horrible, No Good, Very Bad Day.* New York: Aladdin Books, 1972.

Secondary Sources

Chandler, Daniel. Semiotics for Beginners. http://www.aber.ac.uk/media/Documents/S4B/sem02.html (accessed January 29, 2008).
Foucault, Michel. *This Is Not a Pipe.* Translated and edited by James Harkness. Berkeley, Los Angeles, London: University of California Press, 1983.
Gombrich, E.H. *Art and Illusion: A Study in the Psychology of Pictorial Representation.* New York: Pantheon, 1961.
Kennedy, J. M. *A Psychology of Picture Perception.* San Francisco: Jossey Bass, 1974.
Nikolajeva, Maria. "Exit Children's Literature." *The Lion and the Unicorn* 22.2 (April 1998): 221–236.

Nodelman, Perry. "As Canadian as Apple Pie and Old Glory." *CCL/LCJ: Canadian Children's Literature/ Littérature canadienne pour la jeunesse* 111–112 (Fall–Winter 2003): 91–127.

———. *The Hidden Adult: Defining Children's Literature.* Baltimore: Johns Hopkins University Press, 2008.

Ruskin, John. *The Art Criticism of John Ruskin.* Edited by Robert L. Herbert. Garden City NY: Doubleday Anchor, 1964.

Weinreich, Torben. *Children's Literature: Art or Pedagogy?* Frederiksberg: Roskilde University Press, 2000.

Chapter Two
Interpretative Codes and Implied Readers of Children's Picturebooks

Maria Nikolajeva

While we take great efforts in teaching children to read, and in persuading both children and those adults who acts as mediators, of the importance of reading, it is a common prejudice that visual literacy comes natural and does not have to be taught and trained. True, there is vast evidence of very young children responding to images (e.g., Arizpe and Styles 2003); however, response and understanding are not quite identical. Neither do adults automatically acquire visual reading skills, as we all have witnessed our students' rather naïve and primitive discussion of picturebooks when they first encounter these in a children's literature course.

Visual literacy is just as an essential component of a child's intellectual growth as the ability to read verbal texts. And if verbal literacy can be and is trained, so should be visual literacy. Although a vast number of empirical studies have been carried out dealing with four-year-olds responding to this picturebook and six-years-olds responding to that picturebook (see e.g., essays in Evans 1998, 2009; Sipe and Pantaleo 2008), including very sophisticated books and their specific elements (Sipe and McGuire 2006), the very process of understanding and the successively increasing ability to decode the complex synergy of word and image have not yet been studied and theorized sufficiently. It may sound like a paradox when picturebook scholarship has recently expanded like no other field in children's literature research. Indeed, I would claim, and have done so on several occasions, that while we still do not have a comprehensive children's literature-specific theory, we do have a well-developed theory of multimodal communication, including picturebooks. Still, we know too little about how picturebooks are perceived by and make impact on young readers.

I will in this semiotically informed essay not discuss the question whether actual children do or do not understand certain aspects of multimodal texts, but use as a point of departure the concept of the implied reader, the reader that can be extracted and constructed from the text as such (Iser 1974); in picturebook studies, the subsequent notion of implied viewer has been employed (e.g., Nodelman 2000). The concept of literary competence is central in such line of inquiry (Culler 1995). I will thus speak about competent/incompetent and sophisticated/unsophisticated readers, without putting any evaluative or pejorative significance in these terms.

In his ground-breaking work on reader-oriented semiotics, *S/Z*, Roland Barthes suggests that readers need to have access to a number of codes in order to be able to decipher the message:

- the proairetic code
- the hermeneutic code
- the semic code
- the symbolic code
- the referential code

I will consider how these codes are pertinent to visual literacy and how, if in any way, they become specific in a multimodal text.

Yet prior to that, some basics of visual literacy should be reiterated. Like all communication, visual communication is based on encoding and decoding signs. In the scope of children's picturebooks, non-narrative texts, for instance, ABC and counting books, offer the most elementary strategies of visual decoding. Images can range within a broad continuum of representation modes, from photography to abstraction. Visual literacy demands understanding of the connection between the signifier (iconic sign) and the signified. A large variety of images may have the same referent (ball, car, cat), but the viewers are required to understand that the signifiers, the images, can be of different kinds and still connected to the same referent. Images are two-dimensional, although they depict a three-dimensional world. Images can be black-and white. We normally ascribe higher degree of fact to photographic and true-to-life images, while abstract or distorted images will be perceived as fictional. Empirical research shows that even infants respond adequately to shapes, for instance, of human faces. This means that they are capable of decoding iconic signs. An implied reader of a picturebook must possess these elementary skills of visual literacy before we can start speaking about meaning-making.

Decoding the Plot

The proairetic, or anticipatory code controls understanding of the plot. In order to comprehend the plot, the reader must have elementary knowledge of what a narrative is: a text that contains temporal and causal components. It may sound self-evident, yet it should not be taken for granted that young readers necessarily understand that one event takes place after another, and still less that one event may be a result of another event, occasionally outside the text itself. Children's perception of time is still vague, and perception of cause and effect needs certain cognitive maturity. Transferring empirical knowledge onto fictional narrative demands a further effort.

Temporality and causality is the primary organizational principle of a narrative. Even though a story may discursively be constructed in an arbitrary narrative order, the main plot components need to be present: introduction, complication, climax and resolution. Unless these components are tangible, we do not perceive the text as a complete, coherent narrative. We also assume that there are cause-and-effect relationships between actions and events. The lack of causal links makes a narrative less comprehensible. Both temporal and causal aspects are deliberately stronger in narratives than in real life; it is a part of the artistic design. In fact, the stronger these aspects are, the higher the degree of narrativity. Traditional stories (myths, folktales) and formulaic fiction, that children's literature frequently emulates in terms of narrative structure, display the highest degree of narrativity. This explains why these narratives, including children's stories, are often referred to as "simple": the statement refers to the close adherence to a recognizable pattern. Since picturebook format does not normally allow radical deviations from a conventional plot, at least not superficially, picturebooks are often considered to be simple. The alleged simplicity, however, is only manifest on the most elementary plot level and often without taking text/image interaction into consideration.

In using proairetic decoding, readers interact with texts on the basis of anticipation and retrospection, which means that every event points further toward subsequent events, and that each subsequent event may be at best explained and understood through previous events. The understanding of plot components facilitates young readers' anticipation of an imminent conflict, followed by resolution and, in most cases, a happy ending. It also enables readers to make inferences from completed events about earlier planted details, verbal as well as visual; or to understand the characters' actions and intentions.

The most essential code in reading a picturebook is its sequential nature. This is something that art critics often ignore in their analyses when they examine each illustration separately, as an individual work of art, which certainly does not make their approach less legitimate, yet somewhat diminishes the overall understanding. In my experience, even children's books illustrators in training are not always aware of the sequential features of picturebooks.

Unlike a verbal narrative text, images are disjunctive, and the reader must understand that there is a temporal and causal relationship between them, that an event in one image takes place before or after an event in another image and usually is connected to it by some form of cause-and-effect. The reader must bridge the temporal ellipses between images, deciding that the subsequent image refers to a moment which takes place a minute, an hour, a day, or a week later. The verbal text can occasionally fill the visual gap by providing the necessary temporal indices. These can be general, such as "then," "after," "later," or concrete, such as "next morning." In fact, picturebooks successfully utilize indexical verbal signs pointing at images: "He did this . . . and this . . . and this," a device impossible in a verbal narrative. Iterative verbal indices, for instance, "always" or "every day," suggest that the event takes place recurrently, although it is only depicted once. Here, the mutual complementarity of words and images creates complex temporality that demands quite advanced literary competence. Without verbal assistance, empirical knowledge may be sufficient, for instance, to infer that an image of daytime followed by an image of nighttime probably indicates temporality. Page layout, especially the contrast between verso and recto, enhances temporal and causal decoding.

On the other hand, unlike a verbal text, images have the possibility of depicting two or more events, either within the same panel or in a series of panels on the same doublespread, suggesting parallel plots that take place simultaneously or successively. Depending on the readers' competence, they will make the connection between plots, or conclude that they are independent of each other, or get confused. If separate plots conflate, the readers will infer that the previous disjointed images have in fact been connected; a narrative gap is subsequently filled. Frequently, a subplot in a picturebook is employed as a metafictive comment on the main plot. To see the correlation demands sophisticated decoding.

Occasionally, picturebooks depict a chain of episodes with a vague temporal order and without any causal connections at all, the so-called middle narrative; for instance, a child engaged in everyday activities and games. Each episode, often contained within a single image, is a complete, albeit minimal narrative in which the most essential plot components, conflict and resolution, are absent or implied. One can wonder whether such books offer any challenge in training literary competence, but here again text/image interaction becomes a decisive issue. Even such minimal narratives can in their iconotext range from simple and unambiguous to extremely complex, psychologically and philosophically charged. A mature reading may after all reveal temporal and causal aspects, not least though connecting details in images.

The materiality of a picturebook creates further premises. A specific feature of visual anticipatory code is page-turning, where, again, a narrative gap between pages must be filled. A sentence divided between subsequent pages prompts the continuity of the visual narrative (there are picturebooks in which the verbal text consist of one single sentence). A verbal page-turner, such as the question "What do you think happened next?" has a similar effect. In this manner, picturebooks stimulate interactive reading rather than passive ingestion. In fact, a clever picturebook precludes passive ingestion. Picturebooks can further amplify interactivity through flaps, movable parts, cutouts and other purely material features that are all constituents of the proairetic code.

Page layout contributes to plot progression, through a sequence of individual panels, through a balance of verso and recto, and through a dynamic organization of a single image on a doublespread. The non-linear nature of images stimulates various reading directions, even though some details may suggest the order of reading; complex images compel the reader to stop and browse, creating a narrative pause. Here, young children show extreme competence, studying the images carefully, while adults, focusing on verbal codes, feel an urge to go further onto the next doublespread.

Words and images can enhance and complement each other in terms of plot; words can lead readers' attention toward images, not least in the placement of words on the spread, or in the shape of the verbal text reflecting the image. The visual plot can start already on the cover; it can also be developed on title page and the endpapers; it can conclude on the back cover, which can also direct the reader back to the beginning of the story. In other words, the proairatic visual and multimodal code offers considerable further potential as compared to purely verbal.

Meaning-making

The hermeneutic code, adhering closely to the proairetic, involves interpretation on the story level. The ability to follow the plot does not spontaneously lead to a deeper understanding of what the story means, of its underlying layers. To do this, another decoding strategy must be employed. Mastering hermeneutic codes is, however, not an automatic skill. To begin with, readers must realize that there *is* a meaning in a text, which is far from self-evident. Not even all adult readers necessarily engage in interpretation, fully satisfied with the plot itself. For a young reader, the very idea that there is a deeper message behind a story may prove alien. Further, some texts resist interpretation; it is, for instance, pointless to search meaning in a nonsense text, whether verbal or visual. Since many modern picturebooks are playful in a nonsensical manner, trying to extract meaning from them is a futile endeavor. Not least are empty signs, images without referent, abundant in contemporary picturebooks, devoid of meaning. Hermeneutic codes are thus highly dependent on the kind of text we are dealing with.

The concept of the text as *bricolage*, appearing in the works by Jacques Derrida (1978), reminiscent of a more common "montage" or even "collage," may prove useful in approaching picturebooks, in which meaning is created by the mixture, preferably counterpointing, of the verbal and the visual. The central concept of deconstruction posits logocentrism as opposed to différance (a coinage combining "difference" and "deferment"). The model interrogates the presence of one given meaning in a text governed by an extrinsic law ("logos") in favor of viewing meaning as constantly deferred (postponed, or suspended) by further and different interpretations. A deconstructional analysis is thus aimed at discovering the breaches or cracks in the text where new meanings can be detected. Such cracks are especially prominent in picturebooks; yet a successful interpretation presupposes that the reader is aware of the possible presence of cracks and therefore actively searches for them. Since "logos" can also mean "word," rejection of logocentrism implies, in reading picturebooks, that words are not given priority in meaning-making.

Picturebook readers must therefore in the first place realize that in picturebooks, the meaning is produced by the synergy of word and image. To extract meaning from the verbal text alone, which unfortunately is not unusual in educational and scholarly practice, is pointless. Discussing content-related issues such as gender, ethnicity, child/parent relationship, war or death, without paying attention to images, is equally dubious, since images can both amplify and seriously subvert the messages and values of the verbal text.

The specific aspect of interpretation of a multimodal text is precisely its multimodality, where the overall meaning is created on at least two levels; moreover, not by the sum, but the interaction and joint effort of these. This is the basic premise of contemporary picturebook scholarship which needs no further explication. The famous hermeneutic circle can be perfectly elucidated by the process of reading a picturebook, turning from words to images and back, with a new and deeper understanding with every spiral. Further, since images are non-linear, they allow a truly hermeneutic activity of starting with the first overall impression, examining the details, returning to the whole with a more profound understanding, and so on, infinitely. Thus the more profound understanding of the plot, of what actually happens in the narrative, is highly dependent on the level of visual sophistication. The verbal and visual plots can be mutually redundant, complementary or contradictory; they may even be independent of each other. There may be several visual plots to one verbal or several verbal plots to one visual. The verbal plot may be simple, while the visual is complex, and the other way round. The interpretative potentials are endless especially since, in accordance with Derrida, the meaning will all the time be deferred.

In wordless picturebooks, plots are vague and allow multiple interpretations, even if images are relatively simple. When the narrative is made up of a sequence of panels, it may seem easy to read the images in the correct temporal order and to understand the causal links between them (proairetic code); yet there can never be a single unequivocal interpretation. Not least, a visual narrative can be as compact and as extensive as the reader perceives it, which becomes evident in empirical research when children are asked to verbalize their reading of images.

More complex wordless narratives present further challenges. Abundance of details provides infinite interpretative options, and no single hermeneutic code can be applied. Here, the degree of narrativity becomes low, and the only compelling narrative element is the eventual turning of pages. Scholars refer to such picturebooks as difficult or ambivalent, as opposed to simple. However, multiplicity of interpretations does not imply that interpretation as such is impeded. Young readers may not be able to articulate their understanding, but they are certainly capable of meaning-making even in extremely complex images, especially with some training and assistance.

When images are accompanied by words, they can accentuate verbal plot progression, for instance, by the implied movement, expressed through a variety of visual conventions. It has been repeatedly pointed out that in Western picturebooks images are read left to right, in the direction of verbal reading. In cultures where text is read right to left, the reverse is used, and in translations of books between left-to-right and right-to-left cultures, the iconotext frequently gets destroyed. Another convention is depicting a character several times on a page to denote movement and flow of time. A sequence of framed or unframed images also suggests progression. Literal and transferred point of view, alternation between long-distance and close-up images, zooms and panoramic views are among visual devices supporting plots, but requiring hermeneutic decoding.

A frequently overlooked aspect of a picturebook interpretation is setting. Picturebooks depend heavily on visual space. Images are better suited than words to convey all kinds of spatial aspects. Most picturebooks utilize images to create settings that can literally set the plot in a certain surrounding, but also convey narrative time, for instance, by change of seasons; enhance characterization, suggest a mood, or add details not mentioned in the text. Even if the setting is not integral to the plot, it still has a function of contributing to the overall impression. Visual texts have their own conventions that need to be understood. In Western art, there are conventions of perspective, which allow us to interpret, among other things, the mutual size and position of objects, or the distance between them. Further, negative space can be employed, that is, absence of background, blank area around characters or objects, that often emphasizes the central position of the character, a child's self-centralization. Negative space is an artistic convention that needs decoding.

Multimodal hermeneutic code presupposes the mastery of both verbal and visual interpretation, and in addition, a full awareness of how these two interact in the process of meaning-making.

Fictionality

The semic code, in Barthes' model, governs the understanding of literary characters. "Semic" means pertaining to a sign, hence the code refers to the understanding of characters as signs, signifiers, as opposed to living people that they signify.

Here I would like to add an essential aspect to Barthes' definition. Fictional characters are merely one constituent of the fictional topos. The concept of fictionality has been one of the recent hot issues in narrative theory. Young children—and frequently unsophisticated adult-readers—have problems with understanding of fiction as opposed to fact, and of the conventions used in literary works. The semic code should therefore be applied in a broader sense than merely concerning characters, instead encompassing all aspects of fictional texts.

Unlike real life, a text of fiction is a construction, a constructed set of *selected* events and characters, deliberately created by the author to communicate with the recipient/reader (locutionary act), for a specific reason (illocutionary act) and to produce an effect (perlocutionary act). In real life, the immediate understanding of the world is based on sensorial perception: we see, hear, feel, smell, and taste. The mental perception and understanding of reality is more complex and demands abstract thinking, but it is still based on empirical experience, personal or mediated. In fiction, the world is created through language, including visual language. A fictional representation can *evoke* sensorial perception, but not directly affect our senses. From a fictional, linguistically conveyed representation, we construct a mental picture based on our previous empirical and literary experience. More important, if we possess a certain literary competence, we can make inferences from fictional representation.

Understanding fictionality is the key element of literary competence. Even if a narrative is reality-based, it is still an artistic construction. Accuracy of detail, whether verbal or visual, does not automatically make literary space less fictional. A text may create and maintain an illusion of a reality. It may equally subvert this illusion, create cracks to remind the reader of fictionality. It may oscillate between the two strategies. It may depict a world that completely defies our empirical knowledge. On a most basic level, it can be red grass and blue sun. On a more complex level, modern picturebooks often play with "impossible space," inspired by expressionist art. This is not only possible, but legitimate, since authors are free to construct their fictive spaces as they please, without necessarily providing referents for their signs.

Both words and images can be totally devoid of a referent, that is, be empty signifiers. Picturebooks frequently play with such possibilities, either offering non-existing referents or just ignoring the whole issue. Such books are normally labeled as nonsense, while they are in fact incredibly useful implements in visual education. But also imaginary worlds, for instance, in fantasy, demand a different kind of literary competence. On the one hand, a fantastic world enhances estrangement, thus supporting the understanding of fictionality. On the other hand, readers, young and old likewise, lack experience of secondary worlds, and it does take a leap of imagination to enter them, unlike the everyday, perceptible world similar to that we encounter in real life. However, even a verisimilar fictional world is still a construction and can never be as complete as reality, since it is always based on selection. Moreover, language is generally structured (even though it can be fragmentary), which means that a fictional world is inevitably more structured and ordered than real space.

Metafiction is an effective device to draw the reader's attention to fictionality. Understanding metafiction is quite an advanced skill; yet picturebook images have great potential for metafictional games with readers, which go far beyond the radical frame-breaking and mise en abymes of some widely discussed contemporary picturebooks. However, the very awareness of the existence of metafictional visual elements prompts readers to search for them in texts where they are less prominent.

The ontological status of fictional characters, that is, their relationship to real people or other objects outside the text, is highly dependent on our general position towards art as mimetic or semiotic. If we view literature as a direct reflection of reality, we interpret it in a different way as compared to when we perceive it as a pure construction. A mimetically oriented reader will in literary characters seek, for instance, psychological credibility, motivation, and background causality. A semiotically oriented reader will accept that literary characters have no will of their own, that they can lack integrity, wholeness, complexity that real people possess. Characters can be fully subordinate and instrumental to the plot and lack any psychological traits, as for instance fairy-tale heroes. If we put mimetic demands on characters that are deliberately not constructed as mimetic, we will perhaps perceive them as flat and unconvincing. I am not directly claiming that semiotic reading implies higher competence, but the awareness of options certainly does. For instance, the ontological status of imaginary friends, frequently appearing in picturebooks, is decisive for the general interpretation of the narrative.

In their understanding of characters, readers assemble the information that the text provides into a more or less coherent portrait. Some information is direct, such as external description. Some must be inferred, for instance, from characters' actions. Many picturebooks play with ironic counterpoint as words and images offer contradictory information about characters' looks or behavior. It has been debated whether young children understand irony (e.g., Kümmerling-Meibauer, 1999); in any case, understanding irony is a part of literary competence, and the semic code enables readers to assess contradictory information. Here again, the presence of irony stimulates interaction between the text and the reader.

In terms of characterization, picturebooks offer some interesting possibilities as compared to novels. Images can be employed in characterization in different and occasionally more effective ways than words. But they also have limitations. Images are extremely suitable for external descriptions, giving us an immediate portrait of the character. Yet sometimes the verbal/visual interaction can be redundant; for instance if the verbal text describes what a character looks like or supplies information about the characters' size and mutual position that the images are better suited to convey. Images can in various ways indicate and emphasize gender or ethnicity, but they can only indirectly provide information about age, and they have no nominative function, that is, cannot inform us about the character's name. They can, by position on the page, convey power hierarchies, but they cannot express exact relationships, such as mother/daughter or sister/brother. The reader must employ semic codes to interpret and understand characters from the information provided in the iconotext.

Images can reveal that characters are not human. Picturebooks abound in animal characters, yet the fact is not necessarily mentioned in the verbal text. Literary competence includes understanding that anthropomorphic animal figures represent children and adults. This is in fact an incredibly high demand on readers, since they lack direct experience of intelligent and talking animals. On the other hand, children tend to anthropomorphize animals, toys and inanimate objects through play and imagination, which makes them better equipped for accepting such characters, but blurs the boundary between fact and fiction. In some cases there is a fluctuant border between animal and human that once again demands a deeper understanding of the character's ontology. Picturebook characters can even be abstract figures, yet semic codes will clearly prompt relevant interpretation, based, for instance, on color, shape, size, and mutual position.

Images can convey the characters' mood or state of mind (happy, sad, angry. worried), but they have limited possibilities of representing complex mental conditions, unless we move completely from the mimetic to the symbolic level of interpretation, which takes us to the next of Barthes' codes.

Deeper Meaning

The symbolic code assists the reader in understanding the symbolic/non-mimetic meaning of the text. In semiotics, symbols are, unlike iconic signs, arbitrary, connected to their referents in a completely arbitrary manner. Empirical knowledge is of little help in decoding symbols, since such decoding is entirely dependent on convention, on mutual agreement between senders and recipients. It is only through convention that we interpret images of dark forests as danger; images of sailing boats as, for instance, freedom; images of storms as turbulent state of mind; images of rainbows as hope. This is all the more true about young readers who may lack the direct experience of dark forests and sailing boats. On the verbal level, the most elementary symbolic signs are expressed in figurative language, including similes, metaphors and metonymy. On the visual level, there exist both universal symbols (rose for love, moon for sorrow or pensiveness) and occasional ones, that demand wide previous experience of artistic texts. Symbols are frequently vague and self-contradictory. Rain, for instance, can symbolize both gloom and life-bringing freshness.

Interpretative Codes and Implied Readers of Children's Picturebooks • 37

In terms of literary competence, readers must, to begin with, be aware of the existence of symbolic codes. Literary texts are, unlike non-fiction, polysemantic, which means that they have at least two interpretative levels, the literal and the transferred. Unsophisticated readers frequently read texts on the literal level only. This can be best illustrated by the numerous picturebooks featuring a journey to an imaginary world. Literal, or mimetic interpretation views the story as adventure, since the plot is usually built in a conventional manner either as a quest or as struggle between good and evil. Even though fictionality is recognized, readers neglect metaphorical levels of the story which may deal, for instance with fears and anxiety, parent/child conflicts, grief and other strong emotions, not mentioned by words, but emphasized through images. A character's feelings can be visually represented by monsters, dangerous animals (often wolves) or darkness. By coping with these seemingly external threats, child characters manage their own fears and aggressions. Becoming invisible or dissolving into a wall, frequent images in contemporary picturebooks, symbolizes parental neglect. On the symbolic level, the story takes place wholly in the character's inner world, a mindscape or dreamscape.

Also seemingly realistic stories are open to symbolic interpretations, not least in the visual component of the narrative. An empty chair in which a grandparent has been sitting throughout the story symbolizes death, which a less sophisticated reading will probably miss. Imbalanced composition, color scheme, distorted perspective and other purely visual features amplify symbolic decoding. Frames or absence of frames is a powerful artistic device to convey a symbolic imprisonment and subsequent liberation. Certain visual symbols, including colors, are gendered, representing either masculinity or femininity or blurred gender. It is not a coincidence that adults, who are mentioned in the verbal text, appear as an absent sign, a visual omission (paralipsis). The sense of the child's loneliness and abandonment is thus emphasized. The images convey a character's subjective perception, while the words present a more omniscient narrative voice. Characters' position on the page, for instance, occupying the center or crammed in a corner, expresses their state of mind and self-esteem, in addition to more literal characterization, such as facial expression and body language. To understand all these aspects, non-mimetic codes must be employed.

While images, as stated earlier, have limited potential in conveying literal inward characterization, they have vast possibilities in depicting non-verbal and subverbal states, using complex symbols and other visual figurative language. For young readers who are yet incapable of articulating their emotions, this is a superb way of representation, provided that they understand the symbolic code. Images are both estranging, as they render strong emotions less disturbing, and engaging, since they affect readers' perception in an immediate and persuasive manner. In picturebooks, wordless doublespreads are frequently used to convey strong emotions. These can be preceded by a short verbal statement or left without verbal support. A wordless doublespread is, as indicated earlier, a narrative pause. The unarticulated state of mind enables readers to fill the elusive gap almost to infinity, since new connections and inferences can be made over and over again.

Images encourage symbolic encoding, for instance, by adding the sense of hesitation as to the interpretation of events as external or internal, as play, dream or actual happening. The counterpoint of words and images creates a tension that stimulates different levels of reading.

Text, Context, Intertext

Finally, *the referential code* points, according to Barthes, to the cultural context. Here, too, I would like to broaden Barthes' definition by discussing context as such. Socio-historical context is the most elementary, but it is still quite challenging. Readers need to understand that literary texts are created during different historical periods and naturally reflect the time when they were written and published. The simplest example is clothes that point at a specific period. Setting is—or may be—significant to place the narrative in a historical or cultural context, but is lost on readers who do not recognize the markers. The parent/child relationships and social institutions presented in picturebooks must be assessed on relevant grounds. Books from different countries and cultures not only present different narrative and visual styles, which in themselves can alienate the reader, but they also reflect the specific ways, habits and traditions. In all such cases, cultural decoding is essential.

Ideological contextualization is of importance. Picturebooks containing, from today's vantage point, conservative values, can still be appealing to young readers on the plot level. Books that critics consider as artistically high standing can be obsolete in their ideology, especially covert ideology. Views on the child and childhood are of special pertinence. Unsophisticated readers, who apply proairetic or even hermeneutic and semic codes, can still be unaware of ideological messages. Moreover, the verbal and the visual narratives can differ in their ideology. Not least, one of the levels can be ironic toward the other. It is easy to accuse a book of its conservative value system expressed in the text, and miss the counterpoint offered by the images. Theoretically, it can be the other way round, but since words are generally less ambivalent than images we tend to ascribe them stronger authority.

Recognizing literary context is a decisive component of literary competence. In discussing picturebooks we normally speak about intervisuality, visual or pictorial connections between texts, to distinguish from the more established intertextuality. Intervisuality includes direct visual quotations, self-references and parody, extensively discussed in recent criticism (e.g., Beckett, 2001). It has frequently been questioned whether picturebooks abounding in interpictorial images are in fact addressed to children. For my discussion this argument is irrelevant, since adult readers can just as well be uninformed about rich layers of visual references, while children may recognize elements from specific childhood culture that adult readers may miss. As usual, we are dealing with competent versus incompetent readers irrespective of age.

Intervisual literacy is a matter of training. Extensive exposure to picturebooks, as well as other texts, verbal and visual, historical and contemporary, highbrow and mass-market related, stimulates readers to make connections between texts, recognize visual allusions, acknowledge recurrent features in picturebooks by the same author, and not least appreciate parodic play.

Becoming a Reader

It should be clear by now that interpretative codes are hierarchical, starting from the most elementary, the proairetic, to the most complex, the referential. Since literary competence develops gradually, this would seem to be the most natural order in training young readers in visual decoding. Texts construct their implied readers according to the degree of complexity encoded in the text. If the implied reader is expected to read on the proairetic level ("simple" text) it is hardly fruitful to elicit more advanced interpretations. In contrast, a text whose implied reader is supposed to manage symbolic and referential codes can still be read and appreciated by someone who does not have the necessary competence. A text that does not allow proairetic reading will probably be rejected by unsophisticated readers. A normal reaction from an adult, competent co-reader might be: "This is not a book for children." In fact, it can just be a poor, untalented, incoherent picturebook, even if it contains brilliant artwork.

Yet there is some difference inherent to the texts themselves. From his discussion of codes, Roland Barthes identifies two distinct types of artistic texts, readerly and writerly. Readerly texts are consciously based on codes common to authors and recipients. Writerly texts deliberately break conventions and thus defy recipients' interpretations. Obviously, most of children's picturebooks fall under the first category, demanding little effort in the process of decoding. The creators work from their presumptions about what children like, need and understand. In the overwhelming majority of picturebooks, images are either decorative, having no function at all apart from the commercial (making the book appealing to adult consumers), or redundant in the sense that they merely duplicate what the verbal text convey. True, words and images can never be fully redundant since they are after all different types of semiotic signs. However, most picturebooks—or rather children's books with pictures—found in average bookstores hardly promote visual literacy with their symmetrical word/image narratives. A young reader may enjoy the illustrations, yet these will not encourage any substantial effort in meaning-making.

The texts that critics most often take up for discussion are those that offer resistance and encourage readers' interaction. In terms of another theory, readerly texts are monological, while writerly texts are dialogical, based on a creative dialogue between the text and the reader. I am far from claiming that writerly texts in general and writerly picturebooks in particular are unquestionably of higher artistic quality. Yet they doubtless are more suitable for encouraging and training visual competence in young readers.

Bibliography

Arizpe, Evelyn and Morag Styles. *Children Reading Pictures: Interpreting Visual Texts.* London, Routledge, 2003.
Barthes, Roland. *S/Z.* New York: Hill & Wang, 1974.
Beckett, Sandra. "Parodic Play with Painting in Picture Books." *Children's Literature* 29 (2001): 175–195.
Culler, Jonathan. *Structuralist Poetics. Structuralism, Linguistics and the Study of Literature.* London: Routledge, 1975.
Derrida, Jacques. *Writing and Difference.* London: Routledge, 1978.
Evans, Janet. Ed. *What's in the Picture? Responding to Illustrations in Picture Books.* London: Paul Chapman, 1998.
———. Ed. *Talking Beyond the Page.* London: Routledge, 2009.
Iser, Wolfgang. *The Implied Reader: Patterns of Communication in Prose Fiction from Bunyan to Beckett.* Baltimore: Johns Hopkins University Press, 1974.
Kümmerling-Meibauer, Bettina. "Metalinguistic Awareness and the Child's Developing Concept of Irony: The Relationship Between Pictures and Texts in Ironic Picture Books." *The Lion and the Unicorn* 23.2 (1999) 157–183.
Nodelman, Perry. "The Implied Viewer: Some Speculations About What Children's Picture Books Invite Readers to Do and Be." *CREArTA* 1.1 (2000): 23–43.
Sipe, Lawrence and Caroline McGuire. "Picturebook Endpapers: Resources for Literary and Aesthetic Interpretation." *Children's Literature in Education* 37 (2006): 291–304.
Sipe, Lawrence and Sylvia Pantaleo. Eds. *Postmodern Picturebooks: Play, Parody and Self-Referentiality* New York: Routledge, 2008.

Chapter Three
Picturebooks and Changing Values at the Turn of the Century

Teresa Colomer

Of the 250 most distinguished books for child and young people selected by critics and published in Spain in the twenty-first century, half are picturebooks. A third of these deal with topics that tell children about their feelings and emotions. Most of them do this by adopting structures that are poorly cohesive, resembling a list or a catalog.[1]

Taking this situation and the detailed analysis of the selected books as a starting point, two considerations are dealt with. The first is that the new values promoted by children's books during the 1960s and 1970s, are now being significantly modified, even producing a certain shift in the very representation of childhood. As a consequence, there is a particular emphasis on topics that explicitly deal with emotional education—in relation to the development of the personality—and also on an education focused on the more complex values of multicultural coexistence in society. The second consideration is that picturebooks are enjoying a boom, in part due to the suitability of their form to some of the main features of this shift. Thus the broad possibilities they offer of mixing genres and codes allows them to express different levels of disarticulation and specificity in the individual and collective representations of people, which is also a concern of contemporary art.

To illustrate this, we have compared selected recent books with those produced from the mid-1970s to 2000. Certainly, grouping the changing values into these two categories is somewhat artificial, since both groups share the same kind of changes in relation to the values of the previous period; they slip temporally—backward through their published antecedents and forward through the stability of their continuities—while together they subsist as superimposed layers. Nevertheless, both approaches strongly emphasize the predominance of different values in their contexts of production as well as reception.

We will describe this evolution through comparisons of typical examples of the fiction of each period across four areas: the *reflection of social organization* that picturebooks offer, the *dominant values* of each society, which determine their *educational goals*, and the *tools* offered to readers in order to achieve these goals.

The Power of Imagination in the Seventies[2]

As it has developed, literature for children and young people has established itself as an instrument of socialization in our culture. Hence it is necessary to consider the impact that advances made in the sociology of education concerning family and school have made on the ways that educational values are transmitted in postindustrial societies. Basil Bernstein's contribution is especially useful in this area.

As a starting point, Bernstein follows the theories of Durkheim, who states that in advanced industrial societies work relationships are situated in between a social order based on domination and one based on cooperation.[3] Within this macro-sociological frame can be observed changes in education deriving from variations in the division of labor in society produced since the mid-twentieth century. During this period the complexity of the division of labor in relation to culture increased immensely, requiring citizens to develop an ever-greater capacity to operate in the symbolic field, and empowering those sections of the middle classes in information-based professions. According to Bernstein, this has been the most significant phenomenon in recent social change, and has entailed important transformations in education, since the task of social integration entrusted to schools has had to adapt itself to new social needs, shifting from forms of educational transmission based on positional roles (or, in Bernstein's terminology, *closed school*), to forms based on individualized and personalized roles (or *open school*).

The analysis of pedagogical practices derived from this process of change led Bernstein to formulate the concept of *invisible pedagogy* to characterize the diffuse and poorly formulated ways in which the requirements of social behavior are transmitted to children. Invisible pedagogy is defined by having rules of hierarchy that are highly implicit, weak organization of learning contents, and extremely vague and numerous criteria for behavior, in contrast with *visible pedagogy* predominant in the previous period and characterized by a much more hierarchical, delimited, and explicit approach. Invisible pedagogy is related to middle-class ideology, from groups that had already adopted these new forms of socialization in their familial relationships. This can be seen in the emphasis placed on the internalization of relationships of authority, rather than the response to punishment, as a teaching method. To quote Bernstein:

> *This section of the middle classes ... chooses, from among the prevailing forms of socialization of the young, forms that encourage children to show their differences and to learn the niceties and the strategies of inter- and intra-personal control. These forms of socialization are legitimated by a group of theories that are considered progressive within the spectrum of the social sciences. (22)*

The educational approach pointed out by Bernstein implies personal relationships based on the verbalization of problems, their constant negotiation, the encouragement of imagination, the understanding of opposing positions, the internal acceptance of rules, etc. These values and forms of social relationships were translated into the pedagogical propositions of books for children and young people in the sixties and seventies, and they continue to operate now.

Meanwhile, the economic and cultural development of Western societies definitively transformed them into postindustrial societies. In general terms, these can be defined through their being well-off, their democratic political systems, their recognition of equal rights for "different" groups, their emphasis on the management of human resources in the systems of production, and their access to leisure time.

These changes appeared in the *reflection of social organization* presented in books for children and young people. The social context depicted in fiction became that of the middle classes, especially of the liberal arts professions. Thus, the families portrayed in these stories became urbane, predominantly with an only child; meanwhile the access to comfort meant a devaluation of productive work in favor of leisure time, and this filled picturebooks with painters, writers, and poets. Concurrently, the conflicts generated by these types of societies produced a stream of critiques on various themes in these children's books.

The *dominant values* corresponding to these social changes appeared in the demand for democracy and equal rights, in particular focused on relationships of authority at all levels. These were values deriving from the need to know how to manage interpersonal conflicts emerging from more complex work relationships and hierarchical relationships, and from the perception of people as individuals, with their own opinions, will, and actions. The social representation of childhood evolved towards the inclusion of individual rights for children, which led to questioning the absolute authority of adults and blurring the boundaries between traditional ways of behaving and of enjoying oneself in different stages of life.

The *educational goals* that were now projected adjusted themselves to these values. There was a growing awareness of the overriding need for citizens capable of appreciating, establishing, and managing democratic social relationships; for citizens sharing the same rights, and ready to grant or demand those rights to or for others (depending on their social position); and for citizens who would develop a personal independence that would accordingly

44 • Teresa Colomer

lead them to act in an enterprising manner. Democracy, equal rights, personal independence, and the capacity to relate are very widespread values in the children's books produced in this period, in which so-called feminist and anti-authoritarian trends were also developed.

Among the *tools* offered to readers in order for them to develop these attitudes and values, three are especially important: knowing how to underplay conflicts through humor, using creative imagination through fantasy, and encouraging affection for the environment. With these resources, the characters offered as models in fiction had to actively dedicate themselves to the resolution of problems or to the enjoyment of life, and they had to be able to explore the transgression of the rules of coexistence in order to weigh their validity or the limits of their usefulness, even within the heart of the family.

The Desire for Protective Spaces at the Turn of the Century[4]

During recent times societies have evolved towards a globalized system. As in the previous period, the characteristics of these societies correspond to the causes of these changes, so that causes and consequences mutually reinforce each other in a continuous spiral. This produces new forms of the division and exercise of political and economic power (with the impact of phenomena as diverse as the multinational reach of companies or new kinds of terrorism). Technological changes are accelerated, and working hours are increased so that work becomes more and more demanding, and leisure time activities multiply exponentially, and are increasingly centered on consumerism.

These changing patterns also appear in the *reflection of social organization* presented in children's books. The context remains urbane and composed

Figure 3.1 Illustration from Joi Carlin and Morella Fuenmayor. *La cama de mamá*. Caracas, California: Ediciones Ekaré; Volcano Press, 1994.

Table 3.1 Social Representations and Values in the Late 20th Century Children's Literature

Type of society	Reflection (In fiction)	Dominant values	Educational goals	Tools (In fiction)
Well-off societies	Urbane families; single child	Invisible pedagogy	Access to comfort and education	The family questioned
Democracies	New social themes	Hierarchical relationships questioned; the right to equality	Democratic citizens; with equal rights	Exploration of transgression
Management of human resources	Middle classes	Management of interpersonal conflicts; individual rights	Capacity to face internal conflicts; with initiative and independence	External activity (enterprising)
Access to leisure	Leisure contrasted with productive work	Enjoyment of life	Capacity to enjoy and understand art	Dedramatization (humor); creative imagination; affection for the environment

of middle class professionals, but new family forms emerge (with divorce becoming commonplace, the growth of single-parent families, adoption, same-sex couples, etc.) and carefree artistic practice disappears in favor of the consumption of quality leisure time (attendance at the opera, visits to museums, reading, etc.). The contemporary phenomenon of migration also begins to have a notable impact on the ethnic and cultural mixtures presented by fiction in both text and image.

In synthesis, it can be stated that in contemporary picturebooks there is a predominance of urbane children belonging specifically to the middle classes, with access to prestigious cultural and artistic forms, with parents who travel, get divorced and form new families, who live in a society evolving toward ethnic and cultural diversity, and who have access to information about other places with quite different problems, such as wars or homeless children. (Colomer 2004).

But social changes are so deep and occur at such a speed that the social perception of the *dominant values* seems to be passing through a phase of uncertainty which is exacerbated by the question of individuality and the disintegration of the self that was so widespread throughout the cultural thought of the twentieth century and that pervades all forms of contemporary art.

Recently many authors have reflected on the contradiction that exists between the physical well-being achieved by Western societies and the growing signs of social and personal dissatisfaction, stating that we have moved from a need for material objects to a need for meaning. The multiple forms of social disconnection have replaced the traditional sense of belonging to collective projects and shared values, with the simple compulsive possession of goods. But, as it has been stated comically "a supermarket will never generate a community or a sense of belonging." This crisis of structuring institutions and their substitution by a consumption-centered individualism generates apparently incomprehensible explosions of aggression, as witnessed by the bewilderment occasioned by the 2005 riots in the French *banlieux*. Along these lines, the French philosopher Gilles Lipovetsky has stated that postmodernity—a period dedicated to the dissolution of what came before, "without defining what we were going to become, as if it were simply a matter of maintaining a newly-won freedom through the impulse to dissolve existing social, political and ideological structures" (54)—has come to its end. He maintains that a new classification, *hypermodernity*, better suits a period that leaves the past behind and looks forward in an effort to modernize modernism itself, while globalization and market demands bring the world closer and intensify the sensation of fragility produced by the increasing loss of the identities that supported the individual.

The description of a new perception of childhood belongs to this field of interpretation of our present culture. On one hand, the social image of children has developed to include a disquieting form of power, full of ambivalence and complexities. Children are now invested with rights as individuals, inside the family and sometimes *against* the family; we are thinking of the *International Convention on the Rights of the Child*, signed in 1989 and the first document establishing legal obligations for the signatory nations. Children no longer remain inside "the secret garden" but have leapt into the public sphere via new information and communication technologies that they know how to use even better than their elders, reversing the traditional hierarchies in favor of these techno-kids. The market and the guilt of adults at abandoning their children have turned them into economic agents with a huge capacity: in 1968 it was estimated that children worldwide spent (by means of their allowances and their *pestering power*) some 2.2 trillion dollars annually. In 2000 this amount had increased to 35.6 trillion dollars.[5] Children's capacity to transgress is no longer seen as exclusively liberating, but includes malignancy and violence, as can easily be seen in the production of terror films, or in news about school massacres and criminal acts committed by children that have shaken public opinion on several occasions in recent years.

On the other hand, images of children represent them as the victims of conflict par excellence. In its social aspects, this vision comes to be expressed with great harshness, to the point that the limits of using images of children in wars and disasters to express the severity of events, or to disturb viewers, has recently been the subject of wide debate.

On a personal level, childhood has been circumscribed to very limited spaces, practically the bedroom and the schoolyard; so that the space for children to play and move around in is estimated to have decreased to one ninth of what it was throughout during the twentieth century. Childhood is now a much more solitary time, as evidenced by the so-called latch-key children through their self-sufficiency after returning home from school, likewise by the recognition of a very high level of emotional disorders among children.[6]

Transformed in earlier periods into the accomplices of adults who gleefully invaded the realm of children, the image of present-day children has shifted, now shaded with an ambivalence that includes both the powerful issue of being out of control,[7] as well as being the victims of raw emotions and social conflicts. In our societies it has been a long time since children lost the *use value* that they had in agrarian and industrial periods, when they contributed

Figure 3.2 Illustration from Shaun Tan: *The Red Tree*. Port Melbourne: Thomas C. Lothian, 2005.

to the family income or were thought of as old-age insurance. Instead, they have attained a very high *emotional value* that turns them into the objects of adult desires and consumerism: child-objects, expensive to educate—which restricts their number—ready to be adopted, exhibited, relegated to very specific times in the adult schedule, and often appearing as an annoyance because they generate a need for responsibility and commitment that goes against the hedonistic society of their elders.

Considering this situation, the adult discourse presented in these books conveys a desire for the protection of childhood that, in this analysis, is shown in two strands of production. One is characterized by the nostalgia for a return to order and tradition, the temptation to bury the spirit of May '68 (as was expressed recently in the political sphere[8]), and also the need to preserve the time and space of childhood in what could be called a new kind of *children's room,* understood now as a refuge from insecurity. In accordance with this situation, contemporary production is governed by the return to works and forms that have proved effective in the past: reprints of the classics, the use of folk tales as literary models, intertextual references, and high production values in the printing of books. Picturebooks, a modern genre, have little to look back to, but without a doubt their enormous capacity for exploration has found a new area to play in, so that they incorporate these guidelines in very interesting ways, for example, making innovative connections with old folktale forms, playing with levels of intertextual references, or using the material possibilities of the book to their fullest extent.

The other strand demonstrates an awareness of the urgency of providing emotional defenses for children, unprotected as they now are in their emotional lives and their sense of belonging. In this context, the protagonists in picturebooks often feel very lonely and threatened, so that the *educational goals* seem to include the capacity to face the loneliness produced by contemporary life, as well as the failure to reach expectations generated by the excessive value given to success and consumerism. Sadness and depression now invade children's books in a new kind of rupture with thematic taboos. The depth of adult nostalgia and insecurity leads to the contradiction of trying to make today's children learn about all those things that their adults do not do: that they should look beyond the action-packed and chaotic forms of the society of speed and consumerism that surrounds them, so that—following the orders of the picturebooks scattered on the table—they can listen to the silence, distinguish what is superfluous, detach themselves from what is unnecessary, feel satisfied with the simplicity of a job well-done, identify their emotions and the feelings of others, or begin to understand about love and the acceptance of death.

It also seems that once the equal rights issues were resolved in the previous period, the prime educational goals included the legitimating of differences. The fact is that from one period to the next, our societies have changed the composition of their populations, to the point that differences have been displaced from the fields of "gender," already-existing ethnic minorities, or individual characteristics, to problems caused by immigration and the multicultural composition of societies.

The *tools* offered to young readers also present nuances in respect to the previous period. In regard to the three pointed out earlier, there is no doubt that humor, fantasy, and affection still constitute the major tools used by children's literature in order to help protagonists to dedramatize and overcome their problems.[9] But it should be emphasized that imagination has become infused with cultural references rather than being an individual creative expression, which seems to have contributed to the present recovery of and preference for the proven soundness of the classics when facing a fluid and changing world. The imaginative stance leans toward accessing traditional references rather than transgressing them, and it takes refuge in the daydream as a lived experience rather than in imaginative play as a posture.

For its part, the affection for the childhood environment becomes more intimate, using the resource of nearby figures with whom to share urban solitude. The pair of siblings recovers its historical advantage over the only child of the decades immediately prior[10] and it branches out into variants such as pet animals, dolls, and favorite objects that become part of the portrait of the young protagonist. Elderly people, displaced along with children from the rhythms of contemporary life, likewise carry out the function of easing their loneliness. Further, the elderly now tend to be viewed as *people*, apart from their strict familial roles as grandparents, and are shown either in their humorous aspect as resourceful people with fantastic projects (something already present in the previous period), or as the most reflective people, able to face decrepitude or death with dignity, a route very much in agreement with the panorama described. All these figures, then, are convened to give readers the possibility of reflecting on and delegating out their problems, to give them a comforting companion, or a space in which to learn respect and responsibility.

In regard to the family, the affective context par excellence, new forms are accepted without hesitation while as a group it remains more united than ever; when a less idyllic image is shown, it is not in order to put the family into question as such, as in the previous period, but to indicate the unreality of stereotypes of perfection. The family as an institution, and other affective contexts, are approached from an overwhelmingly positive point of view, since the idea is to bring security and hope to childhood loneliness.

Finally, the previous exaltation of the activity and creative initiative of the characters is reduced to give way, as we have already pointed out, to a declaration in favor of an enjoyment more receptive to forms that are traditional, simple, less consumerist, or else in favor of work that is slower, that recovers its value as such, in contrast to the idle critical view of its alienating aspects in the seventies.

All things considered, it can be said that the insistence on more traditional forms of life and the connection of all the members of the family through affection and enjoyment, are triggered equally by the reaction to the abandonment of children in front of the screen, the absorption of time in a whirlpool of productive activity, competitive individualism, or compulsive consumerism.

Besides these nuanced differences between both periods, the intensity with which the reflection about feelings, emotions, and philosophical ideas about the world, has burst out seems spectacular. This feature seems to be the most marked and most innovative part of the representation of the world that is offered in the children's literature of contemporary postindustrial societies, as the exploration of liberatory transgression was in the previous period.

It is a thematic and educational choice that, in many cases, shies away from narrative to employ different types of lists. Thus, several catalog-books have appeared which describe subjects as varied as the things we like, love, or hate; or construct classifications of types of emotions, tears, dreams, causes of affection, or behaviors; or make an inventory of different ways of behaving which in the end, nevertheless, maintain the subject's wholeness, or in the opposite direction, maintain the multiple perspectives that others can have about oneself.

With this choice, picturebooks are presented as the ideal way to explore questions about feelings because of the emotive use of illustrations, the text's proximity to the poetic functions of connotation and metaphor, or the possibility of combining codes in order to articulate different levels of meaning. The experience of poetry and the recuperation of the value of words have become popular, so that young readers have been invited to live within the reflective daydreaming that has taken over a great quantity of books intent on wishing children sweet dreams and on calming them with the cadence of their rhymes. The evocation of an idyllic time of affective, protective spaces is added as a fourth tool to the most overused resources in books up to now (humor, fantasy, and affection), in order to offer emotional escape routes to the implied readers of children's literature.

In short, through the analysis of this panorama, it can be said that, as in any period, children's books really speak about the nostalgia and desires of grownups themselves, and that, through returning to safe ground—to tales that allow social differences, to emotional display in books, and to the daydreaming protection of the home—children's literature seems to want to shield children from today's vulnerability and uncertainty.

This situation suggests new challenges for literary criticism. At the beginning of their development, picturebooks showed themselves to be inclined toward and suited to introducing innovative aspects such as metafiction, ironic distance, or the blurring of fictional boundaries. This led to a broad examination of the limits of this type of exploration of postmodern artistic

Table 3.2 Social Representations and Values in Contemporary Children's Literature

Type of society	Reflection (In fiction)	Dominant values	Educational goals	Tools (In fiction)
Globalized societies	New families (likewise urbane); two siblings	Return to tradition	Well-formed individuals	The family questioned in a nuanced way, but remains united
Individualism; multiculturalism; multinationals; terrorism	Ethnic and cultural mix	Protection of the child	Capacity to face solitude and failure; accommodating collective and personal differences	Exploration of emotions and rupture of thematic taboos
Technological change	Likewise middle class, but professionals	Search for personal security	Resisting the dictates of contemporary life	Reduced activity (anti-consumerism)
Demanding job; consumerism	Quality leisure	Artistic tradition (opposed to technological leisure and consumption)	Knowledge of artistic tradition	Dedramatization (humor); imagination (cultural, day-dreaming, words); affection for siblings, pets, the elderly; exploration of the emotions

forms in relation to children's levels of comprehension. With the current trends, literary criticism again has important topics to consider:

- In relation to the life experience of children, questioning thematic limits in light of books that deal with depression or creative exhaustion, for example
- in relation to children's cognitive capacity, analyzing their ability to process messages that are highly sophisticated, or include new levels of harshness, or messages concerning identity or the complexity of relationships in multicultural societies, that can involve elaborate narrative framing and unresolved conclusions rather than black and white stories and happy endings
- in relation to children's learning of culturally codified forms, debating the advisability of abandoning coherent narrative forms at a stage when children are learning fictional schemes, as was already stated by the linguist Raffaele Simone in 1988 [11]

- or in relation to artistic quality, valuing a production that can adopt these approaches simply due to their advantages in the ease of conveying content to the reader (content which in reality has been poorly elaborated by the author), or because of their commercial appearance of the picturebooks

It is for this task that critics and others in the field now find themselves called together.[12]

Notes

1. According to various sources: the database managed by the research group GRETEL (Grup de Recerca de Literatura Infantil i Educació Literària) at www.gretel.cat which contains all the selections of the magazine *CLIJ, Cuadernos de literatura infantil y juvenil* and of *Peonza*; various selections carried out by CEGAL and the Fundación Germán Sánchez Ruipérez; the most outstanding books of ¿*Qué libros han de leer los niños?*, the bulletin of the Seminari de Bibliografía Infantil i Juvenil of the Rosa Sensat Teachers' Association; the magazines *Lazarillo, Faristol*, and *Notícia de llibres infantils i juvenils* of the Robafaves bookstore; Best Children's Books 2003 of the Banco del Libro (Venezuela); and the books selected for the Premi Protagonista Jove.
2. The works studied in this section were: Carme Solé Vendrell, *Un grapat de petons;* Mercer Mayer, *There's a Nightmare in my Closet*; Helen Oxenbury, *The Restaurant;* Joi Carlin and Morella Fuenmayor, *La cama de mamá;* Kurusa and Monika Doppert, *La calle es libre*; Lois Lowry and Valentina Cruz, *Anastasia Krupnik*; Leo Lionni, *Frederick*; Ivor Cutler and Helen Oxenbury, *Meal One*; Frank Tashlin, *The Bear that Wasn't*; Rosemary Wells, *Noisy Nora*; Chris Riddell, *The Fibbs*; Roald Dahl and Quentin Blake, *Matilda*; Christian Bruel and Anne Bozellec, *Histoire de Julie qui avait une ombre de garçon*; Martin Waddell and Patrick Benson, *The Tough Princess*; Kurt Baumann and Michael Foreman, *Küchengeschichten!*; Florence Parry Heide and Edward Gorey, *The Shrinking of Treehorn*; Hyawyn Oram and Satoshi Kitamura, *In the Attic* ; Janosch: *Oh, wie schön ist Panama*; Heine, Helme: *Die wunderbare Reise durch die Nacht*.
3. A society that is structured on a simple division of labor has forms of integration between its members that Durkheim calls *mechanical solidarity*. On the other hand, a society whose division of labor has become much more complex has forms of integration that he calls *organic solidarity*. To understand the difference between the two we could imagine a society in which the sudden loss of a large part of its population would not alter its continuity, while in a society based on specialized roles, the lack of some kinds of specialists would deeply affect the social functioning.
4. The works studied in this section were: Antonio Ventura and Pablo Amargo, *No todas las vacas son iguales*; Linda de Haan and Nijland Stern, *Koning*

& *Koning*; Armin Greder, *Die Insel: Eine tägliche Geschichte*; P. Fatus, *Papa au bureau*; Elizabeth Spurr and Martín Matje, *A Pig Named Perrier*; Norman Messenger, *Annabel's House*; Silvia Nanclares, *La siesta*; Neil Gaiman and David McKean, *Mirror Mask*; Ian Falconer, *Olivia*; Shaun Tan, *The Red Tree*; David McKee, *Three Monsters*; Frances Wolfe, *Where I Live*; Roberto Innocenti and J. Patrick Lewis, *The Last Resort*; Michael Rosen and Helen Oxembury, *We're Going on a Bear Hunt*; Wolf Erlbruch, *Die Große Frage*; Mark Alan Weatherby *My Dinosaur*; Jutta Bauer, *Opas Engel*; Michael Grejniec, *Wie schmeckt der Mond?*; Angela McAllister and Gary Blythe, *Milo and the Night Marker*.

5. According to data presented by the Diputació de Barcelona, 2007: *El rey de la casa. Adultos a los diez años, niños a los cuarenta. (The King of the House: Adults at Ten, Children at Forty)*.
6. A contemporary study indicates that one-third of Spanish children under the age of eleven appear to show symptoms related to stress. P.M.Pérez, *Estudio sobre hábitos de vida saludable* (Valencia: Instituto de Creatividad e Innovaciones Educativas, Universidad de Valencia, 2007).
7. For example, the success of television programs such as *Supernanny*, which present themselves as assistance for parents in regaining control of the family.
8. On the part of the current French President Nicolas Sarkozy during his campaign in 2007.
9. A side topic would be to analyze whether this humor has become suspiciously banal and evasive, in order to allow the children represented in the books to bring themselves into living the most disparate and surrealistic situations, without any greater subversive claims.
10. Besides, working with a pair of characters offer authors some advantages: having both a female and a male protagonist perhaps supports gender as an educative value; presenting both older and younger characters allows the author to project a perspective that is now responsible, now admiring, or to easily show the tension between both figures; and it also contributes to widening the range of readers for the book as much as possible.
11. Simone graphically contrasts the traditional narrative forms "in the form of a cone", in which the created expectations converge toward the ending, with the emerging forms in form of a "truncated pyramid" in which tension is dispersed, proposing for the first ones for the development of comprehensive schemes during the stage of childhood.
12. Translated from Spanish to English by Olga García Larralde and Helen Gyger.

Bibliography

Primary Sources

Bauer, Jutta. *Opas Engel.* Hamburg: Carlsen Verlag, 2001.

Baumann, Kurt, and Michael Foreman. *Küchengeschichten* Zürich: Nord-Süd Verlag, 1977.
Bruel, Christian, and Anne Bozellec. *Histoire de Julie qui avait une Ombre de Garçon*. Paris: Le sourire qui mord, 1976.
Carlin, Joi, and Morella Fuenmayor. *La cama de mamá*. Ediciones Ekaré; Volcano Press, 1994.
Cutler, Ivor, and Helen Oxembury. *Meal One*. London: Armada Lions, 1971.
Dahl, Roald, and Quentin Blake. *Matilda*. London: Jonathan Cape, 1988.
Erlbruch, Wolf. *Die Große Frage*. Wuppertal: Peter Hammer Verlag, 2004.
Falconer, Ian. *Olivia*. New York: Atheneum Books for Young Readers, 2000.
Fatus, P. *Papa au bureau*. Paris: Éditions Thierry-Magnier, 1999.
Gaiman, Neil, and David McKean. *Mirror Mask*. New Haven, CT: Yale University Press, 2007.
Greder, Armin. *Die Insel: Eine tägliche Geschichte*. Aarau, Frankfurt: Sauerländer, 2002.
Grejniec, Michael: *Wie schmeckt der Mond?* Zürich: Bohem-Press, 1993.
Haan, Linda de, and Nijland Stern: *Koning & Koning*. Haarlem: Gottmer, 2000.
Heide, Florence Parry, and Edward Gorey. *The Shrinking of Treehorn*. New York: Holiday House, 1971.
Heine, Helme. *Die wunderbare Reise durch die Nacht*. Munich: Middelhauve, 1994.
Janosch. *Oh, wie schön ist Panama*. Weinheim: Beltz & Gelberg, 1978.
Kurusa, and Monika Doppert. *La calle es libre*. Caracas: Ediciones Ekaré, 1990.
Lewis, J. Patrick, and Roberto Innocenti. *The Last Resort*. Mankato: Creatives Editions, 2002.
Lionni, Leo. *Frederick*. New York: Pantheon, 1967.
Lowry, Lois, and Valentina Cruz. *Anastasia Krupnik*. New York: Houghton Mifflin, 1979.
Mayer, Mercer. *There's a Nightmare in my Closet*. New York: Puffin Books, 1968.
Messenger, Norman. *Annabel's House*. New York: Orchard Books, 1989.
McAllister, Angela, and Gary Blythe. *Milo and the Night Marker*. London: Puffin, 2003.
McKee, David. *Three Monsters*. London: Andersen Press, 2005.
Nanclares, Silvia. *La siesta*. Madrid: Kókinos, 2000.
Oram, Hyawyn, and Satoshi Kitamura. *In the Attic*. New York: Henry Holt and Co., 1988.
Oxembury, Helen:.*The Restaurant*. London: Walker Books, 1983.
Riddell, Chris. *The Fibbs*. London: Walker Books, 1987.
Ródenas, Antonia, and Solé Vendrell, Carme. *Un grapat de petons*. Barcelona: Barcanova, 2001.
Rosen, Michael, and Helen Oxembury. *We're Going on a Bear Hunt*. New York: Macmillan, 1989.
Spurr, Elizabeth, and Martín Matje. *A Pig Named Perrier*. New York: Hyperion, 2002.
Tan, Shaun. *The Red Tree*. Port Melbourne: Thomas C. Lothian, 2005.
Tashlin, Frank. *The Bear that Wasn't*. New York: Dutton & Co, 1946.
Ventura, Antonio, and Pablo Amargo. *No todas las vacas son iguales*. Caracas: Camelia Ediciones, 1999.
Waddell, Martín, and Patrick Benson: *The Tough Princess*. London: Walker Books, 1986.
Weatherby, Mark Alan: *My Dinosaur*. New York: Scholastic, 1997.
Wells, Rosemary. *Noisy Nora*. New York: Penguin Group, 1973.
Wolfe, Frances. *Where I Live*. Toronto: Tundra Books, 2001.

Secondary Sources

Bernstein, Basil. *Class, Codes, and Control*. 2nd edition. London: Routledge and Kegan Paul, 1977.
Colomer, Teresa. *La formación del lector literario. Narrativa infantil y juvenil actual*. 2nd edition. Madrid: Fundación Germán Sánchez Ruipérez, 2009.
Colomer, Teresa. "Las buenas formas. Tendencias de la literatura infantil y juvenil." *Anuario sobre el libro infantil y juvenil 2004*. 2004. 73–95.
Durkheim, Emile. *La división del trabajo social*. Madrid: Akal, 1982.
Lipovetsky, Gilles. *Los tiempos hipermodernos*. Madrid: Anagrama, 2006.
Simone, Raffaele. *Diario de una niña. ¿Qué quiere decir Maistock?* Barcelona: Gedisa, 1992.

Chapter Four
How to Make Sense
Reflections on the Influence of Eighteenth Century Picturebooks on Picturebooks of Today

Nina Christensen

Picturebooks are among other things used as a means to introduce the child to nothing less but the organization of the world and the representation of this world in words and images. In this chapter, I will discuss examples of how three different principles of organizing the world are presented to children through picturebooks: one based on a Christian paradigm, one based on Enlightenment philosophy, and one based in a modern secularized view of the world. The common denominator of the books discussed is an intent to discuss human nature in relation to classical and Christian ideas of vice and virtue, and that in spite of differences in time and context, they all address a human being with an urge to try to make sense of the world.

The first example is an illustrated book of 252 biblical proverbs for children by one Melchior Mattsperger *Geistliche Herzens-Einbildungen im zweihundert und fünfzig Biblischen Figur-Sprüchen angedeutet* (Spiritual Influences on the Heart in Two hundred and Fifty Biblical Proverbs, 1685). A Danish translation was published in 1710 and reprinted four times during the eighteenth century (1743, 1744, 1756 and 1775). In the book of proverbs, an absolute truth is posited and pictures and texts are supposed to be able to represent this truth.

The second example is a small ABC written by the German educator, writer and philosopher Karl Philipp Moritz: *Neues ABC Buch* (New ABC Book, 1790), illustrated by Peter Haas. In Moritz' book, the truth is mankind's inborn reason, and image and text represent this truth by addressing and referring to the reader's ability to deduct and reason. Interestingly, this text was re-illustrated by German illustrator Wolf Erlbruch in 2000, and in this case a postmodern visual language is combined with the eighteenth-century text with thought-provoking results.

The last example is an extraordinary book by Danish illustrator Dorte Karrebæk. In *Den sorte bog. Om de syv dødssynder* (The Black Book. On the Seven Deadly Sins. 2007), the author presents images and content with relations to the eighteenth century, but depicts a universe with conflicting and destructive individual needs, not a coherent, complete perspective, and an imagetext which does not refer to an inherent truth. Only some individuals who are able to reflect and be empathetic can create some partial meaning in a fragmented, grotesque and egoistical world.

Picturebooks in Denmark in the Late Eighteenth Century

In the late eighteenth century, one of the very few books with illustrations wealthy Danish children had access to, was a small book translated from German, with 252 proverbs or quotes from the bible. In the preface, the publisher discusses the relationship between text and image[1]. According to him, "images are the first origin of letters,"[2] which he argues is evident in, for instance, Egyptian hieroglyphs. Thus, images and letters, words and pictures are linked in a way that resembles W. J. T. Mitchell's concept "imagetext," which is defined thus: "the term 'imagetext' designates composite, synthetic works (or concepts) that combine image and text" (Mitchell 89). The author of the preface writes that children have "always a vast desire to imagine an object alive or depicted in front of their eyes," and therefore the book will be useful for children, particularly when "the images and their explanation are told to them and interpreted in a good manner." The adult has to engage in a dialogue with the child concerning the signification of the images, the process of interpretation of sign and language is supposed to be cooperative, but the message transmitted is not subject of interpretation. The preface states that the book contains "the words of the everlasting truth" (2).

After the preface, the book is divided into two parts: A list of numbered written proverbs is followed by the same proverbs, one per page, in a combination of text and image. The child is supposed to learn to be able to "read" the visual representation of the object, while the adult will read the representation through the verbal text. If in doubt concerning the interpretation, the adult can check the written text at the beginning. Most of the images are easy to decode, even 300 years after. The image illustrates the proverb "It is easier for a camel to pass through the eye of a needle than for a rich man to enter the kingdom of God." (Mark, 10, 25).[3]

In this case, the child can rely on a likeness of image and object. In other instances, the relationship between sign and the object or concept it refers to is symbolic or conventional, as for instance in the visual representations of the word "life," where the quote reads: "Persevere in right conduct and

Figure 4.1 Page from *CCLII Udvalde og med 800 Billeder udlagde Bibelske Hoved-Sprog*. [52 Selected Biblical Proverbs Interpreted with 800 Pictures]. Copenhagen: Nicolaus Møller, 1775, p. 176.

loyalty and you shall find life and honour" (Proverbs, 21, 21) (no. 108). Life is depicted as a young child sitting on a skull blowing soap bubbles, a so-called "homo bulla," a typical seventeenth century allegorical motif showing life as a brief and transitory state. In this case, the child is introduced to a symbolic relationship between sign and concept. In at least one other case, the author/illustrator tries to create a "natural" connection between letter and sound: In number 92, the imagetext reads: "The garlands have fallen from our heads; woe betide us, sinners that we are. For this we are sick at heart, for all this our eyes grow dim." In Danish the letter "W" is pronounced in the same way as the Danish and German word for "woe," in Danish: "ve," in German "weh." The sign "W" appears as an image representing not a letter, but a sound.

In this book, the child is introduced to at least three modes of representation:

- the written text represented by the letters
- the visual text which the child is supposed to learn to decode, both in a symbolic sense and as images referring to objects, concepts and qualities, represented by the images
- the oral text, the sound represented by the adult reading aloud as the child watches the written text.

One could say that the child reader experiences a text consisting of sound, image and written text and that these three forms of representation together represent the Holy Scripture. Thus, the book has one educational aspect, which is to socialize the child into being able to decode certain accepted ways of representing the world in sound, image and letters. Another part of the educational purpose is to transmit information about vice and virtue. The child is introduced to greed by an image of a rich man gathering all his money. Greed is presented as a vice, and gluttony is a sin, according to the representation of Jude, 12 where the gluttonous are "clouds carried away by the wind without giving rain, trees that in the season bear no fruit, dead twice over and pulled up by the roots. They are the fierce waves of the sea (. . .) they are stars that have wandered from their course" (248). Vice and virtue are presented to children through the text from the Bible as well as in small explanatory rhymes or poems on each page. In this way, the text from the bible is adapted to the use of children.

Sense and Sensibility in Children's Literature of the Eighteenth Century

In a Scandinavian and an Anglo-Saxon context there has been a tendency to establish an opposition between educative and entertaining children's literature (Darton 1932, Juncker 2006). In relation to eighteenth-century children's literature, German scholars have presented a more balanced approach. For instance, the editors of *Handbuch zur Kinder- und Jugendliteratur. Von 1750 bis 1800*, Theodor Brüggemann and Hans-Heino Ewers, accentuate the fact that in a German context in the second half of the eighteenth century writers and educators intended not the division between educative and entertaining texts, but the dissolution of the oppositions: "Works should often be both: Educative reader for schools, and textbook and entertaining book for private reading" (8). Writers and publishers of children's books in Denmark and Germany at this time were often educators who wanted to stimulate children's "lust for reading" and "thirst of knowledge" and at the same time provide them with "noble pastime and worthy profit," as the publisher of a newspaper for children wrote in 1779.[4] One aim of literature for children was to participate in the education of virtuous citizens, and a basic principle in stories, dialogues, plays, letters and songs is that vice is punished, virtue rewarded. Children in fiction could portray variations of either the seven cardinal sins or the seven virtues: prudence, temperance, fortitude, justice, faith, hope and charity. The first four virtues have their roots in antiquity, while faith, hope and charity were included by Christianity.

In spite of this explicit interest in the development of the child's character, one cannot interpret these texts for children solely as part of a moral crusade. One must also view them as an important part of the dissemination of ideas and ideals derived from Enlightenment philosophy. One sign of this is that children are not always portrayed as passive victims of or objects to adults' upbringing, but also as individuals who can gain knowledge and thereby authority. Thus, one aim of the progressive educators was to teach children to reason. German philanthropists, like Rochow, Basedow and Campe, organized their own schools and published their own books for children, on the basis of the notion that the child should learn from experience. The so called "object pictures" were thought to be important in order for the child to be able to learn and experience in a joyful manner.

In Germany very beautiful picturebooks for children were thus published towards the end of the eighteenth century, most famous probably Basedow's *Elementarwerk* (Elementary Work, 1774) with engravings by Chodowiecki and Bertuch's *Bilderbuch für Kinder* (Picturebook for Children, 1790–1830) in twelve volumes with text in German and French. Texts in picturebooks from this period show that children were not necessarily expected to be able to decode images, to know the conventions of written text or images, or to decode the combination of the two. This is illustrated by a small ABC from 1790 written by the German writer and educationalist Karl Philipp Moritz (1756–1793). The parallel lives of written text and image is illustrated from the first page: Three different ways of writing the alphabet are depicted and the child has to learn that there are three different signs for the same letter and two different sign-systems for the representation of numbers. Children are apparently supposed to learn them all. After these "imagetexts" follow twenty-six short prose texts, and after that twenty-six copper etchings colored by hand and accompanied by a written letter and a short caption beneath. Interesting questions in this connection is, how children are taught about the relationship between text, sound and image, and which content the "imagetext" is supposed to convey.

The twenty-six prose texts present key thoughts in the philosophy and pedagogy of the Enlightenment. The second text starts like this: "The second image shows a boy, who reads in a book while sitting under a tree." Then follows a description of how books are organized: "Letters are placed by the pictures. Words stand under the pictures. A person who cannot read does only possess the images" and the conclusion is: "Books make young people clever" (7). In the following text, children are introduced to the relationship between text, sound, and image. The text explains that the image shows an organ and that the organ makes a sound because human beings make the organ do so. But a human being can speak whenever he or she wishes, and what the first person narrator reads, he can hear with his ear: "Now I read aloud. And hear with my ears, what I read." What he sees, reads and hears enters his head and it must stay there: "When I close the book, then I must still know what I have read" (9). In this way the child is socialized to the organization of text, sound and image: Representation in images, representation in text and representation in sound.

The images, made by Peter Haas, are generally very simple compared to picturebook illustrations of our age. The intention is apparently primarily mimetic representation: The representation has to be as similar, as close to the object as possible, for the child to be able to identify a real eye from the representation of the object. The written text refers to the illustration: If the written text describes a child sitting under a tree, the illustration shows a child sitting under a tree. The intention is illustrative in both senses of the word: You see and you get information and thereby you can potentially master the world.

A fundamental element of the Enlightenment philosophy is humanism as "belief in human beings," because they are able to reason and to judge wisely, unlike animals. One of the texts ends: "The book can be taken away from me—thinking can not be taken away from me" (13–14). Other texts and images represent the educated citizen and his or her vices or virtues. Vices represented in this case are pride, greed, gluttony, and sloth. It is done in a very simple manner: Gluttony and greed are presented as a rich man who has more than he needs, in contrast to the virtuous temperate man, a wandering man who "is satisfied when he quenches his thirst with water," since "the human being needs little in order to be content" (24).

One of the things a human being does need in order to be able to live happily is reason, defined as the capability to learn, to think and to deduct. The author of the ABC, Karl Philipp Moritz, also published a small 'logic for children', and in this he wrote about the importance of being able to organize one's thoughts. This book opens with a description of the messy boy Fritz, who is unable to organize his clothes, his books or anything else. Fortunately, he gets a new teacher, who teaches him on all occasions to "put together what belongs together and separate what does not belong together." As a reward, his parents want to give Fritz a "Naturalienkabinett," a collection of items from nature, but the teacher suggests that Fritz should make his own and thereby learn how organize such items himself. This story introduces the reader to the aim of the book, which is to teach the reader "the big art of *classification* and *order*, of *comparison* and *differentiation* on which the whole happiness of the reasonable human being is based" (Moritz 1793, 9).

In the ABC the highest good is the human mind. Moritz informs the child about death in a very matter-of-fact way: The human being stops breathing and it is dead. He writes: "Night follows day. Sleep follows being awake. Rest follows work. Death follows life" (Moritz 1794, 27–28). The child's everyday experience is transferred to the course of life. There is no life after death according to Moritz, but exactly because of that must one make use of time, which is presented as the most valuable resource. The argument for this is that only actions live on after death: "Every thing comes to an end. But the works live on" (31).

Thus, fundamental ideas of the Enlightenment are present in Moritz's book: Ideas of education/bildung, of humanism, of secularization. The ideology behind Moritz' book is apparently that human beings can, if they wish, base a society on humanism, reason and virtues. The production of picturebooks made from these principles can contribute to that development. The idealism is almost overwhelming.

The Enlightenment Revisited in Twenty-First Century Picturebooks

A brief comment on the re-illustration of Moritz' text by Wolf Erlbruch will serve as a transition to the last key example. Erlbruch's image of how the world can be visually represented to a child is in many ways different from Haas' small copper engravings. In Erlbruch's case, technical development has made it possible to place text and image side by side, but this is the only way in which a more coherent representation takes form. While the engravings from 1790 were characterized by unity: One central perspective, a well-defined scene with one character and one action, Erlbruch's visual representation is characterized by a combination of simplicity and fragmentation. Fragmentation is evident in the collage-technique, where he places all kinds of images, types of papers, lines, forms of representation (e.g., photo, drawing, and map) together in a heterogeneous depiction of differentiality. For instance, in his illustration of "splendour and abundance," all of the overweight, decadent, engorging people look in different directions and concentrate on their own eating. Except for the woman in focus, who looks appealingly towards the spectator as if wanting to be watched, she herself being either drugged or absorbed in her own world. Or both. This image gives associations to Georg Grosz's Dadaistic depictions of German petit bourgeoisie of the 1920s. Dadaistic inspiration also seem to be present in Erlbruch's depiction of perishableness/mortality: A fork flies about among rocks, houses made out of numbers and lightning made of paper for bookkeeping.

Erlbruch's illustration seems to express a certain disbelief in the firm image of the human being as a person able to reason presented in the text. But at the same time his illustrations encourage the spectator to use his or her deductive abilities. One can, for instance, watch his illustration "Afterthought." The images illustrate the text mentioned before, which says that a book can be taken away from a human being, but that thinking can not, and the text ends: "I cannot see the spirit of the man. For the spirit of the man is in him." Three images show a man sitting at a table. The illiterate child will ideally be able to deduct this message from the images:

1. The man sits with an open book.
2. The man has closed the book.
3. The man has put the book away, and the child will then ideally ask him or herself what has happened.

Underneath the pictures the text reads: "The spirit of man thinks in him." Another example of Erlbruch's belief in the child's ability to read and deduct from pictures is the narrative formed by the first and the last image in the book both showing a reading child. In the first image the child is sitting happily reading with his finger in the book. One does not pay much attention to the fact that his finger is red. On the last illustration the letter in the eye of the boy has moved from A to Z, and a thorny stalk of a rose and a bandage indicates that he pricked his finger on the rose. The eighteenth century text which accompanied the image of a book reads: "An open book encircled by roses. Industry in learning bears its own reward. Who wants to pick the rose, must not be afraid of the thorn" (Moritz 1794, 35). The child in Erlbruch's image has not been afraid of knowledge—his red chins and his smile might, on the contrary, be read as a sign of a twenty-first century child who also represents lust for reading and thirst of knowledge.

An interpretation of Erlbruch's re-illustration of Moritz' text could be that in this case optimism and belief in the capacities of human beings is combined with a certain scepticism and transmission of experiences with less fortunate characteristics in human beings.

Dorte Karrebæk: An Enlightened Child in the Twenty-First Century

In 2007 *The Black Book. On the Seven Deadly Sins,* by the highly esteemed Danish author and illustrator Dorte Karrebæk, was published. The vignette on the title leaf indicates a meta-perspective: A small dog holds a black book resembling the actual black book in its mouth. On the first spread, one notices a man in the left corner, who has a black book in his pocket. A road sign with an arrow leads our attention in the direction of some trees and a road, and on the next picture we find that he drops the book. The arrow on the road sign points away from the straight road and in the next picture in the direction of the boy who receives the book from the dog. The cover of this book is depicted, and one will almost instinctively compare it with the cover of the physical book, which is thinner and lacks the name Dorte Karrebæk on the cover.

A brief text by a first-person narrator explains that the book is the notebook of a scientist: He writes: "For many years I have been cultivating special characteristics of insects. I have isolated seven that are predominant in the world we live in, and I have inoculated them in seven different species, which I will describe thoroughly on the following pages. All that is left is to watch how they will develop" (s.p). He has named the species after the seven deadly sins: Pride, greed, lust, envy, anger, gluttony, and sloth, and the species are first described visually in sepia pen drawings. Animals in different stages of development are numbered and explanations given below them so that together with the pink paper the layout resembles an old natural science book or an encyclopaedia. The species bear names derived from the Latin words for the seven deadly sins: "Greed" comes in the shape of "the Avaritians," and this creature is depicted as egg, young, male and a female enlarged, and natural size.

Gluttony also appears in the shape of "the gulans": Male, female, young one, natural size. The reader is introduced to the magnifying glass, and a map of the habitat of the species is presented. In the next spread the boy from the first pages returns. Arrows lead him and the reader in the direction of a forest,

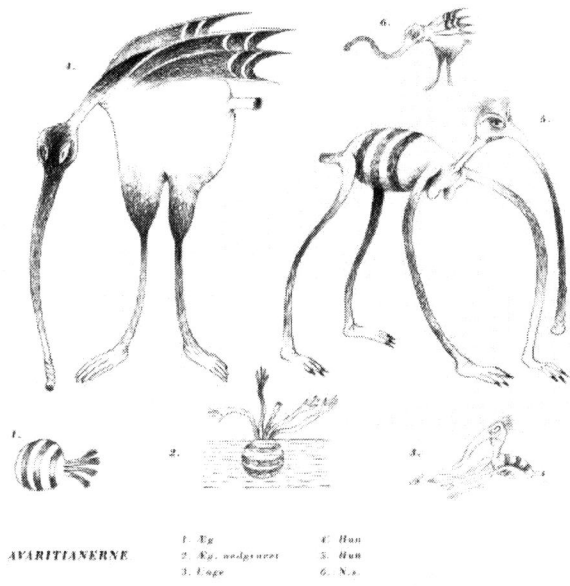

Figure 4.2 Illustration from Dorte Karrebæk: *Den sorte bog. Om de syv dødssynder.* Copenhagen: Alma, 2007.

the boy carrying a small box that resembles a "Naturalienkabinett" or boxes with collections of insects. He starts watching the "superbians," the proud ones, and then moves on to the "avaritians." In a comic-like sequence, the reader sees what the boy sees: that the angry-looking creature collects items, repeatedly saying: "I can use that." The loot is carefully stored behind barbed wire, fences or bricks, and the message to those who tries to get near is "Go away." The portrait of Greed ends with an illustration showing a specimen killed and archived in the boy's box. Lust, envy, anger, and gluttony are portrayed in a similar allegoric and caricature-like manner. Finally, sloth is presented as a naked male and female figure standing absolutely passive without any expressions on their faces and without mouth or eyes. A young one of the sloth species is unable to get the attention of his parents and cries out "Help," while he looks appealing towards the boy-scientist and the reader behind the magnifying glass. The boy collects the full-grown specimen of the species for his collection, but the young one gets out alive: "It is good one is a human being" the human boy thinks. But behind him "homo sapiens" or the man who lost the book—and who maybe wrote it—is lying as if dead on the area which belongs to human beings. The book ends with a depiction of the dead incarnations of sloth, a written list of the seven deadly sins and the name of the species which represent the qualities in the book.

Compared to the collection of biblical proverbs and the message of idealistic humanism of Karl Philipp Moritz the message of Karrebæk is more ambiguous. Basically, the book represents a narrative with a beginning, middle and an end: A boy finds a book, he reads the book, wants to find what is in the book and does so. He collects the items depicted in the book and brings them home. But this narrative is my reconstruction: there are no written words to interpret the meaning of the images and not a narrator in a written text to organize the narrative. The illustrator is the organizing principle: she sees to that the spectator can construct a narrative from the images, and in the beginning she places the spectator in a third person perspective. The motif is repeatedly seen from the same perspective at a certain distance of the main character. She uses shadows—as Karrebæk often does—as a kind of subtext to the main image, and the shadows in this case lead the spectator in the direction of the boy: He is the main character, not the man who ran away. Then the story within the story, The Black Book of the boy, is opened, and the written text of this book has an explicit first-person narrator. This narrator is apparently a scientist, a person who knows "The big art of classification and order, of comparison and differentiation" as Karl Philipp Moritz put it. And so Karrebæk's scientist classifies and differentiates the species. The written text in this book is the imitation of a non-fiction publication, and the reader in this part of the book seeks in vain for a traditional narrative. Furthermore the "book" by the scientist plays on the convention of identity between sign and object in scientific books: If number one says "egg" one looks for number one and must suspend disbelief and accept that this is the image of an egg of an "avaritian". But at the same time, the illustrations are so grotesque and strange, that one does not come to think of actually existing animals, but rather on the extraordinary, scary, funny, and larger-than-life creatures in paintings by Hieronymus Bosch. The reader will decode the images as a fantasy or parody of a science book, in spite of—or perhaps also because of—the cautious effort to mime a scientific way of thinking, all the way down to the image of the magnifying glass and how it functions.

Scientists—especially during the Enlightenment—make maps, and so does the first-person narrator. Maps represent the world. So the boy can take the map from the book and apply it to his reality. And he too can organize, classify, and compare, and when he does that, the reader of the book sees with his eyes through the magnifying glass. As readers, we become scientists ourselves, but unfortunately what we see is exactly the opposite of order: We watch stupid, ignorant, selfish, angry, violent beings, in relation to which a common denominator is the dysfunctional relationship between the sexes and parents and offspring. The greedy are too busy guarding their property to take notice of their children, and they even steal food from them. The envious are so absorbed in fighting that they rip their offspring in parts, the gorging eat their offspring, and the indolent simply do not notice that they have been reproduced, while their child looks appealing at the boy scientist and thereby at the spectator. After that the perspective changes back to a third person point of view, where the boy is seen from outside as a young scientist back in a world characterized by order. The only disorder is that apparently homo sapiens—the author or at least carrier of The Black Book—is dead. In the next-to-last image, the boy scientist looks appealingly towards the spectator, who is placed above him, as if he is viewed by an adult close to him. His thought "I am glad I am a human being," is counterpoint to the dog: "I am glad I am a dog."

The visual language, which includes changing points of view in text and image, and many visual codes from different sources (e.g., comics, picturebooks, science books, paintings) is apparently addressed to a very competent reader—or spectatorship. Karrebæk trusts the reader to be able to decode the complex narrative in images, where words are added only when absolutely necessary, for instance in the representation of dialogue. The supremacy of the written text is gone and handed over to the image. Therefore it is also apparently a silent book that one will and can read alone—or a book that creates a need to speak and try to articulate the readers' surprise and confusion after having watched the narrative.

Karrebæk's book can be read as an allegory over the human species. If one looks at the main character, the boy, he looks at himself as a human in contrast to the animal-like creatures he studies: he is able to read, to study, to investigate and systematize, but he is also empathetic, since he is the only one who tries to save a young one from its gruesome parents. The man who drops the book and who in the end lies dead as Homo sapiens is apparently "the knowing human," but he does not survive. Apart from these two figures, the rest of the characters in the book are mixtures of human beings and animals, they are the scientist's mutants of human and animal. Though these anthropomorphic animals represent vices, the representation follows the traditional pattern of depictions of vice and virtue in children's books: Vice is punished since the creatures die. In this way, one could claim that Karrebæk's book is a reaction towards the Romantic image of the child. She depicts the child, the boy scientist, as the most mature person, and the adult creatures as irrational, vicious, and depraved. In Freudian terms they are driven by the "id" attributed to the infant, while the child is apparently driven by curiosity *and* empathy, reason and emotion, and that makes him survive, while the human being who only tries to control and order but does not possess empathy dies.

Conclusion

The books analysed in this chapter reflects different ways in which picturebooks from different periods of time try to educate the child. On a basic level, the books instruct the reading child to master various forms of visual and verbal codes. The books help to teach the child visual and verbal literacy. The case of the eighteenth-century examples show that the visual code in particular is supposed to be unknown to the child; the child is not supposed to know how text and image can interact, which is evidently related to the scarce number of illustrated books for children from that period. The implied child reader of the twenty-first century on the other hand is expected to be visually literate. A number of complex visual codes are used, both in Erlbruch's and Karrebæk's work. The implied child reader is definitely expected to be a skilled reader of images.

The three books discuss ideal human behavior in very different ways, but all three books play on the opposition between vice and virtue. The first example presents a God-given order of vices and virtues. Moritz describes a "human" order in which the virtuous citizen can tell vice from virtue by using his or her inborn reason. Karrebæk, and to some degree Erlbruch, present a society characterized by the blurring of boundaries between vice and virtue, where the child has to educate him- or herself by the help of books. Though the most recently published examples show less belief in the reasoning of human beings, picturebooks apparently still encourage the child to try to make sense of the world by reflecting on the order, or lack of order, of the world.

Notes

1. The Danish preface is a prose version of the original German preface that is written in rhymed verses.
2. When no other translation is available, translations of quotes in Danish and German are mine.
3. Translations of quotations from the Bible are from *The New English Bible*. Oxford: Oxford University Press, 1970.
4. Preface to *Adresse-Avis for Børn*, (Newspaper for Children), no. 1, 1779.

Bibliography

Primary Sources

CCLII Udvalde og med 800 Billeder udlagde Bibelske Hoved-Sprog. Copenhagen: Nicolaus Møller, 1775.
Adresse-Avis for Børn, no. 1, 1779.
Karrebæk, Dorte. *Den sorte bog. Om de syv dødssynder*. Copenhagen: Alma, 2007.
Mattsperger, Melchior. *Geistliche Herzens-Einbildungen im zweihundertundfünfzig biblischen Figur-Sprüchen angedeutet*.[Augsburg 1685] Reprint: Hildesheim: Georg Olms, 1965.
Moritz, Karl Philipp. *Versuch einer kleinen praktischen Kinderlogik, welche auch zum Theil für Lehrer und Denker geschrieben ist*. Berlin: August Mylius, 1786 [second edition, 1793].
Moritz, Karl Philipp. *Neues ABC Buch welches zugleich eine Anleitung zum Denken für Kinder*. Illustrated by Peter Haas. Berlin: Christian Gottfried Schöne, 1790, second edition 1794. Reprinted by Insel Verlag: Frankfurt am Main, 1980.
Moritz, Karl Philipp, and Wolf Erlbruch. *Neues ABC-Buch*. München: Kunstmann, 2000.

Secondary Sources

Brüggemann, Theodor, and Hans-Heino Ewers. Eds. *Handbuch zur Kinder- und Jugendliteratur. Von 1750 bis 1800*. Stuttgart: Metzler, 1982.
Darton, F. J. Harvey. *Children's Books in England. Five Centuries of Social Life*. London: British Library Board, 1999 [first edition in 1932].
Ewers, Hans-Heino. "Einleitung." In *Kinder- und Jugendliteratur der Aufklärung* edited by Hans-Heino Ewers. 5–59. Stuttgart: Reclam, 1980.
Immel, Andrea, and Michael Witmore. "Introduction. Little Differences: Children, Their Books, and Culture in the Study of Early Modern Europe." In *Childhood and Children's Books in Early Modern Europe* edited by Andrea Immel and Michael Whitmore. 1–19. London: Routledge, 2005.
Juncker, Beth. *Om processen. Det æstetiskes betydning i børns kultur*. Copenhagen: Tiderne Skifter, 2006.
Mitchell, W. J. T. *Picture Theory. Essays on Verbal and Visual Representation*. Chicago and London: The University of Chicago Press, 1994.

Chapter Five
"All this book is about books"
Picturebooks, Culture, and Metaliterary Awareness

Evelyn Arizpe

> *I don't think this book is for like little children. The story is for little children but the way it's written is like for adults because, because it's quite shocking where the words are.*
>
> **Abdul**

What exactly was it that 11-year-old Abdul found shocking about "where the words are" in Oliver Jeffers' picturebook, *The Incredible Book Eating Boy*? Abdul was from a Muslim Algerian family and spoke both Arabic and French. He had been in the United Kingdom for approximately four years and his English was quite fluent. As he and his classmates read and talked about Jeffers' picturebook, Abdul laughed at the jokes in the text and at the illustrations. He did not seem to have any problems understanding the postmodern features of this book—the comic-strip features, metafiction, fragmentation, open-endedness, and the use of different fonts or the open ending. Once we talked further, his comment became clearer: he was referring not only to the spatial arrangement of the text on the spreads, but also to the way the artist has placed both text and illustrations on backgrounds of different types of paper and book materials, some of which have words printed on them. Like most of his peers, Abdul was both surprised and fascinated by the way the artist has "used" bits of old books and other materials to create his picturebook but he was the one who expressed his feelings most strongly about it.

In 2007, James McGonigal and I worked with a group of immigrant children, pupils in a Scottish primary school, to find out how literacy experiences and questions of cultural identity influenced their understanding of Scottish children's fiction (McGonigal and Arizpe 2007). In 2008, I invited some of these children to take part in further research using two (non-Scottish) picturebooks: *Traction Man is Here* by Mini Grey (2005) and *The Incredible Book Eating Boy* (2006). My aim was to explore how they made sense of postmodern features that are not usually present either in more traditional storybooks or in textbooks for learning a new language. My original intention for this chapter was to describe and discuss this exploration and, for the most part, that is what I have done. However, as I listened once again to the children's observations, I also began to get a sense of their reaction to the picturebook as a cultural object: a reaction—such as Abdul's—which seemed to stem from their experiences and expectations of what a "Picturebook" was supposed to be like, how it was made and what it was meant for. Practitioners and researchers seldom consider this "metaliterary" understanding when children respond to picturebooks. This chapter traces evidence of this understanding, discusses what it might mean in terms of children's literary meaning-making, and concludes with suggestions for further research.

Previous Research on Culturally Diverse Pupils and Literacy

Writing about conflicting home-school literacies, Eve Gregory and Jean Biarnès (1994) described the case of a young British Chinese boy who was starting school, Tony, in which the contradictions between the approaches to teaching reading and writing of his British teacher on one hand, and his traditional Chinese grandfather on the other, led to a radical negative change in his behavior in the classroom and a refusal to look at or to take home any "school" books, including picturebooks. In the section entitled "The Talismanic Value of Books" Gregory and Biarnès recount how the teacher's visit to Tony's family home revealed that, in Chinese culture, books are highly valued and given to children as a reward *after* learning to read. Therefore, for Tony's grandfather, "to provide a supply of books before this, devalues both the book itself and the concept of hard work" (22). The researchers remind us of the findings of psychologists, anthropologists and ethnographers which show that children make sense of the world and interpret their experiences according to familial social and cultural background. *Ways with Words*, Shirley Brice Heath's seminal study from 1983, clearly illustrates how this includes an understanding of literacy learning. The concept of a "book," as well as a "picturebook," falls within this understanding.

Within her wider work on syncretic literacy, Gregory has analyzed how bilingual children construct and negotiate meaning in a new language and how picturebooks invite interaction with text (Gregory 1994). More recently, she and a team of researchers have looked at the syncretic literacy practices that occur within ethnic minority families. Although different from Western practices at a number of levels, these domestic cultural/literacy practices can provide a wealth of knowledge and interpretation strategies (Gregory et al. 2007). This coincides with Kate Pahl's (2004) ethnographic research on ephemera and other responses to popular culture and the media in multilingual homes that highlight the children's hybrid experiences and narratives. Hybrid responses were also evident in the findings of Arizpe and McGonigal (2007), where children interpreted and connected Scottish stories within their previous experiences of texts. None of these studies, however, focused on picturebooks in particular and on how they might be linked to the understanding of what a 'picturebook' is and their relationship to expectations of literacy learning.

Where contemporary, multi-layered picturebooks are concerned, there is now a helpful and growing group of studies on reader-response (among others, Arizpe and Styles 2003, Pantaleo 2008, Sipe 2008, and the essays in Evans 2009). Some studies have focused on picturebooks to explore the influence of culture on interpretation and how they can aid in the adaptation of culturally diverse children to their new communities, particularly through language (e.g., Bromley 1996, Colledge 2005, Laycock 1998, Mines 2000 and the essays in Enever and Schmid-Schönbein 2006). Findings confirm that cultural literacy experiences are involved both in the reading of the words and in the discussion of the visuals—both at a cognitive and at an affective level.

In Kathy Coulthard's chapter (in Arizpe and Styles 2003) on the responses of bilingual children to Anthony Browne's *The Tunnel* and *Zoo*, she describes the ways in which children from diverse ethnic backgrounds and at different (English) language levels were able to access some of the more complex layers of meaning in these picturebooks. However, it was clear that for some of them, the differences between home and school practices meant that, first, the visual was of less importance than the written word and second, that the text was not meant to be questioned or discussed. Coulthard gives the example of Funda (the child of Turkish immigrants who were not literate in English), who was more concerned with decoding the words and labelling what she saw in the pictures than with exploring their relationship. This resulted in her responses being predominantly literal.[1] Yet when Funda is moved by an image of the solitary boy in the cage at the end of *Zoo*, "she is able to draw on life experiences to see beyond the literal" and respond more empathetically, thus "moving into the readerly gap" (183, 184). To take pupils "beyond the literal" was precisely the aim of another project, carried out by Jane Bednall and Leanne Cranston with Eve Bearne (2008), by understanding how bilingual pupils' reading experiences were shaped by their cultural experience. Supported by the teachers, the children explored various picturebooks; they came up with questions for particular images, wrote poems and took digital photographs. Interviews at the end of the project revealed that the pupils had developed a sophisticated understanding of how these multimodal texts worked.

The Context for the Picturebook Project

The immigrant pupils involved in the picturebook project described here were aged eleven through twelve and in the last year of two primary schools in working-class areas of Glasgow with a high proportion of asylum-seekers and refugees. The children who participated in the study were Abdul (Algeria), Gabriel (Congo), Soraya (Malaysia), Andzej (Slovakia), Neylan and Umay (Turkey), Sirwa (Iraq), Mohammed (Pakistan) and Eshan (second generation Pakistani).[2] In addition, I had the opportunity to interview Cecilia, a recent immigrant from Argentina. Abdul, Gabriel, Neylan, and Umay had been in Scotland for between three and five years; their English was therefore more fluent and they tended to be the more experienced readers. Soraya, Andzej, Sirwa, Cecilia and Mohammed had been in Scotland for less than a year and were more hesitant to articulate their responses.

In order to introduce the project to them in a way that would not make them feel they were being given books for "little" children, I asked them to imagine what would need to be explained to a younger child so that they would understand the picturebook and if there were any clues in the book that would help them. Each hour-long session with up to three children involved reading the picturebook, asking questions (based on the interviews carried out by Arizpe and Styles 2003) and encouraging discussion. The interviews proved to be challenging in a number of ways, particularly because of the time required for dealing with language difficulties.[3] However, all the children were intrigued by the picturebooks and, as the session progressed, the amount of comments and interruptions increased, the volume rose and there was a great deal of backward and forward movement through the pages. This signalled their excitement and enjoyment of the picturebooks and also their attainment of a level of comfort which allowed them to manipulate the books and to express their opinions. In what follows I shall describe their responses to each of the picturebooks and then the comparisons they made between the two, before ending with a discussion of these findings.

"This Book is All Jokes": *Traction Man Is Here*

Traction Man Is Here is about the adventures of a toy: a male "action" doll that has different outfits for different missions, whether he is in the jungle, in space or "Sub-Aqua." Wearing distinctive combat boots, "warfare" shirt and "dazzle-painted battle pants," he saves his pet, Scrubbing Brush, from the Mysterious Toes at the Bottom of the Bath and the Dollies from Wicked Professor Spade. His courageous deeds are, as he says himself "all in a day's work." However, when Granny gives him a new outfit for Christmas, "an all-in-one knitted green romper suit and matching bonnet," even the Cupcake laughs at him. Fortunately, in saving the Spoons that have fallen off the kitchen counter, he also manages

"All this book is about books" • 73

to rescue his own dignity and earn a medal. Although he and Scrubbing Brush relax after their last mission, "they know they are ready for Anything."

Grey won the Boston Globe-Horn Book Award in 2005 for *Traction Man*. Another of her books, *The Biscuit Bear* won the Smarties Prize in 2004 and that same year *The Pea and the Princess* was shortlisted for the Kate Greenaway Award. Her picturebooks include metafiction, fragmentation, intertextuality and non-traditional textual and spatial arrangements. They subvert traditional genres such as nursery rhymes, fairytales and, in the case of *Traction Man*, the "superhero" narrative, destabilizing its connotations to masculinity and power. These unexpected subversions and incongruities are the main sources of the humor that pervades her books.

Superheroes, Masculinity and Power

In order to appreciate the romper suit joke (and the book as a whole), readers have to have an understanding of the characteristics of superheroes, such as their (clean-cut) good looks, bravery and power, but also a high level of "masculinity" which is then undermined by the babyish suit implying powerlessness and effeminate behavior. Several children spontaneously used the word "superhero" to describe Traction Man and were able to explain why the book was "a superhero kind of thing": it has adventures and missions, he saves everyone from danger and he is very brave.

These ideas seemed to be mainly gathered from popular culture—from comics, films and computer games about the superheroes the children referred to, such as Spiderman, Superman and Buzz Lightyear. *Traction Man* prompted some of them to begin to question these predictable narratives: "[the author] makes Traction Man want to be the hero; like in lots of movies, the aim is always some girls. I don't know why" (Gabriel seems to have perceived the fallen Spoons as "female"). However, although the children appreciated the irony of the superhero having to wear "a silly costume" (Abdul), they did not see this in terms of the author's intention to challenge the superhero narrative. When asked why the author had created the book, the children's answers reflected mainly educational aims, such as "for small children to learn to read" (Andzej).

Structure, Voice and Humor

Eshan had grown up in the UK and was a keen reader, but like the other pupils in the study, he was clear that *Traction Man* was different from other books because of its episodic narrative and a structure that implies continuity rather than closure:

Eshan: I think it's different because it is imaginative and differently set out from the books that I read.

Evelyn:	How is it differently set out?
Eshan:	It's all these different missions [. . .] and like in the books that I read it's just like all one big story, or like coming to the end at the end . . . I think it just has like different missions and there's no like beginning and end . . .

Another postmodern feature that surprised and puzzled the readers was the narrator's identity. There were some unexpected answers to the question, "Who is telling the story?": "the person who's reading it to you," "Santa," "Traction Man," "a wee bit the author, a wee bit the boy." It was the writing on the scraps of graph paper that, after lengthy discussion, led some of them to the conclusion that the boy had written it. Gabriel and Abdul discussed this issue in more depth:

Abdul:	I think it's the third person because [. . .] if it was Traction Man that was saying, he'd be like "**I** jumped on the pillow," "**I** was wearing these trousers, **I** was wearing my boots" [his emphasis].
[. . .]	
Evelyn:	Or could it be the boy?
Abdul:	No, it couldn't possibly be the boy [. . .] but I think so they tried to make it sound like it's the boy because like they wouldn't want like an old man telling the story or something, they'd want somebody their age.
Gabriel:	I think it's the boy 'cos the toys can't move themselves [he goes on to compare this to how movement in film is created by computer]. I think it's the boy telling the story but the author is moving the toys.

Later, Gabriel went back to the letter to Santa on the title page, which seems to have been written by the boy on the same graph paper as evidence to support his argument.

Like several of the other children, Andzej's favorite spread was the last one, where Traction Man and Scrubbing Brush are "floating" on a blue carpet after their last mission next to a pair of scissors that look like a lurking shark. Although none of them used the word "irony," the readers recognized that the humor in this picture comes not only from the scissors but also because it is clearly going to lead the hero and his pet into yet another adventure. As Mohammed said, "it's funny because they are relaxing and scissors coming to get them and they don't even know it." Andzej's knowledge of English was limited (just as his knowledge of British books) but he was able to grasp the way in which humor permeates the picturebook: "This book is just all jokes!"

Imaginary and Creative Play

The action doll's movement was one of the aspects that caused debate: whether Traction Man was "really" doing all those heroic things, whether the boy was "taking it around," whether it was the boy's imagination or even a dream. Like Gabriel, several children referred to the film *Toy Story*, where toys have a life and adventures of their own. Eshan, however, thought it was different: "I don't think the Traction Man is really coming to life, I think it's just like imaginative, whereas in *Toy Story* they were really coming alive." Three of the other interviewed boys decided the child was imagining Traction Man's actions because they remembered their own imaginary play: "When I was small I watched *Toy Story* and I had the action man Woody and I used to think he would come to life in the night" (Eshan).

For the girls, the drawings on the floor by the boy's bed provided a clue as to what was "really" happening, allowing them to make the cognitive leap from a first level of interpretation to a more complex level. Their excitement at recognizing this clue is evident in their expression:

Neylan: Oh, I know! He's drawn! He's drawn the pictures [. . .] and he's trying to cut them out. I think he's just imagining . . .
Umay: Oh!
Sirwa: He's just drawing them and he's only making up the story.
Neylan: Maybe someone that really likes drawing and likes the artist thing and he's a little boy 'cos some boys they've got imaginative things and they draw . . .
Umay: And he's cut them out and sticked them on his drawing!
Neylan: Maybe he got a photograph [of the animals] and like brought the things together [. . .]
Umay: You can feel these are like Maths jotter pages [touching the graph paper . . .]
Neylan: Can you see this bit, it's been gluing that bit here . . .

Neylan is saying that the boy is actually imagining, writing, and illustrating the story, based on his toys and objects in his house, on bits of graph paper which he then glues onto "normal" paper, maybe "sticking in" some photographs as well (this interest in the process of "making" the story later transferred to how the author had created the whole book). The appearance and perceived texture of the "bits of paper" prove her point and Neylan's companions seem to agree with her.

The "Wee Ones"

Not surprisingly, these children's first concern about how younger children would respond to the picturebook was about language. They mentioned that some of the "difficult" words would need explaining, especially if they were children "who come from another country." What surprised me was how clear they were about how this audience would react, citing their observations of siblings or cousins. They argued that little boys in particular would like it because they like superheroes and action. I would suggest that their perceptions of a younger audience's response also reveals their own cognitive processes in understanding this picturebook, given they had to "figure out" the jokes that relied on language as they read the book themselves. As they described it, this process involved, first, understanding the language, then looking closely at the pictures, appreciating the action sequences, viewing the transformation of real objects from the "superhero" perspective (i.e., "jet-powered trainer," "Planet Duvet") and finally, "getting the jokes" such as the irony of the superhero relaxing when danger is approaching.

Their perception of younger children's response to *The Incredible Book Eating Boy* also took into account the differences in language, narrative, and format but they were more uncertain about whether they would enjoy it as much as *Traction Man*.

"It's quite shocking where the words are": *The Incredible Book Eating Boy*[4]

Jeffers' 2006 picturebook was selected as a Richard and Judy Christmas book. It was the Irish Children's Book of the Year for 2007 and in the same year the book's young protagonist, Henry, appeared on postcards and book tokens celebrating the 2007 World Book Day. As the title suggests, this picturebook is about a boy who loved to eat books. He becomes very smart until he eats too many too quickly and has to give up. Throughout the book, text and image are clearly linked and for the most part, the illustrations show everything in the relatively simple text. However, the illustrations expand the words in many senses, creating the mood and the humor in the book.

The last page of the picturebook shows Henry eating a mound of broccoli as he reads, next to the words: "Now Henry reads all the time … although every now and then […]" The printed sentence breaks off into tooth marks, suggesting that the missing bottom right-hand corner of the book has been bitten off by Henry himself. In this way, not only the story and the illustrations, but also the design, play on the interlinked ideas of books as objects of "consumption" and of conveyors of knowledge.

Jeffers adds another metafictive layer by recycling backgrounds materials such as discarded pages and covers from books, paper from ledgers and notebooks, and maps. The materials are mostly old and sometimes torn; they would normally be considered rubbish, but in his book the artist has given them new meanings by placing them within his story: dictionary pages and accounts are now wallpaper and the cover of a volume of the Encyclopaedia Britannica has become a theatre stage. These collages also often play on the text: for example, the cover of a book published by the "Board of Education" becomes a school blackboard—a joke for more experienced readers.

Both the final "bite" and the intertextual fragments with which Jeffers has created his book, draw readers' attention to the status of books as material artifacts, made of paper and cardboard as well as other materials such as textiles, wood, and glue. This self-referentiality works at different levels: it is a book about books which is made of books and paper, it is a source of humor but it is also thought-provoking and raises questions about the status of books as sources of learning and knowledge as well as potentially ephemeral objects.

"This book is weird"

Most of the immediate answers to the main question of what younger children would make of the picturebook and what they might find difficult to understand, were based on literal readings of the texts and illustrations. As Neylan said: "This is a book [that's] weird. 'Cos in real life you can't actually eat books. No. Even if you eat it you will be in hospital." They thought the "wee ones" would enjoy the book and think it was "cool," however, they were worried that they might imitate Henry and start eating books or that they might paint and scribble on them (as the author has done on the back cover).

"The writing at the back" (Eshan) provoked much speculation and they spent some time trying to decipher some of the tiny print. After doing this for the first pages, they all decided that this writing did not affect the story although they thought younger children might find it confusing. Eshan concluded that these backgrounds were "very imaginative" and "added more detail" while Soraya said they were more like "patterns" made of letters rather than flowers. Later, after we finished reading and the children were going back to look at it more carefully, they began to pick out some of the intertextual references which made the backgrounds more significant. Although they were unable to grasp the more subtle ones, such as the "Board of Education" book cover and needed help with the "fish and chips" joke (Henry eats *Moby Dick* with chips), they did recognize others: Henry was painted on a map because "maybe he was travelling" (Andzej) and on graph paper because "it's like paper you'd use in class" (Neylan). Eshan and Cecilia came closest to describing the metafictional result: "[Jeffer's done that] to call attention that it was about books, because it was all about books" (Cecilia)[5] and "all this book is about books" (Eshan).

The children also speculated about the way Jeffers had actually put the book together: whether he had stuck the photographic images (which they were quick to point out) and the drawings on the pages or whether he had used a computer. They remarked on the use of fonts for making things "stand out" or have "effect" and "expression." Even with a limited vocabulary, they drew on their knowledge of comic book conventions to name aspects of Jeffer's technique such as "speech bubbles" and "onomatopoeia." Several compared his style to "comics" or "cartoons" because they were "simple" (some said they could draw figures like that themselves). Because of this apparent simplicity, most felt that younger children would have no problems understanding the visual techniques, such as the use of four arms to show movement when Henry juggles books.

The most obviously metafictive device of the book is the "bite" at the end. The fact that the bite also appears on the back endpapers and the cover not only confuses fiction and reality but it also provides the "ending" for the book in place of the words that should be there to finish the sentence. The children reacted to the "bite"(which I had kept out of sight while we read the book) with surprise, incredulity, and finally, laughter. Gabriel realized readers might be confused, but said this would not detract from their enjoyment:

> *You think it looks normal, but when you look at the back there you find somebody who ate the book [. . .] I think that's a good idea because [Gabriel reads the ending] if you read that to the wee ones they'll say "the guy ate this book" and they're gonna go "Oh that's so cool!" [. . .] They'll think Henry ate the book!*

It was at this point that Abdul made his comment that it's "quite shocking where the words are." I would suggest that this observation is a result both of his cultural background and because he had probably never come across a book like this, however, more research would be necessary to explore this hypothesis further.

Comparing and Contrasting

Sometimes the children made spontaneous comparisons between the two picturebooks, particularly about their comic book features, fonts and the way in which they had been put together. Speaking of the main characters, Andzej said that Traction Man was stronger, while Eshan argued that Henry was smarter. Andzej then claimed that Traction Man was also smart because, as the book says, "he was always there" (when needed). Mohammed found the images in *Traction Man* were more attractive because of the use of "bold" colors while Neylan found *Traction Man* had more "details" and was more "decorated" (she disliked the bare spaces and lack of objects in Jeffers' book). Abdul noticed that both picturebooks had images that covered the whole of the page [bleeding into the margins] and Gabriel pointed out that both used bits of "real" paper stuck on the picture.

These two boys also compared the endings, revealing their expectations about the way stories traditionally end but at the same time showing they were familiar with cliff-hangers—a feature of many superhero narratives:

Gabriel:	See the end of this one [*The Incredible*]? It doesn't really end [. . .] they could have wrote something else [also] like in *Traction Man* [. . .] Like they could say, 'he gave up', you just could say 'after, he just walk[ed] away' [. . . it's like a] cliff hanger so you don't really know what was the end.
Evelyn:	But aren't they both a bit like cliff-hangers because . . .
Both:	[interrupting] Yes!
Abdul:	That's a kind of cliff hanger because of the bite mark!
Evelyn:	And in this one?
Gabriel:	There they're not saying anything about the scissors so that's a kind of cliff-hanger as well.

Both picturebooks were described as "funny," probably both in the sense of "weird" and in the sense of causing laughter. The perception of incongruity as humorous has to do with a social and cultural repertoire of expectations: it is the reader's ability to deal with the unexpected that makes a text "funny." The more we read and reread the books together, the more we all laughed, perhaps because of the experience of appreciating it together (as in Pantaleo 2006). Perhaps they began to get "into" the books or they felt more relaxed as I laughed with them. Spontaneous involvement in the text in the form of performance became their way of extending the humor: "doing the voices," making the relevant sounds and mimicking the sounds (for example, the ones Henry makes as he eats a book—including being sick!).[6]

Two peritextual features of the picturebooks caught the children's attention. One was Jeffers' autobiographical blurb on the back flap, where he appears as a child in the photograph, which says he once fed a book to his younger brother. The other was the dedication at the end of *Traction Man* "To my big brother Tony." This led back to the question of why the authors had written/illustrated the books, a question which most children interpreted as what "the point" or "moral" was. Jeffers' intentions were interpreted at a basic didactic level: "to teach children to read," "to tell children not to eat books," "to tell children to get smart by reading" and "to tell children to eat healthy food/vegetables." Only Neylan replied from a more creative perspective when she said she thought the author was trying to say to her brother that if he wants "something real to happen you can imagine and draw it yourself and write your own ideas."

Further Possibilities

I would hypothesize that the didactic view of books and reading is a result of traditional cultural approaches to children's texts which stress the "instructive" rather than the "entertaining" function of books. It may also be linked to cultures where few children's books are available or accessible except for textbooks and where the purposes of reading are principally instructive or religious.

In terms of the visual, researchers and teachers need to consider the way some pupils privilege the status of written text over image, according an authority to the words which may mean they are not using pictorial cues to help their interpretation and thus failing to recognize any ironical mismatch. Understanding and developing pupils' visual literacy also means taking into account previous visual experiences and the influence of popular culture and peers.[7] Finally, further research would be needed to explore how certain ways of 'reading' images in different cultures might make a difference when reading 'Western' images. For example, in Mohieddin Ellabbad's fascinating text *The Illustrator's Notebook* (2006), he points out that not only do Arabic cultures read text from right to left, they also read images in this way and he gives the example of heroes from both cultures that are moving 'forward' in opposite directions.

Do readers of picturebooks 'code-switch' when reading images, like they do when reading words? What is the impact of non-traditional, postmodern features on immigrant and ethnic minority children's meaning-making and on their responses? Despite the humor and irony, these children took the moral of the texts and their educational potential very seriously. Several of the ethnic minority readers I have worked with have been particularly concerned with distinguishing between what is 'true' and what is 'fiction' in the books we read. Like the Roadville children in Heath's study (1983) and the Maktab students in Brian Street's study (1984) these children had also learnt to think of stories as 'true' and to look for the morals in them.

More work needs to be done on the book/picturebook and its links to educational, recreational or religious contexts.[8] Some readers might find the playfulness and irreverent tone of some contemporary picturebooks hard to accept during their first encounters with them, for example in the case of *The Incredible Book Eating Boy* which includes scribbles, torn paper and other 'desecrations' of the book. In the same way, references to the author that undermine his or her authority (such as a picture of the author as a child or confessions of naughtiness) or the appearance of generally 'unacceptable' images such as faeces or vomit (as in Jeffers' picturebook) can be shocking in the first instance, although they seem to quite quickly become a source of humor. Would it be true to say that ethnic minority children who have been in the UK for longer find these images less shocking and are more able to enjoy the jokes?

In the end, all the children rose to the challenges of the text and were able to enjoy the humor, revealing at the same time an understanding of audience and the ability to make connections to their own experiences. This deeper meaning-making was achieved within a context of dialogue and discussion where these meanings were negotiated with attention to textual evidence and the opinions of others. The implications encourage us to consider how the interplay between different literacies and cultures affects and creates metaliterary awareness of verbal and visual texts and how this awareness might be developed further. That, of course, is our cliff-hanger.

Notes

1. Coulthard compares Funda to Maruf (Gregory 1997), from a Bangladeshi background, who was not used to the type of exploratory talk around books in the classroom and suggests that like him, Funda was responding to text and image in a way that reflected her home literacy practices.
2. Although not strictly an "immigrant," Eshan asked to participate in the project and, in the event, it proved interesting to compare his comments to the others.
3. It is worth noting that being an immigrant to Britain myself was helpful in putting them at ease. In the transcriptions, I have tried to keep a balance between respecting their words and giving a flavor of the way they spoke and making their comments intelligible. Despite these challenges, working with these children was very stimulating and I am very grateful to them and to the schools for allowing me the opportunity to do so.
4. A brief summary of these findings appears in Arizpe and Styles (2008), but in that essay I was focusing mainly on the response to the postmodern features of this text.
5. Cecilia was interviewed in Spanish. This is my translation.
6. The paperback edition of this book (which appeared after these interviews were conducted) comes with a CD that includes all these sounds.
7. In Arizpe (2009) I attempted to take this approach to some of the data from Arizpe and McGonigal's study (2007) as well as from the project described in this chapter. Comparing illustrated books from different cultures could be a thought-provoking exercise.
8. Sipe (2008) cites Lopez-Robertson (2005) and Ballenger's (1998) studies which found different response styles among young Latina and Haitian readers respectively, as examples of studies that reveal "how culture, race, ethnicity, and socioeconomic status both enable and constrain response to literature, and thus shape literary understanding" (241).

Bibliography

Primary Sources

Ellabbad, Mohieddine. *The Illustrator's Notebook*. Toronto: Groundwood Books, 2006.
Grey, Mini. *Traction Man is Here*. London: Red Fox, 2005.
Jeffers, Oliver. *The Incredible Book Eating Boy*. London: Harpercollins, 2006.

Secondary Sources

Arizpe, Evelyn. "Sharing Visual Experiences of a New Culture: Immigrant Children's Responses to Picturebooks and Other Visual Texts." In *Talking Beyond the Page: Reading and Responding to Picturebooks* edited by Janet Evans. 134–151. London: Routledge, 2009.

Arizpe, Evelyn and Styles, Morag. *Children Reading Pictures*. London: RoutledgeFalmer, 2003.

Arizpe, Evelyn and Styles, Morag with Cowan, Kate, Mallouri, Louiza and Wolpert, Mary Anne. "The Voices behind the Pictures: Children Responding to Postmodern Picturebooks." In *Postmodern Picturebooks: Play, Parody, and Self-Referentiality* edited by Lawrence R. Sipe and Sylvia Pantaleo. 207–222. London: Routledge, 2008.

Ballenger, Cynthia. *Teaching Other People's Children: Literacy and Learning in a Bilingual Classroom*. New York: Teachers College Press, 1998.

Bednall, Jane and Cranston, Leanne with Eve Bearne. "The Most Wonderful Adventure . . . Going beyond the Literal." *English Four to Eleven* 32 (2008): 19–26.

Bromley, Helen. "'Madam! Read the Scary Book, Madam'—The Emergent Bilingual Reader." In *Talking Pictures* edited by Victor Watson and Morag Styles. 136–144. London: Hodder and Stoughton, 1996.

Colledge, Marion. "Baby Bear or Mrs. Bear? Young English Bengali-Speaking Children's Responses to Narrative Picture Books at School." *Literacy* 39 (2005): 24–30.

Enever, Janet, and Giselle Schmid-Schönbein. Eds. *Picturebooks and Primary EFL Learners*. Munich: Langenscheidt, 2006.

Gregory, Eve. "Negotiation as a Criterial Factor in Learning to Read in a Second Language." In *Researching Language and Literacy in Social Contexts* edited by David Graddol, Janet Maybin and Barry Stierer. 48–61. Cleveden: Open University Press and Multilingual Matters, 1994.

Gregory, Eve, and Jean Biarnés. "Tony and Jean-François Looking for Sense in the Strangeness of School." In *First Steps Together* edited by Henrietta Dombey and Margaret Meek Spencer. 17–29. London: Trentham, 1994.

Gregory, Eve. *One Child, Many Worlds*. London: David Fulton, 1997.

Gregory, Eve, Tahera Arju, John Jessel, Charmian Kenner and Mahera Ruby. "Snow White in Different Guises: Interlingual and Intercultural Exchanges between Grandparents and Young Children at Home in East London." *Journal of Early Childhood Literacy*, 7.1 (2007): 5–25.

Heath, Shirley Brice. *Ways with Words*. Cambridge: Cambridge University Press, 1983.

Laycock, Liz. "A Way into a New Language and Culture." In *What's in the Picture? Responding to Illustrations in Picture Books* edited by Janet Evans. 79–95. London: Paul Chapman, 1998.

Lopez-Robertson, Julia. "Young Latina's Response Styles during Literature Discussions: Personal Life Stories as Meaning-Making Devices." National Reading Conference, Miami, FL, 2005. Paper.

McGonigal, James and Arizpe, Evelyn. *Learning to Read a New Culture: How Immigrant and Asylum-Seeking Children Experience Scottish Identity through Classroom Books*. Final Report. Edinburgh: Scottish Government, 2007, http://www.scotland.gov.uk/Publications/2007/10/31125406/0 (accessed October 30, 2009).

Mines, Heather. "The Relationship between Children's Cultural Literacies and Their Readings of Literary Texts." PhD Diss. University of Brighton, 2000.

Pahl, Kate. "Narratives, Artifacts and Cultural Identities: An Ethnographic Study of Communicative Practices in Homes." *Linguistics and Education* 15.4 (2004): 339–358.

Pantaleo, Sylvia. "Young Children Engage with the Metafictive in Picture Books." *Australian Journal of Language and Literacy* 28 (2005): 19–28.

Pantaleo, Sylvia. "Pickles, Pastiche and Parody: Exploring Humour in an Undone Fairytale." *The Journal of Reading, Writing and Literacy* 1.3 (2006): 43–62.

Pantaleo, Sylvia. *Exploring Student's Response to Contemporary Picturebooks*. Toronto: University of Toronto Press, 2008.

Sipe, Lawrence R. *Storytime: Young Children's Literary Understanding in the Classroom*. New York: Teachers College Press, 2008.

Street, Brian. *Literacy in Theory and Practice*. Cambridge: Cambridge University Press, 1984.

Chapter Six
Artistic Allusions in Picturebooks

Sandra L. Beckett

One of the most striking trends in contemporary picturebooks is the frequent, and often highly sophisticated, visual allusions to art works. Many of today's picturebook creators are master recyclers of art. Yet, in spite of the fact that this is a widespread phenomenon that can be found in books from many countries and for all age groups, the subject has received surprisingly little critical attention, as I first discovered when preparing a paper on "Paintings, Parody, and Pastiche in Picture Books" for the Children's Literature Association Conference on "Children's Literature and the Fine Arts," held in Paris in July 1998.[1] More than a decade later, this situation has not changed. In her ground-breaking book, *A Theory of Parody: The Teachings of Twentieth-Century Art Forms*, Linda Hutcheon has argued quite convincingly that parody, in the broad sense of any "revisiting" or "recontextualizing" of previous works of art, is a characteristic shared by all the arts in the postmodern world (11).[2] Although Hutcheon doesn't mention children's literature, picturebooks are certainly no exception. In many countries, unconventional, innovative works by picturebook artists challenge habitual thinking about the picturebook and explore and develop the potential of the genre as its own unique art form, one in which artistic allusion and metadiscourse on art play a significant role.

Many picturebooks contain allusions to the stylistic conventions of an entire genre or to the style of a period or movement. The first doublespread in Jean Claverie's rendition of Charles Perrault's *Riquet à la houppe* (Ricky with the Tuft) introduces the viewer into a classic "Artist's Studio" scene. It evokes the general atmosphere of traditional Dutch paintings from the period of Rembrandt and Vermeer of Delft through details such as the clothing (large, white collars and tall, black hats), the artist's red beret and palette reminiscent of self-portraits by Rembrandt, and the subtle play with a hidden light source that throws Riquet's shadow on the curtain. Claverie's pastel watercolours manage to evoke the richness of the oils of the Dutch masters. A group of adults are gathered around a portrait of the young Riquet: in the foreground are a woman playing a musical instrument, a dog, the artist, and a second seated man who bears a striking resemblance to the artist, but holds a pen and paper rather than a palette. Like many artists, Claverie often playfully represents himself in his pictures. Here the artist and his scribe double seem to constitute a double self-portrait that cleverly alludes to the dual role of many picturebook makers who, like Claverie himself, are both author and illustrator. In this parody of the common "Artist's Studio" theme, the adults' eyes are all riveted on the child prodigy who has become the centre of attention, a playful reminder of the fact that picturebook illustrators have placed high art in the service of the child.[3]

What several critics have referred to as the "scavenging" of styles, is characteristic of picturebook artists (see Nodelman 83). The illustrations of an entire book may evoke a specific artistic movement. Some versatile picturebook makers mimic a wide variety of styles, depending on the mood or atmosphere they want to create. Maurice Sendak, "a frank and enthusiastic scavenger," in the terms of Barbara Bader (498), borrows styles ranging from nineteenth-century engravings to romanticism to cartoons. Others tend to adopt a single style. Certain artistic movements are more popular with illustrators than others; impressionism and surrealism are among the favourites. Anthony Browne's penchant for surrealism has made it a distinctive feature of his own style. The delicate illustrations that evoke Sleeping Beauty's dreams in *Songes de la Belle au bois dormant*, by Frédéric Clément, are decidedly impressionist. Nodelman rightly observes that "illustrators of fairy tales frequently choose styles that evoke periods of history not particularly related to the tales but that they perceive to share the values they find in the tales" (86).

Some illustrators cleverly blend two or more styles in the same book. Mitsumasa Anno's books are described by Nodelman as a "charming blend of the American primitive and the Japanese traditional, of Hokusai and Grandma Moses" (85). His magical tale *Kagebōshi* (English trans., *In Shadowland*), inspired by Andersen's *Little Match Girl*, juxtaposes Western-style watercolour-and-ink paintings, which represent the "real" world, with black-and-white pictures executed in oriental paper cut technique (each one cut from a single piece of paper), which symbolize the world of shadows.

Illustrators may refer to the characteristic manner of the entire oeuvre of a particular artist. Although Browne uses the general iconic conventions of surrealism, he most often adopts the manner of Magritte. His works frequently quote and requote specific Magritte paintings (allusions to Dalí are present, but are much less common). Familiar Magritte motifs such as lampposts, bowler hats, and stylized trees trimmed in unusual shapes haunt Browne's pictures. One illustration in *Voices in the Park* includes bowler hat lampposts, trees, and clouds, not to mention the one in the shadow that humorously turns Charles's mother into "The Woman in the Bowler Hat."

One of the most frequently quoted artists is Henri Rousseau, undoubtedly because the primitive, instinctive, childlike quality of his art is seen to have particular appeal for children. Illustrators often appropriate Le Douanier's "exotic landscapes" when the text evokes the jungle. In one of several Rousseau-like jungle landscapes in the intriguing wordless picturebook *Den röda tråden* (English trans., *The Red Thread*), Tord Nygren incorporates the manner of a second artist: in an opening in the dense foliage, Van Gogh can be seen painting in the yellow cornfield. Nygren has introduced the artist himself into this parody of *Crows in the Wheatfield*s. A huge Van Gogh sun replaces the large red disk with which Rousseau punctuates the centre of several of his canvases. The eccentric bird that mimics the shape and color of flowers in *Exotic Landscape* is wittily replaced by a blue flower. The tropical bird from *Exotic Landscape* has taken flight and wings its way over the cornfield where Van Gogh paints his crows, so that the bird, as well as the sun motif, link the two artists juxtaposed in Nygren's illustration. The intertextual play in *The Red Thread* is quite sophisticated and sometimes perplexing even for critics. Carole Scott puzzles over the juxtaposition of Van Gogh and Linnaeus lecturing two children on botany amid a field of giant plants (105). Linnaeus's presence can only be explained if the reader recognizes the allusion to Rousseau, who drew inspiration from illustrations in botanical books.

Illustrators commonly use the style of a particular artist to illustrate a fictional work inspired by the life or work of that artist. This includes the new genre of art books that W. Nikola-Lisa refers to as "art fantasy," that is to say, fantasies that exploit an artist and his works for fictional purposes (53). Miles Hyman appropriates Van Gogh's palette to illustrate Jean-Luc Fromental's fanciful story about a pig that loses an ear and becomes a famous artist in *Le cochon à l'oreille coupée* (The pig with the cut ear). Rigo and Ricardo Alcántara's *El caballo acrobático* (The horse acrobat) borrows the colurful horse from Chagall's *Cantique des cantiques* to tell the story of Colorin, a musical horse who leaves his farm to join the circus. There he is discovered by a famous artist, who remains unnamed in the text but is transparently identified in the subtitle, "A Fantasy with Marc Chagall." Although all of the illustrations are inspired by Chagall, the only faithful rendition of one of the artist's paintings occurs on the very last page. Inspired by his new animal model, Chagall has just put the final touches on the *Cantique des cantiques*. The humorous implication is that Chagall is appropriating Rigo's colorful visual world, in which Colorin preexisted. This is underscored by the mise en abyme of a minute Chagall at the circus painting Colorin, as he appears on the cover with Rigo's signature immediately below.

Pish, Posh, Said Hieronymus Bosch, by Nancy Willard, is a highly imaginative poem about the poor housekeeper who is being driven to distraction by the odd creatures that come to life under the brush of one of the world's most eccentric painters. Willard's fantastic images are complemented by the visual interpretation of Leo and Diane Dillon, whose playful look at the artist's bizarre, often grotesque creatures is the result of a longstanding admiration for Bosch. The "pickle-winged fish" on which the housekeeper rides back to her relieved master recalls, in a comic mode, Bosch's strange flying fish, especially the winged fish mounted by a fat man and a lady in *The Temptation of St. Anthony* triptych. On the cover, a smiling monk, undoubtedly St. Anthony himself, and a strange creature, whose bird head capped with a funnel mimics "The Devil's Messenger" from the left panel of the triptych, watch with rapt admiration as the master who created them paints contentedly while his housekeeper wrestles with their counterparts in the kitchen. A heavy, ornate frame, whose strange creatures seem to have escaped from within, was fashioned by the Dillons's son, Lee, to contain each illustration. It is as if the viewer is looking into a mirror in Bosch's mad household that reflects a different scene each time and turns it into a kind of framed painting that includes the artist. The mirrored scenes are reminiscent of the kind of mise en abyme that André Gide so appreciated in the works of Memling and Quentin Metzys. They could almost be the canvases that sit on Bosch's easel in so many of the illustrations, but remain invisible to the reader.

Children are more apt to decode allusions to specific works of art or parts of them than general allusions to an artistic movement or an artist's style, so it is not surprising that the former are most common in picturebooks. Allusions to the works of well-known European artists figure prominently in the profusion of minute cultural icons that make up the wordless picturebooks of the Japanese author-illustrator Mitsumasa Anno. In the first award-winning *Journey* book, inspired by his trip to Europe and published in Japan in 1977 as *Tabi no Ehon* (My journey), the solitary, enigmatic little traveler on horseback encounters many figures from French paintings. As one would expect, Anno's second Journey book, published in English as *Anno's Italy*, contains numerous references to famous paintings and sculptures by great Italian masters. The three Muses from Botticelli's *Primavera* join in a street procession, Fra Angelico's *The Annunciation* and Leonardo da Vinci's *The Last Supper* are set in the Italian countryside, and in a teeming Renaissance square the Venus de Milo is being offered for sale along with pop art portraits of Sophia Loren in the shadow of Michelangelo's *Pietà*. Anno's artistic allusions nonetheless move freely through time and space. He does not hesitate to include Cézanne's *Card Players* sitting at a table outside a farmhouse in the Italian countryside.

Although Anno's quotations are not generally parodic, they often have a ludic function. In the first book, a nude bather in a tub, reminiscent of Degas's *The Tub* or one of Renoir's bathers, is hidden from view to all but the reader by a wall, against which Anno wittily places a ladder that a man is just starting to scale (the reader is left to imagine the outcome). The recontextualization of elements from specific paintings is often quite sophisticated. Another page cleverly combines scenes from two of Seurat's best known paintings: the figures from the foreground of *A Sunday Afternoon on the Island of La Grande Jatte* are positioned close to those of his *Bathers at Asnières*, which was painted about the same time. Sitting in the field between the two groupings is the artist doing one of the preparatory studies for *La Grande Jatte*. In a doublespread depicting daily life on a large farm, the women from Millet's *The Gleaners* can be seen gathering grain in one of the fields close to a dense forest where Little Red Riding Hood is gathering flowers. The reader may not immediately notice that Anno's illustration also includes the cart loaded with hay and the two large haystacks from the background of Millet's painting, because, although they remain in the same position, the bird's eye view greatly alters the perspective and therefore the proportions. The rider approaches the scene from the left like a mirror image of the man on horseback that can be seen in the distant right background of Millet's painting. The scene in the entire doublespread is reminiscent of the vicinity of the village of Barbizon near the Forest of Fontainebleau, where the painters of the Barbizon school worked. It was Millet in particular who documented the daily activities of farm laborers. In the final doublespread, which seems to continue the plains of Barbizon, the peaceful scene contrasts with the teeming life that spills over most pages and the eye is immediately drawn to the two figures bowed in prayer from Millet's *The Angelus*. Anno seems to be particularly fond of this icon, which recurs unexpectedly fifteen years later in the delicate watercolor that closes *Anno's Magic Seeds*. In the multi-layered tale and mathematical tour de force about Jack and his magical seeds, Anno borrows Millet's icon to depict Jack and his wife, with their heads bowed, praying for a good crop after planting the seeds. The presence of a new element, Jack's son, who, hat in hand, comically mirrors his father, does not make the scene any less recognizable. This self-referentiality is perhaps a tongue-in-cheek attempt to appropriate definitively Millet's icon. Several years before publishing *Anno's Magic Seeds*, the artist admitted during an interview: "I await the day when today's children will be adults. They will go to see the paintings in the Louvre and will say: 'Millet did that after Mr. Anno!'" (Anno 56).

Nygren also incorporates many artistic allusions into the fantastical tableaus of his wordless picturebook *The Red Thread*. In the very disparate-looking crowd from the opening doublespread, the easily recognizable Mona Lisa (her creator stands on the other side) should alert young readers to the presence of other familiar figures from paintings, although they will certainly not decode them all. Against a backdrop reminiscent of a Vasarely painting, Mona Lisa is joined by Jan van Eyck's Giovanni Arnolfini, one of Rousseau's *Football Players*, one of Renoir's *Two Little Circus Girls*, Modigliani's *Leopold Zborowski* and a woman in a blue dress who resembles *Elvira*, as well as a number of figures from Picasso's works, including his young son Paulo in Harlequin costume, his *Child with a Dove*, and *Igor Stravinsky*. Another illustration depicts Picasso's *Three Musicians* playing under a tree while a Pierrot entertains a group of children. *The Red Thread* offers an excellent example from the genre of picturebooks to support Linda Hutcheon's claim that the *Mona Lisa* and paintings by Picasso are among the most parodied works in the visual arts (8). The entire group of children and adults is engrossed in watching a large egg hatch, and the egg itself may be a multi-layered artistic allusion. A few years earlier, another Swedish author-illustrator, Lennart Hellsing, published *Ägget* (The egg), in which an egg is dreaming about what it will become when it grows up, one of the many possibilities being to become an "artistic egg." The illustration by Fibben Hald shows the interior of a museum, undoubtedly the old Stockholm Museum of Modern Art, where several people are standing around Constantin Brancusi's egg-shaped sculpture entitled *The Newborn*. In order to help young readers decode the parody, an egghead is reading about the sculpture in a catalogue on which the name Brancusi is clearly written. In Hellsing's book, the artistic allusion is limited to one illustration and one particular episode, in which the egg protagonist fantasizes about an artistic future. The situation is reminiscent of *Willy the Dreamer*, in which Browne's chimpanzee protagonist dreams that he's a painter. However, in Browne's case, even though this is the only episode that is directly related to the topic of art, artistic allusions occur throughout the book, as they do in all of Browne's works.

Allusions to individual works of art tend quite often to be parodic. In *Hier is ek* (English trans., *Here I Am*) by Ann Walton and Piet Grobler, the whimsical, fantastic story of a grandmother who journeys, by means of assorted wild animals, from South Africa to Holland to visit her new grandchild, Piet Grobler's jungle scene is a parodic reworking of Rousseau's *The Dream*, in which the nude Yadwigha lounging on a sofa is replaced by Gran scantily clad à la Jane in a leopard-skin. The old lady retains the same pose but her hand is slightly raised pointing at a gorilla that has been added in the upper right corner. He seems to have swung in from one of the Douanier's other jungle paintings (which include simians) to provide the grandmother's next means of transportation. Piet Grobler plays cleverly with Rousseau's painting, extending the reddish-colored serpent, attracted by the snake charmer in the original, across the entire illustration (his tail ends on the far left) and onto the next page. Browne's reworking of the same painting in *Willy the Dreamer* is particularly appropriate since Rousseau was painting Yadwigha's dream. It is not surprising that Browne was attracted to the forerunner of the surrealists, whose paintings draw us compellingly into his dreams. Browne's playful treatment of the snake motif superposes details from another painting producing an ingenious *bricolage*. The snake twined around the trunk, holding a banana in its mouth, echoes parodically the serpent that proffers the apple in Rousseau's earlier *Eve*. Another snake slides down one of the ladders cleverly worked into the foliage in an obvious allusion to the game of *Snakes and Ladders*. Children's games and fine art are given equal status in Browne's illustrations. He replaces the wild cats, retained in Grobler's illustration, by a house cat—perhaps foreshadowing the Cheshire cat-ape in the following dream sequence—the couch occupied by a rather conventional family watching television—an image that evokes vague reminiscences of the opening scene of *The Simpsons*. Browne targets adult readers in another allusion that links the couch scene to psychotherapy: the man sitting opposite Willy is a portrait of Sigmund Freud.

When illustrators use what René Payant refers to as "*citation*" (quotation) in painting (5), the choice is seldom random. Unlike the representation of other objects in a room (a vase on a table or a cushion on a chair), paintings evoke a multitude of intertextual associations dependent upon the viewer's experience. When the artistic allusion is contained within a frame and hangs on a wall, young readers will likely sense that they are being called upon to make what Umberto Eco calls an "inferential walk" outside the text, even if they do not have the competence to identify the works of art and decode the parody. In the sparsely decorated living room of Fam Ekman's parodic retelling of *Little Red Riding Hood, Rødhatten og ulven* (Red Hat and the wolf), three familiar paintings immediately draw the reader's attention. The color has been taken out of the paintings (which now reflect the black and white tile floor) and applied to the walls. The paintings are all French, a reminder perhaps that the original literary version was Perrault's, although Ekman's story, like so many retellings outside France, is more closely modeled on the Grimms' version. Carefully chosen for their subject matter, the paintings constitute a mise en abyme of themes in Ekman's retelling that may only be decoded by a cultured elite. Picasso's painting of Marie-Thérèse asleep in a chair, titled *The Dream*, reveals the fresh, naive sensuality and erotic appeal of a budding young woman and it is thus that Little Red Riding Hood has often been represented by male authors and illustrators. Perhaps Ekman is even suggesting that Picasso, who painted *The Dream* at the little château of Boisgeloup, was a wolf who seduced the naive, young Marie-Thérèse. Chagall's painting, *I and the Village*, in which the green head of a youth and the whitish head of a cow stare fixedly at each other, reflects the subject of Ekman's retelling, in which a naive young boy named Little Red Hat encounters the wolf when he goes to the city (this painting dates from Chagall's first trip to Paris). Degas's pastel *The Tub* announces the scene in which the wolf surprises the grandmother taking a bath in an old-fashioned tub filled to the top, a comic contrast with the original's young nude bather.

Although Ekman has used artistic allusion deliberately and to great effect in other picturebooks, when I asked her about these particular paintings, she admitted, in an e-mail dated January 19, 2001, that the choice had been based largely on the fact that they would be "fun to draw" and would lend themselves well to her simplified manner of "re-doing" them. However, she did find the theory about the tub scene in particular "very interesting" and admitted that what she "thinks" does not necessarily reflect what she is doing "unconsciously."[4] When illustrators pay homage to specific artists and art works, it is not always in the visibly intentional manner of Anthony Browne.

The paintings hanging on the walls in Browne's *The Big Baby* generally quote specific paintings fairly accurately, as did Ekman's, but one is deliberately and playfully misquoted. In both cases, however, the allusions nonetheless have a parodic function and constitute a playful mise en abyme of events and themes in the story. The paintings that are reproduced faithfully are entirely dependent upon the recontextualization for their parodic effect. Munch's *The Sick Child* hangs above Mr. Young who, when he feels the least bit ill, becomes, in his wife's terms, "a Big Baby." Unlike many of his better-known expressionist paintings, the one of Munch's sick sister remains anchored in reality, as does the scene it mirrors below of John's father sick in bed. In contrast, Dalí's famous painting, *Sleep*, which depicts a large face sleeping propped up on crutches, is used to reflect the surreal situation that results when Mr. Young drinks a whole bottle of "Elixa de Yoof" tonic in his obsessive desire for eternal youth, and awakes to find a baby's body attached to his disproportionate, adult-sized head. The last painting is much less celebrated, but the manner in which Browne misquotes it assures that it will catch the attention of viewers of all ages. When John's father calls Mrs. Young into the bedroom later to tell her about his "TERRIBLE dream," it is no longer the Munch that hangs over the bed but a playful reworking of John Henry Fuseli's romantic work titled *The Nightmare*, in which John's baby-father has replaced the little, grinning demon which sits on the sleeping woman.[5] In *Piggybook* Browne reworks Gainsborough's *Robert Andrews and His Wife* in a similarly playful and simple manner. Once again, the composition respects the original, but Robert Andrews now has a pig's head and only the blank form of his wife's contour remains on the bench. Children do not have to recognize the painting to deduce that the absent feminine figure represents Mrs. Piggot, who has finally walked out on her chauvinist pig husband and sons.

Often Browne's picturebooks contain sophisticated, multi-level parodies. The portrait hanging in the Piggots' living room at the beginning of *Piggybook* is an immediately recognizable rendition of Hals's *The Laughing Cavalier*, but when this scene "*en rose*" is repeated toward the end of the book "*en bleu*,"[6] the laughing cavalier has been replaced by a pig in the same dignified pose, just as Mr. Piggot and his sons have been transformed into "real" pigs rooting around on the floor for scraps. "The Laughing Pig" portrait is a parody "in the second degree,"[7] as it mimics Browne's earlier version of *The Laughing Cavalier*, itself an ironic recontextualization of the Hals's masterpiece. Browne's double-coded parody provides a second level accessible to the many readers—adults as well as children—who will not recognize the Dutch master's most famous painting. Browne uses a similar technique in *Willy the Dreamer*. In the first illustration Willy dreams beneath a faithful quotation of Magritte's *Castle in the Pyrenees*, but on the last page the huge rock has taken on Willy's features. As in *Piggybook*, the second picture offers a kind of surrealistic parody not only of Magritte's painting, but also of his own illustration (the carpet has become grass, the lines of the armchair are visible through

Willy, a Willy pattern has replaced the flowers on the wallpaper, etc.). The cover illustrations add further layers to the parody. On the front cover, Willy floats in an armchair that has partially turned to stone, the seascape below is now full of bananas (a banana lighthouse, banana sailboats, banana fish), and a full-scale boat in a bottle floats on the water. On the back cover, Willy, still dreaming, flies off into the sunset on his rock-armchair. The remarkable success of Browne's picturebooks is largely due to their ability to appeal to readers at opposite poles of sophistication.[8]

Often illustrators are not content to include one or more isolated paintings. Yvan Pommaux goes much further than Ekman when he uses artistic allusion in his parodic retelling of the same fairy tale in *John Chatterton détective*.

A doublespread depicts Little Red Riding Hood being held hostage by the wolf to obtain from her mother the one painting he needs to complete his "collection of wolves," "Le loup bleu sur fond blanc" (Blue wolf on a white background). It is noteworthy that the wolf is dressed entirely in blue. This wolf seems to have a narcissistic obsession with his own image. Although the originals are not depicted with the same degree of faithfulness as Browne's, cultured adult viewers are able to label many of the paintings in the wolf's very eclectic art collection, including a Magritte word-image (here *loup* rather than *cheval*), a scowling wolf (rather than a smiling pig) à la Hals, a wrapped wolf by Christo, a wire wolf by Alexander Calder, a "Walking Wolf" by Giacometti. The purposeful stride of the latter mimics not only the well-known sculpture, but also the stance of the wolf himself as he talks on his cell phone.

In Ekman's *Kattens Skrekk* (The cat's terror), the story of a cat with an obsessive fear of dogs, the museum is full of parodied artworks with canine subjects: the *Mona Lisa*, Gianlorenzo Bernini's marble sculpture of *David*, etc. The cat's anguish is appropriately suggested by Munch's *The Scream*, the most famous example of the expressionist movement, art "born out of anxiety" (Tansey 390). In the same manner that the "pure feeling" of Kasimir Malevitch's early Suprematist works such as *Black Square* and *Black Circle* is expressed in black and white, "the cold, paralyzing intensity of the . . . feelings" of the terrified cat peering in the doorway is communicated visually in stark black and white wood engravings (Birkeland 12).[9]

These contrast strikingly with the colored illustrations of the cat's dream embedded in the middle of the story, for which Ekman appropriates three of Rousseau's best-known paintings. For the sequence in which the cat dreams that he is a shepherd bit by a large dog while asleep in the desert, Ekman parodies *The Sleeping Gypsy*. The position of the feline has been playfully inverted by superimposing the cat protagonist's head on the sleeping gypsy who is now a wide awake shepherd. The parody is continued in a second illustration that suggests the ambiguity inherent in the Norwegian title *Kattens Skrekk* which, like *kattesrekk*, could mean "being afraid of cats," as well as "what cats are afraid of." Instead of reacting with fear, as readers anticipate, the cat, fully awake and upright, uses the shepherd's staff, conveniently provided by the

Figure 6.1 Illustration from Yvan Pommaux. John Chatterton détective. Paris: L'École des loisirs, 1993.

Artistic Allusions in Picturebooks • 93

Figure 6.2 Illustration from Fam Ekman. Kattens Skrekk. Oslo: Cappelen, 1992.

original artist, to beat the crying dog for disturbing his peaceful sleep. The substitution of a shepherd for the gypsy in the original reminds the reader of the dog/*David* sculpture in the museum and seems to cast the cat in the role of the fearless, young conqueror of Goliath in his dream. A parodic rendition of *Portrait of a Woman* accompanies the next sequence, in which the cat protagonist, occupying the same position as the tiny cat in the original, tells his mother what happened. The yellow hat is borrowed from the painting parodied in the following sequence, when the angry mother decides that the dog's punishment will be to take them and all their relatives on a ride through a particularly hilly region in *Old Junier's Cart*. The original painting was a cat's nightmare, as it contained three dogs, but Ekman retains only the black dog that Rousseau insisted on painting under the cart in spite of suggestions that it was too large; she playfully makes it even larger to replace the mare hitched to the cart.

The very same year, but on the other side of the Atlantic, the author-illustrator Dav Pilkey published a book about cats that plays with artistic allusions in a strikingly similar manner. Like Ekman's book, Pilkey's *When Cats Dream* begins and ends in black and white, evoking the world as cats see it when they are awake, and uses color in the central illustrations to evoke cats' dreams. In a black and white "softwarm lap," that turns out to be that of Whistler's Mother, from the stark, ascetic canvas titled *Arrangement in Gray and Black No. 1: Portrait of the Artist's Mother*, Pilkey's cat falls asleep and the world becomes increasingly strange and more vividly colored as the cat moves into fantastic, Chagall-like dreamscapes. The final doublespread is a bricolage of motifs from different paintings: the cat and window from Chagall's *Paris Through the Window* join a feline version of one of his violinists. To evoke cats dreaming in the jungle, Pilkey shifts temporarily to Rousseau's visual world. The book's open ending has the cat falling asleep in Mona Lisa's arms, to return to its colorful dreams.

The title page of Browne's *Willy the Dreamer* is a reworking of a Magritte *Dream Key*, in which, as in the original, only one of the words below (the banana) actually corresponds to the object. Readers are certainly not surprised to learn that when Willy dreams that he's a painter, he is in a studio surrounded by parodies of several of Magritte's most famous paintings, each bearing Browne's characteristic signature. A close look at Magritte's famous pipe reveals that it is actually a banana. Bananas replace the apple that dissimulates the face in *The Great War*, the enormous nose in *The Philosopher's Lamp*, and the bread in *The Golden Legend*; although he retains the shape of the apple in *The Postcard*, it has nonetheless taken on the color of a banana, suggesting another work, *This Is Not an Apple*. Magritte's reworking of the Venus of Milo, *The Flying Statue*, has received the head of a gorilla. On the top left Browne reproduces the painting titled *Not To Be Reproduced*, adding chimpanzee-like ears to the reflection in the mirror. Nor is Browne content to reproduce it only once, but develops it into another of his clever multi-level parodies. When Willy dreams of fierce monsters toward the end of the book, the reflection with the oversized ears has now stepped out of the mirror and looks at an even more frightening reflection whose ears have been transformed into bananas that give the monster a Viking look. The book in the original is still sitting on the mantelpiece, but now we can clearly read the title: *Beauty and the Beast*. The "strange landscape" in which Willy finds himself is the vast desert-like expanse of Dalí's *The Persistence of Memory*, which a plague of bananas has rendered even stranger. With one exception, they have replaced even the artist's characteristic soft watches; the rock in the background now has the face of a sleeping gorilla. Into the landscape Browne introduces motifs from other famous works by Dali: *Slumber* is now a sleeping banana, *Burning Giraffe* is a flaming banana, and hanging from one of Dali's open drawers is a banana peel.

Like other forms of intertextuality, artistic allusions would seem to be inaccessible to most children in light of their limited cultural heritage. But why would illustrators increasingly use these references in their picturebooks, even making it a hallmark of their style, if they felt that their young readers/viewers were not proficient at decoding them? I argued in " Parodic Play with Paintings in Picture Books" that children of the Simpsons generation are more proficient at decoding parody than baby boom children (191–192). Illustrators like Browne obviously believe that today's children are quite capable of appreciating parody. They can ensure the complicity of their young viewers by choosing paintings that have become popular icons in children's literature. Munch's painting was familiar to many young people even before the image became an icon of popular culture thanks to the 1996 film *Scream*. Children cannot miss the parodic intention in Hyman's illustration of a woman screaming in the museum, as he also quotes Munch's painting on the same doublespread. A similar allusion in Browne's *Voices in the Park* is less transparent and more complex. The mouth of a woman (or rather a female simian) is wide open as she screams. It is only in a later illustration, which provides a close-up of the newspaper the gorilla is reading on the park bench, that we notice the reproduction of *The Scream* on the front page. When we turn back to the original illustration, we see that the trees also seem to be screaming in the background. It has been suggested that such visual allusions address the adults who mediate children's books (parents, librarians, teachers), and certainly some are there for the amusement of adults, either in their role of co-readers or as readers of picturebooks in their own right. Some critics feel that artistic allusions may be directed at an elite audience whose opinion carries weight—notably reviewers and critics—with the intention of winning acclaim from the adult children's book establishment. However, many adult viewers may be as unlikely to understand the more subtle references as children. The duskjacket of *Willy the Dreamer* states that Browne's pictures "pay homage to great painters." Perhaps some illustrators are simply engaged in a personal (and sometimes highly complex) dialogue with those artists and care not a whit if it all goes over the head of their viewers.

It is also possible that picturebook artists practice this type of parody as a form of playful revenge against the world of high art. When *The Laughing Cavalier* is depicted as a wolf or a pig and the *Mona Lisa* as a dog, high art loses its sacred aura and is made to look pretentious and ridiculous. Perhaps parodic allusions are a form of revenge on "fine artists" who do "real art" and are paid as much for one painting as an illustrator might obtain for the entire print-run of a successful picturebook. Tohby Riddle certainly seems to poke fun at high art when he depicts the four animal protagonists from *The Great Escape from City Zoo* in an art gallery wearing the disguises they believe will allow them to fit in. The four animals standing in front of Magritte's *Ceci n'est pas une pipe*, totally ignoring the paintings on the walls, "are not four people" appreciating fine art in a gallery; they have no idea what they are supposed to be doing there. Browne also seems to poke fun at high art in *Voices in the Park*, where the two paintings displayed for sale in a garbage-littered street beside a panhandling Santa with the sign "Wife and millions of kids to support" are a very sad-looking *Mona Lisa* and *Laughing Cavalier*. Browne will free these miserable-looking figures from their frames in a later illustration which shows them dancing in the street. Riddle's quotation of *Ceci n'est pas une pipe* may allude more to Browne, who has made it a popular icon in children's literature, than to Magritte. Perhaps these allusions constitute an invitation to view picturebook illustrations as high art and just as important as the art works they appropriate. Whatever their reasons for parodying works of art, illustrators have created a new brand of sophisticated picturebooks that target all ages, a trend that has been identified as one of the survival techniques of children's books in the electronic age.[10]

Notes

1. A revised version of the paper, "Parodic Play with Paintings in Picture Books," was published in 2001 (see Beckett, 175–195). The present paper refers only briefly to the picturebooks examined in the earlier study. A chapter in my book in progress, *Crossover Picturebooks*, is devoted to artistic allusion.
2. Because the term "parody" is commonly used to imply that the purpose of the reference is primarily to ridicule the work evoked, I will use the more neutral term of "allusion," reserving the former for references with a comic or satiric intent.
3. Jean Perrot (1991, 42–53, 184–186) examines Claverie's works in the context of his study of the influence of baroque art in children's literature.
4. This scene is examined in more detail in Beckett (2002).
5. The substitution of a dragon's head for the luminescent horse's head is no doubt simply because children will consider it more nightmarish.
6. This reflects the evolution of the work of the Dutch master, whose colors were bright in the earlier works and sober in the later ones.
7. I refer, of course, to the subtitle of Gérard Genette's *Palimpsests: Literature in the Second Degree*.
8. For a more detailed study of Browne's work, see Doonan (1999).
9. Malevitch himself defines the style as "the supremacy of pure feeling in creative art" (Arnason 1986, 187).
10. At a forum I organized in 1997 for the Modern Language Association titled "The Status of Children's Books in This Millennium and the Next," Wendy Lamb, executive editor in the Books for Young Readers Department at Bantam Doubleday Dell, speculated on the types of books that would make children want to continue reading in an electronic age, and mentioned in particular sophisticated dual-audience picturebooks (172).

Bibliography

Primary Sources

Anno, Mitsumasa. *Tabi no Ehon* (My Journey). Tokyo: Fukuinkan Shotan, 1977. Published in English under the title *Anno's Journey*. London: Bodley Head, 1978.
———. *Tabi no Ehon II*. Tokyo: Fukuinkan Shotan, 1977. Published in English under the title *Anno's Italy*. London: Bodley Head, 1979.
———. *In Shadowland*. New York: Orchard Books, 1988.
———. *Anno's Magic Seeds*. New York: Putnam, 1994.
Browne, Anthony. *Piggybook*. London: MacRae, 1986.
———. *The Big Baby: A Little Joke*. London: MacRae, 1993.
———. *Willy the Dreamer*. London: Walker, 1997.
———. *Voices in the Park*. London: Walker, 1998.
Claverie, Jean. *Riquet à la houppe*. Paris: Albin Michel, 1988.
Clément, Frédéric. *Songes de la Belle au bois dormant*. Paris: Casterman, 1997.
Ekman, Fam. *Rødhatten og Ulven*. Oslo: Cappelen, 1985.
———. *Kattens Skrekk*. Oslo: Cappelen, 1992.
———. Email to the author. January 19, 2001.
Fromental, Jean-Luc, and Miles Hyman. *Le Cochon à l'oreille coupée*. Paris: Seuil Jeunesse, 1994.
Hellsing, Lennart, and Fibben Hald. *Ägget* (The egg). Stockholm: Raben & Sjögren, 1978.
Nygren, Tord. *Den röda tråden*. Stockholm: Raven & Sjögren, 1987. Published in English under the title *The Red Thread*. Stockholm: R & S Books, 1988.
Pilkey, Dav. *When Cats Dream*. New York: Orchard, 1992.
Pommaux, Yvan. *John Chatterton détective*. Paris: L'École des loisirs, 1993.
Riddle, Tohby. *The Great Escape from City Zoo*. Sydney: HarperCollins, 1997.
Rigo [Martín Martínez Navarro], and Ricardo Alcántara. *El caballo acrobático*. Barcelona: Ediciones B. 1991.
Walton, Ann, and Piet Grobler. *Hier is ek*. Cape Town: Juta, 1996. Published in English under the title *Here I Am*. Cape Town: Juta, 1996.
Willard, Nancy, and Leo and Diane Dillon. *Pish, Posh, Said Hieronymus Bosch*. San Diego: Harcourt Brace Jovanovich, 1991.

Secondary Sources

Anno, Mitsumasa. "Anno 85–Anno 87." Remarks collected by Geneviève Patte and Annie Pissard; Catherine Germain and Elisabeth Lortic. *La Revue des livres pour enfants* 118 (Winter 1987): 53–57.
Arnason, H. H. *History of Modern Art*. 3rd edition. New York: Harry N. Abrams, 1986.
Bader, Barbara. *American Picturebooks from Noah's Ark to the Beast Within*. New York: Macmillan, 1976.
Beckett, Sandra L. "Parodic Play with Paintings in Picture Books." *Children's Literature* 29 (2001): 175–195.
———. *Recycling Red Riding Hood*. New York: Routledge, 2002.
Birkeland, Tone. "At the Crossroad—the Norwegian Picture Book." In *Norwegian Books for Children and Young People*. 10–13. Lillehammer: Lillehammer Olympic Organizing Committee, 1994.
Doonan, Jane. "Drawing Out Ideas: A Second Decade of the Work of Anthony Browne." *The Lion and the Unicorn* 23 (1999): 30–56.
Eco, Umberto. *The Role of the Reader*. Bloomington, IN: Indiana University Press, 1979.
Genette, Gérard. *Palimpsestes: la littérature au second degré*. Paris: Seuil, 1982.
Hutcheon, Linda. *A Theory of Parody: The Teachings of Twentieth-Century Art Forms*. New York and London: Methuen, 1985.
Lamb, Wendy. "Strange Business: The Publishing Point of View." *Signal* 87 (September 1998), 167–173.
Nikola-Lisa, W. "I Spy: A Place for the Arts in Children's Picture-Books." *Journal of Children's Literature* 21.2 (Fall 1995): 52–56.

Nodelman, Perry. *Words about Pictures: The Narrative Art of Children's Picture Books.* Athens, GA: The University of Georgia Press, 1988.
Payant, René. "Bricolage pictural: l'art à propos de l'art; I—La Question de la citation." *Parachute* 16 (1979): 5–8.
Perrot, Jean. *Art baroque, art d'enfance.* Nancy: Presses Université de Nancy, 1991.
Scott, Carole. "Dual Audience in Picturebooks." In *Transcending Boundaries: Writing for a Dual Audience of Children and Adults* edited by Sandra L. Beckett. 99–110. New York: Garland, 1999.
Tansey, Richard G., and Fred S. Kleiner. *Gardner's Art Through the Ages.* 10th edition. New York: Harcourt Brace, 1996.

Part II
Picturebooks and Storytelling

Chapter Seven
Frame-making and Frame-breaking in Picturebooks

Carole Scott

Borders and boundaries are of great significance in our lives. Our bodies establish our physical domain, tethering us to this world in space and in time and marking the edges of our being. Our minds replicate these boundaries: psychology studies the division of self from not self, and self from "other"; sociology and anthropology note the way we structure our communities and divide ourselves into "us" and "them"; political science looks at the lines we draw to balance and control power and to create borders around our nations. And philosophy, ethics, and religion help us set the boundaries between right and wrong, sacred and profane, the saved and the damned. So, in our art, the borders we draw are invested with far more than aesthetic judgment. They become "the ordered application of a certain belief system" (Steele 6) "packed with contextual and historical meaning, inspirational [and] confusing" (28). Thus, exploring the purposes and effects of framing in picturebooks involves not only consideration of the aesthetic aspects and graphic design or graphic-narrative metafictive devices as literary constructs. We must also delve into social commentary and psychological states of mind, and the way that frame-making and frame-breaking comment upon social and psychological boundaries and distinctions in our lives.

Over the past few years, our experience with the world's borders and boundaries has changed dramatically. Two examples come to mind immediately: the internet and email have altered our perception of time and space; and terrorism's random atrocities have dimmed the line between war and peace and destroyed our sense of sanctuary and safe places. Both of these developments challenge our former visions of borders, boundaries and order, breaking some and creating others. The artist reflects these shifting perceptions and, for picturebook artists, the dynamic interaction between graphic and verbal text multiplies their significance, and communicates to us and to our children an understanding of boundaries and how they might be broken. This, of course, includes the boundary between imagination and real-life experience, and the notion of fictionality.

My interest in borders and framing has made me increasingly aware of two approaches to the way they function in picturebooks. I note that in his ground-breaking book *Words about Pictures* published almost twenty years ago now, Perry Nodelman tells us that "a frame around a picture makes it seem tidier, less energetic"; "symmetry . . . creates a sense of tidy order"; and frames within pictures "heighten the dramatic focus; they force us to pay attention to specific parts of pictures" (50–51). Though he does not say so explicitly, he is suggesting that framing can serve a dual purpose, so that frames border pictures, and frames organize pictures.

This sense of dual purpose is, I believe, fundamental to the understanding of how framing functions, and has led me to distinguish between what I term "perceptual" framing and "structural or architectural" framing. I will exemplify my distinctions by looking at two older books, Beatrix Potter's *Peter Rabbit*, the most innovative and experimental of her books as regards framing, and Daisy Utemorrah's and Pat Torres' *Do Not Go Around the Edges*, before turning to some more contemporary works.

Potter's use of white space has been pointed out by more than one critic, myself included,[1] noting that the area around the picture frequently takes up a great deal of the page, sometimes more than half. While image is emphatically separated from text by the gutter, the framing is always subtle as the various-shaped pictures merge gently into the surrounding space; the soft edges of her pictures often fade into such light colors that the delineation between image and white page is hard to see. The framing suggests a perceptual approach, giving the impression of peering through a peephole. Furthermore, the shape of the picture responds to the images it includes. For example, as Peter squeezes under the gate (19), the holly bush defines the right-hand side of the picture, and the image of Mr. McGregor attempting to put his foot on Peter (40) distorts its shape to include Mr. McGregor's boot.

Most interesting is the framing device of a color wash or even of the boundaries of objects themselves. Thus, when Mr. McGregor chases Peter with intent to kill, the two are without background or frame, except for the faint suggestion of wash defining Peter's path and highlighting the overwhelming significance of the passionate relationship between the two figures, in contrast to which all else becomes irrelevant. In another instance the lens is placed simply upon the watering can in which Peter seeks sanctuary. The border of the picture is defined by the shape of the can itself, as Peter tries to become one with it. Only the drops of water, the result of Peter's intense desire for obscurity, extend beyond the borders of animal and object. The effect is enhanced by a pale, shadowy circle that includes the body of the can, and part of Peter. The tension between this hint of a frame, and the stark outline of the can and the rabbit offers some insight into frame-making and frame-breaking. Does the wash fail to encircle the rose of the can and Peter's rump which break its line, or does the shadow draw the eye to spotlight the image? The relationship between frame and image fluctuates and serves to intensify the emotion expressed in the story and experienced by the reader. The framing does not serve to bring order to the picture; rather it responds to the image that the eye and emotions perceive, and provides us with a good example of what I term perceptual framing, which selects what is pertinent to be included, and what is not.

To clarify this idea, I will introduce a popular view of landscape painting in the late eighteenth and early nineteenth centuries. Many held that the artistry of the natural world could most readily be transformed into a painting simply by putting the right part of it in a frame. Thus the would-be painter in pursuit of a subject carried around a wooden rectangle on a stick, rather like a giant lollipop, holding it up before his eyes as he faced the view, to see which part would best be imprisoned in the frame. Though this may appear a little foolish to us now, we use the same concept when we compose a photograph, or when we turn to photoshop to cut and discard the parts that mar the composition. Quite recently, I saw a well-known potter use the same technique to select the best piece of her decorated slab of clay. The approach depends on framing by cutting away what is not of significance.

In contrast to this approach, is one I term structural or architectural. Instead of the image of the landscape painter, I offer a portrayal of the Creation, in which God, holding a pair of compasses, leans down from heaven to draw a circle in the midst of chaos. This circle places a boundary around the newly formed Earth, and encompasses a space within which order, life and beauty may be introduced. This notion of framing is a more structural one, and we use it when we talk of framing a house or using a frame for bees to make their honey, or even in earlier usage, a weaver's loom on which cloth is created. We also use the word "frame" when we talk of framing a question, or framing a story. All have to do with order and the construction of a pattern to sustain it.

In this context I suggest the Australian book, *Do Not Go Around the Edges*, which is highly structured with multiple frames dramatizing the intersecting of cultures, perspectives, and stories. The book is the autobiography of an Australian aboriginal woman whose life was shattered by the intrusion of the white man's culture. Her family is broken; she is put into a boarding school, given a basic education and trained as a domestic. Torn between her aboriginal identification, beliefs and world-view and those of the dominant culture, she expresses her life story in a brief, rather objective narrative of the incidents, and in a series of poems which offer her emotional comments and yearnings, and observations of her natural surroundings. The illustrations, by another hand, reproduce design elements of aboriginal culture and support the poems' observations, providing a strong statement of the life and culture from which the author was removed.

Each doublespread is set with the top edge of the paper acting as the border, while the other three sides are marked with a thick frame of solid russet, outside a white border, and then a thin russet line marking the edge of the picture. Since, across the bottom of each doublespread there is also a strong line with two intricate edges, rather like mounts for photographs, this lack of balance between top and bottom gives the impression of a larger page cut across horizontally, with the top lost or discarded. This framing principle echoes the book's basic premise, of a person whose life has been cut in two with one part rejected. This deliberate rejection introduces one element of perceptual framing into a work that is predominantly structural.

The page layout provides a counter to this force, for the poem, the feeling heart of the book, is prominent on either the recto or verso page of the doublespread, mounted with a double frame within the illustration that reflects the focus of the poem and the strength of the native culture. The vivid earth tones of the picture and the force of the designs further press the factual events of the more objective narrative toward the bottom edge of the book, away from its center. The complex layers and dynamic thrust that the frames present provide a visual commentary upon the acculturation process and its fallout of loss and damage. Here the framing, and the absence or breaking of the frame across the top of the page, establish a series of borders that separate and encapsulate elements of a fractured life, and set a hierarchy of worth where perspectives, beliefs and cultures are balanced one against the other, but not made whole.

Dorte Karrebaek's *Pigen Der Var Go' Til Mange Ting (The Girl Who Could Do Many Things)* not only offers her readers a complex and emotion-charged framing structure, she also provides outstanding innovative and highly dynamic instances of frame-breaking which carry subtle meanings. In a sense one might consider the interaction between frames as a kind of graphic intertext, or of "layering used for semiotic effect" (Steele, 172). This is a tale of the relationship between a young girl and her parents, focusing upon her state of mind and perception of the situation. With a few notable exceptions, Karrebaek employs one square central frame superimposed upon a second square double its size. The two are separated by a 4 mm border in red, blue or yellow, and the whole reaches almost to the edge of the paper, with a white half cm border.

The interplay between the two panels is intricate and dynamic, effectively suggesting the shifting relationship between parents and child. The first image reveals the girl as a rigid, doll-like figure standing within the inner-square which depicts in deep perspective the central room of a house. The outer square behaves as a simple frame, with a pattern repeating the fabric of the girl's dress. In the next four images, the room in the inner frame remains, though the perspective and the movement of the curtains blowing in the wind do alter. The girl, however, has moved into the outer frame where she is employed in various tasks: ironing, scrubbing the floor, washing dishes, attempting to sleep, or just standing with her eyes rolled upward to the central frame where her parents chase one another, have pillow fights, pass out drunk and dance.

This commentary on the role reversal where the parents play irresponsibly and the girl is left with all the work is broken momentarily on doublespread 6 where the three sit together around the table in the room which has expanded to fill the page, obliterating the outer square altogether, and framed only by the small white edge. However the division returns immediately: this time the girl is with her parents in the inner picture, but her shadow already moves strongly into the outside square, and on doublespread 8 she is completely back in the outer panel.

The red, yellow, or blue border that divides the inner square from the outer one is not always impermeable. The girl's head and TV screen jut over from outside to inside on doublespread 2 and 3; mother's hair penetrates from inside to outside while feathers from the pillow fight drift over the line into the outer panel in doublespread 4 (see figure); and waves and zigzags of light of sound emanate from the inner square into the outer panel on 2. All of these framing devices reveal the tensions in the dysfunctional family: the girl's sense of alienation, the parents' neglectful lack of attention and their expectation that their child be their housemaid, and the general impingement of their lives upon her wellbeing and sense of self.

The verbal text certainly reinforces this visual depiction: for example,

> "'Self-learning is good learning' said the father and the mother. And they went on playing while the girl thought that they themselves had apparently learned to quarrel a lot."[2]

These few words provide us with the parents' self-righteous defense of their neglectful attitude to their daughter, their own volatile life-style, and the cynical attitude of a young girl who has had no childhood and whose only formal instruction in life appears to have come from the television. Notably on the second doublespread, the finger of the TV instructor breaks through the framed picture of the television set into the girl's space.

Frame-breaking is used to make another subtle comment on the impact of the parents' behavior upon the child in doublespread 5 depicting the girl lying awake in bed, while the parents in the frame above have passed out on the floor, an empty wine bottle and glass providing the reason for their insensibility. The girl's bare feet stick out from the quilt which is too short for her, and the outer frame in which she lies is full of large blue and yellow stars, suggesting the turmoil that has taken place and perhaps the reverberations in the parents' wine-battered minds. Most telling is the empty bottle which, lying on its side, penetrates the frame between the drunken parents and the girl. It could be conceived as dripping wine onto the girl's bed, but suggests even more strongly the barrel of a rifle pointing at her head.

106 • Carole Scott

Figure 7.1 Illustration from Dorte Karrebæk: *Pigen Der Var Go' Til Mange Ting* [The Girl Who Could Do Many Things]. Copenhagen: Forum, 1997.

After a final party where the parents dress as animals and metamorphose into them, the girl breaks the frames altogether, growing suddenly into three progressively older and larger images of herself each superimposed upon the other so that the largest frames the other two. She becomes too large for the squared room and steps out through the top, her magnified self breaking through onto the surface of a new land where her dress is reflected not in a frame, but by a ladybird, and by a magnificent flower that surges from the shadow of her footsteps. The movement of the book is from architectural framing to perceptual, in this case replicating the growth from a boxed-in life to one of freedom.

An interesting contrast to Karrabaek's book is Matteo Pericoli's *Stellina* (2006) which tells the story of a baby bird, fallen from its nest in a New York traffic light post, and rescued to spend its life enclosed in an apartment. In this book it is the outdoors that is framed and boxed in, while the apartment is pictured as open and free. Thus, when the wild bird looks out of the window, the outside world is rigid and enclosed and in no way tempting, while the inside is colorful and enticing. Even where there is an indoor frame, such as piano keys, Stellina is in no way bound by them; instead she perches on top of any structure, and the top of the picture is always open and borderless. While simple in comparison to Karrebaek's complex depiction of relationships, the use of borders and frames provides some interesting comments on the nature of the freedom, particularly the freedom for self-expression, possible in a safe, though contained space, as opposed to the oppression of the outside world. One image that reveals this idea in some detail shows Stellina perched on the pencil that draws the city captured on a bordered roll of paper.

One more book that portrays inner barriers is Jimmy Liao's *The Sound of Colors* which explores the experience of a girl who has recently gone blind, and traces her first sightless journey out of the house. Though subtitled *A Journey of the Imagination*, Liao's images juxtapose the concrete world of the city, highly structured by rectangular and diagonal lines configured with geometric precision, with metaphoric whimsical shapes that are clearly fanciful. For example, while she descends mathematically constructed stairs into the subway, plodding up the stairs to the exit "As slowly as an elephant . . . , peacefully, patiently, one step at a time," the metaphor catches her imagination and the image presents the accompanying elephants clad in remarkably patterned jumpsuits in a tunnel fantastically surrounded by textured boulders in a surreal landscape cross-section.

In his depiction of his narrator's search for her lost light and color, now to be found only in her memory and in her heart, Liao, like earlier illustrators, does use the technique of diminishing borders to correlate with her emotional involvement in her journey.[3] But his counterpoint between perceptual and architectural framing is extremely complex as it charts the barriers of blindness and the accompanying alienation and loss against the spirit's persistent search for wholeness. The girl's journey is by subway, and she taps her white cane up and down innumerable staircases, visioned in multiple geometric squares, rectangles and diagonals, as she travels from station to station. The stark architectural frames that comprise her underground environment may be lightened with whimsical features, but the intricacy of the repetitive boxes and the way they channel her direction is overwhelming. Even above-ground experiences present nature as crafted structural barriers–though there is at least one example of triumphant frame-breaking–or accentuate a grid-like format. The happy colorful destination once again is highly structured, but the stained-glass is shaped of curves, rather than geometric lines, cross-cut to create a more chaotic, informal design.

The combination of intricate lines and structures with whimsicality most significantly echo the architecture of deconstruction with its "casual relationship between lines and form without premeditated rational intention" (Steele, 219), one in which "the dream of pure form has been disturbed. Form has become contaminated . . . [with] forms placed in conflict to produce an unstable, restless geometry" (Wigley and Johnson quoted in Steele 202–203.) The result effectively simulates the deconstruction of the world of sight into the Sounds of Color.[4] Although the stained-glass window presents Liao's picture of the girl's final destination, his penultimate image, one that I consider much more perceptual in its framing and conception, captures for me the process of revisioning the world through different senses.

David Wiesner's *The Three Pigs* must be included in this discussion for its delightful use of framing to dramatize the notion of fictionality. Like Louis Kahn's mid-twentieth-century postmodern architecture,[5] Wiesner's book is characterized by "layering, intentional disjuncture, and deliberate ambiguity in plan, elevation and scale [which] generate a level of playfulness and humor" Steele 173). Wiesner breaks the boundaries of narrative structure and genre, and print setting and book making (in which his characters take part). And he deconstructs the borders of pictures and pages by elimination, realignment, folding, crumpling, and even reshaping them into paper planes on which the characters can take flight. He plays with the notion of perceptual framing, particularly using the notion of cutting out and discarding elements of pictures, as well as the idea of pages as static, discrete entities which can be creased up and then straightened out again.

In contrast he also introduces images not from book manufacture, but from the Hollywood film set where pages are represented as giant flats of scenery which must be maneuvered into an appropriate place in the unfolding drama, and whose precarious balance may render them liable to unexpected toppling. While aspects of the depicted images on page or on scenery flat are often static and structured with firm borders and edges, they can simultaneously be represented as evanescent bordered boxes whose boundaries can be penetrated and escaped from, depending on the volatility of the characters.

Wiesner's metafictive disassembling and reassembling the notion of a recognizable narrative recalls mid-century American architect Charles Moore's[6] "all-out assault on the modernist tenet of the integrity of the external wrapper" and its implicit attack on a dividing line of what lies inside and what lies outside (177).[7] The pigs have taken charge of their own story, and in so doing have released and recruited other figures—notably the dragon and the fiddle-playing cat—from their stories and their roles, so that the boundaries of the narratives, like the frames of the pictures, become fluid and semi-permeable. The final construction of the happy ending is made from the selection of the page bearing the sturdy brick house of the original story, and re-inhabiting it. "It's my place," says the third pig. "Notice the brickwork. I did it myself." The creators of the new narrative are also into DIY (Do-It-Yourself) house construction, architects of their lives and of their dwelling.

The dimensionality of the images further dramatizes the metafictive sense of standing outside the story, for in "the old story" the characters seem very flat in contrast with the higher texture, the shadows and other graphic features that render the higher dimensionality of the figures that escape the bordered images. The first pig is "bl[own] right out of the story" when the wolf huffs and puffs, and the metanarrative that takes place outside the depicted page frames continues this increased dimensionality, even to the point of threatening to come right out of the page into the reader's world and sensing our presence. And in the escape of the dragon, the dimensionality of the pigs and the emerging monster is increased through the use of color against a black and white background. In all of these actions, the sense of frame-breaking is one of freedom and power over one's own destiny, just as the girl in Karrebaek's book finds a good place to be. Nonetheless, when surrounded by friends in one's own house, it seems as though the structured life can be very enjoyable. The pigs sit happily in their enclosing square frame, on square stools around their square table, while the wolf sits thoroughly framed by a picture frame or a picture frame window, small and insignificant. I guess it all depends on who constructs the frame!

In *The Lost Thing* (2004) Shaun Tan, like Wiesner, foregrounds the use of frames and borders, though he favors Liao's use of internal framing to create a highly structured effect. He employs a simulated collage technique to depict the multiple borders and boxes of modern life and the dilemma of things that do not fit and have no place, but he offers no escape but the power of cynical humor. The general impression of his book's organization is that of a scrapbook whose text and images are pasted onto the pages of a recycled science or engineering treatise or textbook packed with definitions, diagrams, tables, and calculations. This background reaches to the edge of the page, and appears to be a patchwork of pieces, yellowed with age, and oriented in different directions. Unframed, random, and apparently tangential to the narrative, the entire page may be considered as a framing medium for the images and formal text of the story, although it interferes with rather than enhances the focus of the supposed work. It does, however, suggest not only the buzz of information that creates a constant noise in our lives, but also the bricolage that provides a theme of the book: old, useless things in which some people find value—a valuation made on whimsical rather than on thoughtful or aesthetic grounds. The narrator of the events himself collects bottle caps, rows of which are depicted on the book's end papers.

"Pasted" upon this noisy background is a wide variety of cut-outs. The verbal narrative is hand-written upon yellow, lined paper or cards, each cut to accommodate the length of the sentence it bears. These are framed by a dark, shadowed line which gives a three-dimensional effect to the inserts. Larger in size are the pictures and images, some an inch or two square or round, some filling an entire page or a doublespread, or crossing over the gutter to take up part of the facing page. And there is often a layering of scraps one over the other: images and or verbal text thus appearing framed by cut-out pieces of pages of scientific text, less yellowed than the general background page. The many-framed organization of the page—multiple layers of newer and older scraps of paper, large and small, many of which appear randomly taken from the detritus of others' lives—conveys a feeling of confusion and of loss. A vast sea of information swallows the valuable and the irrelevant without discernment, and the ability to perceive what is significant grows harder as we become "too busy doing other stuff, I guess."

Besides the images and text directed toward the story line are random pieces of often humorous commentary, advertisements, formal documents, and printed announcements that refer tangentially to the theme of the book. While some of these notices are from suppliers of such goods as "flywheels, gears, sprockets . . . and hard-to-find alternators," tying in with the background emphasis on mechanical things, many point toward a bureaucratic jumble that values tidiness over creativity, routine over thought, and process over judgment. One full page of Tan's book is dedicated to such notices, whose central feature is The Federal department of Odds and Ends, which finds a pigeon hole for anything that doesn't fit, and whose motto is "sweepus underum carpetae."

While foregrounding the use of framing, using discarded printed words to frame comments on the useless boxing of life into meaningless categories and pigeonholes, and the pursuit of goals whose value is more than questionable, Tan's work subtly subverts the notion of the frame, both perceptual and architectural. What is cut out and preserved would appear to be no different from what must have been discarded. Perception of what is significant and what is not is evanescent like "something [I see] out of the corner of my eye that doesn't quite fit [and] I see that sort of thing less and less these days . . ." as Tan's protagonist tells us at the end of the book. The order and structure that architectural framing brings is similarly challenging to discover: the narrator's confusion is endemic to the inscribed text, the connection between the text and the graphic images and the relationship of one image to another is frequently uncertain, and the images themselves, while often mechanistic or surreal, offer little illumination to the reader. Rather, the notion of boxes and borders is itself pre-eminent, implying that our perception is itself fragmented by them and that, like the lost things, perhaps our only freedom is to find the place where other lost things go.

As we might expect, the picturebook illustrators discussed have chosen styles of framing that are most consonant with the themes the books express. Beatrix Potter's rebellious Peter is not a respecter of the boundaries human beings fashion to mark ownership of their natural environment. The artificial borders Mr. McGregor has shaped to enclose his own vegetable empire are readily permeable by natural creatures, so it is logical that Potter's images are not characterized by strongly marked frames. In contrast, the architectural framing of *Do Not Go Around the Edges* stresses the dominant, rigid divisions of the post-colonial experience which have fragmented into bordered parts the self of those born into the aboriginal culture. The "edges" between the two emphasize the difference between the artistic representation of the natural world as experienced through aboriginal perception and the rules and regulations of the post-colonial power that imprison the person in a series of limited roles and social aspirations.

This contrast between freedom and constraint, wholeness and fragmentation is also apparent in both *Pigen Der Var Go' Til Mange Ting* and *Stellina*. In *Pigen*, architectural framing presents the fracturing of family experience and expulsion of the child from the parents' relationship. At the end of the story, the girl steps out of the heavily framed constraints of the family situation into the perceptual freedom of the final pages with their absence of borders and their Art Nouveau tendrils. Here the framing offers comments on the social and psychological aspects of the girl's maturation. *Stellina* simply presents the notion of freedom and constraint in what appears to be an ironic reversal of the usual contrast between framed civilization and unframed nature. In the city environment, the outside is so heavily ordered and oppressive that indoors becomes the place of freedom.

In *The Sound of Colors*, the intensive use of architectural shapes, stairways and tunnels implies the sense of imprisonment that the loss of sight portends. The movement toward freedom is indicated by the possibility of breaking barriers, but more emphatically in the nature of the framing, and the sensation of falling into imagination, which has no barriers. While whimsicality is injected into the architectural presentation, structure is nonetheless dominant. Extrapolating from this situation, one might suggest that, besides the notion of moving into borderless imagination, the experience of sound itself is without edges, offering a possible future that is less broken and more whole.

The Three Pigs makes a direct assault on architectural framing, but this assault is conceived in the sense of remaking the frame to express one's own sense of order. Deconstruction leads to reconstruction as the pigs create their own environment which involves the safety and freedom they desire, rejecting the premises of the roles in which they were originally cast and reframing both their environment and their place in it.

Finally, and most cynical, *The Lost Thing* offers us frames within frames, a meaningless ordered environment without a sense of escape. Nonetheless, within the boxing and framing of lives, co-existence is presented as possible.

The notion of perceptual and architectural framing in its simplest form necessarily moves into more complex permutations and combinations as the artists use the techniques to express their perspectives on the stories they tell. While there is often a correlation between unstructured or perceptual framing and freedom or natural existence, and heavily structured framing and the sense of being boxed in and limited, the two approaches may be combined in sophisticated ways. For example, Tan's creation of frames from elements that are perceptually derived serves to emphasize that the balance of freedom and limitation, whether political, social, psychological, or expressive of other aspects of human experience, is in continual ferment and devolution. This turmoil of life is captured in frame making and frame breaking, and in the gentle demarcation techniques of perceptual framing that contrast with architectural framing's imposition of a strong sense of order in the delineation of borders and structures.

Notes

1. Cf. Scott (2002), Perry Nodelman (1988), Peter Neumeyer (viva voce).
2. English translation by Maria Nikolajeva and Carole Scott.
3. The existence of and absence of frames has often been used by illustrators to mark the difference between objective and subjective experience, reality and dream, or to note the increase of emotion or of imagination of

characters and events. A well-known and often-cited example is Maurice Sendak's *Where the Wild Things Are* (1963) where, as Max moves into his imaginative journey, framing disappears and the illustrations stretch to the page borders.

4. Three images of modern, post-modern, and deconstructivist buildings are of interest here. They are:

   a) Renzo Piano & Richard Rogers: Pompidou Centre, Paris 1977 (modernism).

   b) Alan Greenberg: News Bldg. Athens, GA 1992 (postmodernism).

   c) Coop Himmelblau, Groninger Museum, Netherlands 1994 (whimsical architecture of deconstructivism).

5. Louis Kahn (1901–1974), Professor of Architecture at the University of Pennsylvania 1957–1974, played with notions of functionality and its absence, and conceived of buildings expressing human emotions in their construction. He is considered an early post-modernist.

6. Charles Moore (1925–1993) shared many of Kahn's post-modern tendencies, and is particularly known for his concern with the public realm and the diverse cultural population that it serves.

7. An architectural deconstructivist image is relevant here: Peter Eisenman: Max Reinhardt Haus, Berlin 1992.

Bibliography

Primary Sources

Karrebaek, Dorte. *Pigen Der Var Go' Til Mange Ting*. Copenhagen: Forum, 1997.
Liao, Jimmy. *The Sound of Colors: A Journey of the Imagination*. Translated by Sarah L. Thomson. New York: Little Brown, 2006.
Pericoli, Matteo. *The True Story of Stellina*. New York: Alfred A. Knopf, 2006.
Potter, Beatrix. *Peter Rabbit*. London: Warne, l902.
Tan, Shaun. *The Lost Thing*. Vancouver: Simply Read, 2004.
Utemorrah, Daisy, and Pat Torres. *Do Not Go Around the Edges*. Broome, Western Australia: Magabala Books, 1990.Wiesner, David. *The Three Pigs*. New York: Clarion Books, 2001.

Secondary Sources

Nikolajeva, Maria, and Scott, Carole. *How Picturebooks Work*. New York: Garland Press, 2001.
Nodelman, Perry. *Words About Pictures*. Athens, Georgia: University of Georgia Press, 1988.
Scott, Carole, "An Unusual Hero: Perspective and Point of View in *The Tale of Peter Rabbit*." In *Beatrix Potter's Peter Rabbit: A Children's Classic at 100* edited by Margaret Mackey. 19–30. Lanham, MD: Scarecrow Press, 2002.
Steele, James. *Architecture Today*. New York: Phaidon, 1997.

Chapter Eight
Surprised Readers
Twist Endings in Narrative Picturebooks

Brenda Bellorín and Cecilia Silva-Díaz

> Tell you a secret. The last act makes the film. You can have an uninvolving, tedious movie, but wow them at the end, and you've got a hit. Find an ending.
> **Robert McKee in Adaptation.**[1]

The endless debate about how children's books should end has primarily focused on the psychological and emotional fulfilment of expectations. However, little has been said about the cognitive mechanisms that challenge readers to strive for meaning as they reach the end of a story. We believe that a description of the patterns as well as the textual and graphic strategies which characterize surprise endings in picturebooks can allow us to go deeper into defining levels of complexity according to the type of cognitive functions that twist endings can trigger. Therefore, in this chapter we will look at several picturebooks to study the forms, effects, and implications of surprise endings. We will attempt to show how the patterns of concealment and revelation appear in the narrative, and how the interplay of text, image, and the physical dimension of picturebooks can help children develop both their narrative thinking and their understanding of how a work of art creates meaning. We will draw parallels with cinema in order to illustrate more clearly what these narratives, which also use images to convey meaning, and to share. This will allow us differentiate those elements which only appear in picturebook narratives.

Aristotle Also Said: A Story Must Have a Beginning, a Middle, and an End

As human beings we constantly seek to give closure to specific episodes of our personal experience. This propensity appears not only in our personal lives, but also in the core of narrative thinking and storytelling. Writers such as Aristotle have recognized this tendency since ancient times. We believe that the way we anticipate endings affects how we read the present: we allow ourselves to add anticipated meaning to our "now" assuming that the expected "then" will give meaning to the plot. Even the capricious *tick-tock* that distinguishes two identical clock sounds is an attempt to create a minimal plot that can shape and organize the passing of time (Kermode 53). In creating such narrative structures we expect coherence between the beginning, the middle, and the end, because the first two elements are reshaped by the last.

Once we infer the explicit and implicit information that will condition our reading of reality, we predict an end and, almost immediately, experience an urge to confirm our inferences. If we find out that our predictions were less than accurate, we strive to correct them by reconstructing the sequence of events in order to restore meaning. By doing so, we accomplish a sense of closure (Goodman 55–58). The retrospective signifying process of the whole experience is what allows us to achieve cohesion and coherence. This need for conclusion is not exclusive to personal experience; it is also a part of the process of reading and, of course, rereading texts.

When we read random events as a story, we synthesize dissonant elements to attain closure. Expectations are reshaped and modified and attention is fixed "on the reverberations or implications that result from fulfilment and frustration of those expectations" (Rosenblatt 54).

According to the Aristotelian canon, *peripeteia*, the turning point that brings about unexpected changes in the story, is located at the climax or the middle point. Stories that have their *peripeteia* in the middle are enjoyable because readers are able to adjust their predictions, meet their expectations, and thereby attain closure. However, in contemporary literature—and picturebooks are no exception—surprises can take hold at any point of the story. Pleasure does not necessarily derive from confirming what one expected at the end, but from being surprised. In twist endings the desire to reach the end prevails, but there is also pleasure in reaching the end in unexpected ways.

Don't You Dare Bring in a Deus Ex Machina

Twist endings usually surprise readers by concealing an important part of the narrative. Characters or facts turn out to be different from what they previously seemed to be. Geoff Haggerty describes it well: "It was a dream./He was a girl./She was a guy./He did it./He wasn't real./He was dead the whole time./

She was dead the whole time./It was an alien./It was a robot./It was science fiction./God did it." (Haggerty)

The history of cinema shows that twist endings can make excellent blockbusters. *Psycho* (1960), *Planet of the Apes* (1968), *The Usual Suspects* (1995), *Fight Club* (1999), *The Sixth Sense* (1999), and *Memento* (2000), are just a few examples. Although these films—just like those with traditional endings—place the resolution at the end, their narrative structure transforms the viewer's desire for closure into anxiety by making the *pereipeteia* as an aesthetic game of playful divergence in which a first examination does not necessarily clarify things, but instead leaves them more confused or in need of a second round of disclosure.

In most of these films—the exception being *Planet of the Apes* in which the last image, the Statue of Liberty, not only freaks out Charlton Heston, but surprises us all—the twist ending is encoded in the *anagnorisis* or the recognition of the true state of things by the main character. Hollywood is not very fond of the escapist deus ex machina, as Robert McKee says emphatically to Charlie Kaufman in *Adaptation* (2002).

Twist endings in picturebooks are not necessarily based on *anagnorisis*; the character can be aware of the *peripeteia* while the reader can remain clueless until the end, when he or she can finally acknowledge the turning point. Because of picturebooks' nature as *icon text*,[2] as defined by Nikolajeva and Scott (6), the game of deception can be a matter of perspective and points of view: a narrative that plays with the layout and the frames used from one doublespread to another. The game's strategies usually depend on the fact that highly relevant information is concealed in the text or in the pictures or, sometimes, in both. In most cases, key elements remain literally out of sight of the reader, suggesting that the story can continue one way or another. Can picturebooks with twist endings be aesthetically engaging and cognitively stimulating for young readers? We believe that the answer can only be affirmative if the game of diversion allows for an adjustment of the reader's predictions in order to attain closure.

If the surprise brings about recognition of the deception and invites the reader to put together the entire story's hints and clues in a second reading, both the reader and the story's conceit have won the game. If the pictures or the text are able to suggest the deception without giving away enough elements for the re-configuration of the story then, perhaps, the picturebook only offers a win-lose scenario. When this happens, the feeling is somewhat similar to the laughter induced by a joke in which the resolution is not entirely funny because the punch line is unclear and, therefore, does not offer closure. Finally, if the surprise only brings about perplexity and frustration both the reader and the story have lost. In this sense, a proper compliment for an ending would not be "I didn't see that coming," but rather "I can't believe I didn't see that coming—it was so obvious."

Oh, Wow. That's Kind of a Twist, Huh?

Film critics have established narrative patterns in twist endings. Nicholas Turner suggests that the plots of films with twist endings can be broken down into various categories. In this section we will look at Turner's categories in an attempt to adapt his findings to picturebooks. Analogies with cinema are useful in order to understand the nature of the endings and other fictional strategies. However, information about the process of reconfiguration of a story through rereading is perhaps better mirrored in literature. Picturebooks—as with any other kind of book—allow us to go back and look closely at the word choice; they allow us to use fast-forward and replay, like watching a DVD at home, in order to look carefully at any details we might have missed while trying to get a full understanding of the plot on the first reading.

Five of Turner's categories are of particular relevance to the current discussion:

1. The Puzzle

Like in an old *Twilight Zone* episode, something seems odd throughout the story, but it is hard to put your finger on what exactly it is. The reader of Van Allsburg's *Bad Day at Riverbend* (1995) has a similar experience. The black and white cowboy with color strokes seems awkward, but the enigma is solved when it is revealed that the story takes place within a coloring book that a girl is painting.

2. The Menace Returns

This kind of ending, often used to set up a sequel, is very common in horror films like *Friday the 13th* (1980). With this device the ending claims to start all over again and the pleasure seems to lie in recurrence, in repetition. It is also used in picturebooks. The text in Ungerer's *Le Géant de Zeralda* (Zeralda's Ogre, 1971) tells the story of how Zeralda tames and marries the terrible giant who eats children and manages to live happily ever after with him. However, the last image suggests the recurring menace by showing the giant's offspring hiding a knife and attentively watching his baby brother.

3. The Reversal or Double-cross

The character's motivations in this type of plot are not what we imagined. A movie like *No Way Out* (1987) reveals only at the end that Kevin Costner has been a Soviet spy all along. In a picturebook named *Loup* (Wolf, 2000) by Olivier Douzou, something similar occurs. In the first page the text says, "I put my nose on" and a rectangle appears in the corner of the page in blank. In the following doublespreads the text continues: "I put my eye on," "I put on my other eye," "I put my ears on," "I put my teeth on."³ In each doublespread the right page progressively fills in with geometric figures which stand for every feature if the wolf's face. The tension begins, first, by understanding who is putting what, and then, once the reader can recognize the character, it increases with the expectations it raises of what will be eaten by the wolf. Finally, the ferocious wolf ties a napkin around his neck; he is ready to . . . eat a carrot! The wolf has been vegan all along.

4. The World Is Not What We Think

This sort of ending is exemplified by *Planet of the Apes* (1968): having believed throughout the film that is was about another planet, thanks to the view of the ruins of the Statue of Liberty we discover that it was our planet, but hundreds of years in the future. It is from this image that the character loses all hope of returning home, because, his home, as such, no longer exists. In stories like this expectations are betrayed by a deceptive narrative. These types of narratives only reveal themselves at the end of the story in a gesture that introduces or confirms absurdity. In Lane Smith's *Glasses, Who Needs 'Em?* (1991) a wacky doctor tries to convince a boy that he needs glasses by giving him even more wacky arguments. The doctor's surreal point of view—which, logically, the patient has disregarded as nonsense—turns out, in fact, to be correct and truthful once the boy has his glasses and is able to see the real world. This picturebook plays with what is subjective and what is part of reality.

5. He Was Dead All Along

Popular films such as *The Sixth Sense* (1999) and *The Others* (2001) used this device. Though we have not found equivalent existential twist endings in picturebooks, in Antonio Ventura's *Cuando sale la luna* (When the Moon Rises, 2005) the character does change ontologically: right up to the end, the reader believes that the narrator is the owner of the teddy bear and not the teddy bear himself.

Before moving on to the classification of picturebooks by their endings, we would like to reconsider, once more, the role that surprise plays in narrative picturebooks.

Wow Them in the End

Expectation and *surprise* are important in learning about literature, especially for inexperienced readers. Children learn to fill in the gaps of concealment, to make predictions, and, in the process of rereading, to confirm and correct these predictions in order to achieve closure. The surprise created by unfulfilled expectations can allow children to explore the way conventional stories work and to think about what literature can offer.

Surprising plots contribute to activating many cognitive functions in children. They learn to read stories by using the knowledge they have acquired from previous reading. In addition, they adjust their expectations to the new information or, in what amounts to the same thing, they become aware of the fact that the elements in the text and pictures are not there casually, and that hints and clues are there for the later reconfiguration of the story just waiting for the reader to recognize them as such. Experienced readers know that surprises can be very conventional when they are part of genres such as thrillers or heists. The readers of this type of fiction expect to be surprised by a twist ending. Therefore, the unfulfilled expectations are part of the conventions of such genres.

Another type of surprise is experienced when conventions are broken in experimental stories: in metafictional fiction this can make the reader aware of how convention works (Silva-Díaz). As a consequence, children can experience pleasure in spite of the potentially unfulfilled expectations. In the metafictional twist ending, the re-composition of what has been broken can be challenging and exciting. It also allows the reader to learn how to deal with the temporary sense of disorientation that results from surprise endings.

In the game of concealment-revelation that exists in picturebooks with surprise endings, the position of the reader is very active, although quite different from that described by Bettina Kümmerling-Meibauer in her work about ironic picturebooks (157–183). Thus, while ironic picturebooks invite the reader into the story to see what the characters are unable to see, stories with twist endings limit the reader's view until the end, when the whole picture is finally shown.

The cunning ambiguity and unclear intentions of picturebooks with surprise endings are somewhat devious, all of which can be quite appealing. They might include literary devices and tropes such as red herrings, and simulated realities. They might also include pictorial devices of denotation and exemplification (Doonan 15),[4] which offer complex aesthetic experiences to children by allowing them to learn about how visual art communicates. The need for re-composition created by picturebooks with surprise endings can make children aware that every mark matters: they can internalize, for instance, the fact that framed pictures can communicate focalization and that bleed illustrations are a sort of zoom-out utilized to give a broader contextualization of the scene in the image.

These devices encoded in both pictures and text—or in the relationship established between them—imply complex conceptual figures such as irony (Kümmerling-Meibauer) and the use of metonymic images that force the reader to access information gradually (Bajour).

The End[s]

At this point, we will attempt to demystify the idea that picturebooks that do not fulfill the reader's expectations at the end are necessarily considered to have a bad ending.[5] We will look into some picturebooks and classify them according to their endings. In an informal testing out of our ideas, in Venezuela in August 2007 we spoke to a total of seven children ranging in age from six to ten, and we have included some of their comments here. Paradoxically, and contrary to our interest in endings, neither the classification nor the children's responses to the picturebooks always offer closure in the matter of twist endings. Nevertheless, we expect to bring about a very slight twist in the way we think about picturebook endings.

1. Disturbing Epilogues

In this type, regardless of a positive or negative ending, it is the last image or sentence that drastically changes the outcome. The epilogue becomes a kind of new beginning that takes the conclusion of the story to another level, to a different point in time and space.

In disturbing epilogues the reader might not be able to acknowledge the extreme detour at the end. For example, *Foxtrot* (2002) is about a misunderstood fox who wants to become a musician in spite of his quiet and conventional family environment. The epilogue discloses itself both in the text and illustrations, suggesting that Foxtrot's son will have to deal with the disapproval of his tuneful family because, instead of following in his father's footsteps, he wishes to become an artist. When we asked Yalin and Sofía if the book had a happy ending, neither of them hesitated in saying yes, and neither of them acknowledged the possible problems that Foxtrot's son could face in the future.

As we mentioned previously, in *Le Géant de Zeralda* the epilogue is in the image, not in the text. Ten-year-old Cristina thought the story had a satisfactory ending. But, when questioned again about this, she admitted that it might not be such a good thing to marry an ogre and cook for him forever after. Looking one more time at the final illustration she said: "Don't tell me he is going to eat the baby."

2. Concealed Intentions

Concealed intentions occur when the reader is clueless about the character's intentions. In picturebooks with no text like *De Verrassing* (The Surprise, 2003), the illustrations can only show the actions of the character but cannot tell the reader about the motivation for these actions (Kress and Van Leeuwen 76). In this sense, *Loup*, alluded to before, is similar to *De Verrassing*. Though the text is written in the first person, the character does not reveal his intentions until the end. This book is a good example of how unexpected endings may break down the expectations that readers have built up about the story based on literary knowledge acquired in prior reading. Don't we all get frightened when a wolf starts naming its body parts one by one?

3. Hidden Characters

The concealment of a character or one of a character's relevant features can be accomplished either by focusing the text or by framing the illustrations. *Susan Laughs* (1999) offers a rhymed list of the things she can do or feel. Both the textual focus and visual framing conceal until the end that Susan is in a wheelchair. The ending suggests that if the reader felt just like Susan throughout the narrative, perhaps it is because there are no substantial differences between the character and the reader.

Figure 8.1 Illustration from Jeanne Willis and Tony Ross: *Susan Laughs*. London: Andersen Press, 1999.

Surprised Readers • 121

Figure 8.2 Illustration from Jeanne Willis and Tony Ross: *Susan Laughs*. London: Andersen Press, 1999.

After reading this book, six-year-old Suria felt the urge to correct her first impression by confirming with a second reading that Susan was never on her legs in any of the illustrations. In contrast, Cristina had a much more complex interpretation: "Those are all the things Susan thinks she can do but actually can't."

Another picturebook that plays with a hidden character is *You're All Animals!* (2000). The elephant Billy Trunk wishes to find someone like him in his new school. Feeling lonely among his freakish classmates, he begins to exchange emails with Frank, with whom he apparently shares everything: grey skin, big nose and ears, and a love for donuts. The surprising final illustration shows Frank, Billy Trunk's pen pal: a tiny mouse. During the story, character and reader have shared the same expectations but the illustration reveals the differences between those who are seemingly so alike. Since the revelation does not contradict the coincidences between the characters, Sofía elaborated on how the story plays with the concept of likeness to create expectations and humor.

4. Restricted Reality

Le drame (2000) has a suggestive title that encourages the reader to expect all kinds of drama and disaster, and right from the start, the reader encounters it. However, it is not until the end that the reader discovers that the disaster, more than a drama, is a mess. The omniscient narrator lists catastrophes, one after another: "Everything began with an accident ... A truck was unable to stop on time and hit a car ..." (6).[6] The text is displayed in variations of the serif typeface—changing size and color according to the expressive function. The illustrations are overlaid invaded with other fonts to denote onomatopoeia.

In this extremely noisy picturebook, the apparently unlimited running chain of catastrophic events becomes unbelievable, or at least overwhelming. At the end there is an overpowering scream that is followed by a zoom-out revealing the entire narrative situation to the reader. It is the moan of an angry mother complaining about the mess that the children have made while playing out the disaster. The game of deception clearly plays with the framing. The illustrations have been focused inside frames that reduce the reader's view to a portion of the narrative. The reader then becomes aware that the typographic games were used to denote the voices of the players and that the omniscient narration was subordinated to a playful dialogue in the main story. The story allows the reader to readjust their expectations and correct the original inference and predictions in both the text and the pictures.

Another example in this category would be *Bad Day in Riverbend*, although in this book the suspicion that something is odd is there right from the beginning. The strokes of color are the elements that cause the reader, once he or she has reconfigured the twist ending, to think "I should have seen it coming, after seeing all the black and white in the landscape."

5. Sneaky Narrator

Surprise and confusion can surface from not knowing who is telling the story. This is what happens in the picturebook *Cuando sale la luna*. Readers tend to assume that human characters are protagonists in stories in which inanimate objects, animals, and humans coexist. In this picturebook, the narrative is written in the first person. The first picture shows a child and his teddy bear; the reader assumes that it is the child who is telling the story, especially because at the beginning the voice says, "When the moon appears and it's time to go to bed, the toys from the box come out to play"[7] (4). However, as the narrative progresses the reader is surprised by the fact that it is the teddy bear that has been telling the story all along: the subtlety-implied fact that the teddy bear is a toy from the bed has made this very difficult to perceive. Since the surprise is only dealt with in the text, the possibilities of correcting first impressions in a second reading are slim. Perhaps it would be more explicit—and less of a win-lose situation—if the surprise had been reaffirmed in the illustrations as well by playing with the frame or focus. By doing so the book could have represented a change of perspective that mirrored the changed perception of the narrator's identity.

6. Non-Explicit Turning Points

In the narrative game of divergence, information relevant to anticipating an ending can be concealed, requiring more or less expertise from the reader in understanding what and how this information has been hidden. The tricky game of concealing *peripeteia* by ellipsis is complex indeed. When something as important as *peripeteia* is hidden, making sense at the end of what one has read and looked at in order to restore meaning and achieve a composite text can be difficult.

Giggle, Giggle, Quack (2003) is a picturebook with this level of difficulty. Farmer Brown goes away for the holidays and leaves his brother in charge of the farm. Before leaving he warns him to be vigilant of the mischievous duck and to follow the instruction sheet he has left for him regarding the care of the property and the animals. The duck gets hold of a pencil and swaps the farmer's instructions with his own, which include strange arrangements for the animals: pizza night, bubble baths for the pigs, and extravagant musicals for the cows. The duck appears in all the illustrations with a pencil—some even show him sharpening the pencil or positioning himself in front of the instructions. Although the narrative is given in the omniscient third person, the book also has plenty of dialogue, which expresses conversations that are taking place over the phone or the noises made by the animals—the latter denoted with different fonts. The instructions are also represented graphically as part of the illustrations with a different typeface than those used to express the other levels of discourse.

In this picturebook there are elements for a win-win scenario, but it could easily become a win-lose scenario depending on the reader's experience because the *peripeteia* is not explicit: the turning point is alluded to by ellipsis and is not expressed in a clear way. To infer that the duck has replaced Brown's instructions for others that suit him better is only suggested by clues that appear in crescendo. The game calls for a reader who is very skilled in deduction. When the farmer screams "Duck!" and is shown in the final illustration furiously grabbing his bag, both the scream and the image can be interpreted as an invitation for the reader to go back and look for clues that could have been missed on the first reading.

Ten-year-old Cristina knew the duck was the author of the mischief from the first note. She thought it was the funniest of all the books we shared. Sofía and Yazlin, both seven-year-olds, had the impression that it was a very funny story because the duck was mischievous but they were unable to point out what specifically made this character scheming and devious. Yazlin thought the farmer was angry because the duck didn't answer the phone. She did notice the duck was grabbing a pencil all the time but was unable to make the necessary connection. At the beginning, she was even doubtful of which farmer had written the notes. When the conversation was about to end, the interviewer offered her version. Yazlin was amused and, without thinking twice, said: "Maybe the duck took the pencil away from the farmer." When we asked seven-year-old Sofia who wrote the notes, she pointed to the authors' names on the book's cover: Doreen Cronin and Betsy Levin.

This picturebook challenges the reader to infer a decisive element of the plot through persistent but not explicit clues. Additionally, to understand that there is an impostor, the reader must be able to acknowledge the duck's motivations, which are very complex if we consider that the inference has to be based on the context—which means the reader has to know what the farmer considers as regular efficient farm functioning. In other words, the deduction cannot be derived from the notes alone, which express the animals' childlike desires. The reader must infer that perhaps the notes are falsifications made by a character that has a different agenda from the farmer.

Surprise endings based on any sort of concealment can offer clues as well as red herrings to "wow" the readers with signs that are planted throughout the story in order to have the reader make inferences. The reader might find this kind of story unsettling: confusion can result from playing with reality and fiction, intention and expression, being and seeming.

7. Fabricated Endings

This kind of ending is anchored in metafictional strategies that make the reader aware that endings are constructed throughout the story. The reader's attention is fixed on the book's physical dimension: the front matter, the doublespread pages, and the binding are all revealed as units of meaning.

For instance, in *Wolves* (2006), the story of a rabbit that goes to the library and checks out a book about his predator, offers two endings. The first creates dissonance for the sensitive reader: the wolf is vegetarian and becomes friends with the rabbit. The second—suggested by ellipsis with a torn page—takes the reader to the last page, in which a three-dimensional due notice from the library allows the readers to deduce that the rabbit has been eaten by the wolf. Though the ending is literally revealed in the margins of the story, it's much more convincing and powerful. It is also much more consistent with other aspects such as the tone used by the narrator which invalidates the politically-correct ending.

Another example that fits this category is *Le jardin de Babaï* (Babaï's Garden, 2004). This aesthetic artefact offers two endings, belonging to two versions of the same story presented in two different languages (and even in two different alphabets). The two trajectories cross over in the middle and allow the reader to understand that the same sequence of pictures read backwards does not necessarily offer the same story. In this beautifully crafted book the reader becomes aware that all elements—including the copyright page—can bring meaning to a story.

End of Story: An Inconclusive Note about Twist Endings in Picturebooks

As Perry Nodelman suggests in *Words about Pictures: The Narrative Art of Children's Picture Books* (15–21), young readers need clarification. Since, in a way, the ending summarizes the story, the reader's ability to understand it fully is very important. Therefore, when an ending does not offer closure by clarifying the narrative situation or giving the readers a hint that they will find the clues in the rereading of the picturebook, the concealment-revelation game may become a meaningless gag. This gag can drain the rich aesthetic experience encoded in the ending, as well as the core learning experiences involved in the reading process, including deduction, inference, and filling in gaps. As we have shown, games of concealment-revelation that are part of stories with twist endings are empowered by the multimodal nature of picturebooks. These games invite readers to experience one very powerful emotion: surprise, which is just one of the many pleasures that literature can offer.

Notes

1. All of the section titles for this article (except for "End of Story: An Inconclusive Note about Twist Endings in Picture Books") are quotations from Spike Jonze and Charlie Kaufman's film *Adaptation*. The film concerns a screenwriter who experiences difficulties in adapting the book *The Orchid Thief* for the cinema. His writing crisis overlaps with the story he is attempting to translate. Confronted by his twin brother, who decides to also become a screenwriter, he reflects on what makes an effective film (for example, the importance of the ending).
2. Nikolajeva and Scott define it as the "inseparable association between text and image that cooperates to transmit a message" (6). An icon text is equivalent to what Jane Doonan refers to as a composite text, which she defines as a "work that is made from the union of what the words say and what the pictures show. Properly speaking, it exists nowhere but in the reader/viewer's head" (83).
3. "Je mets mon nez," "Je mets mon oeil," "Je mets mon autre oeil," "Je met mes oreilles" Authors' translation.
4. As Jane Doonan says: "Pictures have two basic modes of referring to things outside themselves: denotation and exemplification. Denotation is simple. A picture that represents an object and refers to and denotes it . . . The meaning of the symbol is attached to the object . . . denotation doesn't depend upon truth to physical likeness . . . The other main mode

of referring is called exemplification, which means that pictures show, by example, abstract notions, conditions, ideas that cannot be pointed to directly but can be recognized through qualities or properties which the pictures literally or metaphorically display. Meanings do not come attached to symbols that denote. You have to select your meaning from a variety of possibilities and apply those which best suit the image(s) and the context" (15).

5. According to many psychologists, stories addressed to children must have a satisfactory ending. In a study on children's books published during the 1970s, 1980s, and 1990s, Teresa Colomer concluded that 60% of them had satisfactory endings. The rest either ended with the acceptance but not resolution of a conflict, had open endings, or unhappy endings. Negative endings go against expectations. How can the main character die? How can characters in fairy tales not live happily ever after? Unfulfilled expectations can strongly impact readers.

6. "Un camion qui n'a pas freiné et la voiture se retourne," authors' translation.

7. "Cuando aparece la luna y llega la hora de dormir, los muñecos de la caja salen a jugar," (4), authors' translation.

Bibliography

Primary Sources

Allan, Nicholas. *You Are All Animals!* London: Hutchinson, 2000.
Cronin, Doreen, and Betsy Levin. *Giggle, Giggle, Quack*. New York: Simon and Schuster, 2002.
Dozou, Oliver. *Loup*. Rodez: Éditions Rouergue, 2000.
Frank, Claire. *Le Drame*. Paris: Rouergue, 2000.
Gravett, Emily. *Wolves*. London: Macmillan, 2006.
Heine, Helme. *Foxtrot*. Munich: Carl Hanser Verlag, 2002.
Ramos, Mario. *¡Soy el más fuerte!* Barcelona: Corimbo, 2003.
Sadat, Mandana. *Le jardin de Babaï*. Paris: Grandir, 2004.
Smith, Lane, and Jon Scieszka. *Glasses, Who Needs 'Em?* New York: Viking, 1991.
Ungerer, Tomi. *Le Géant de Zeralda*. Paris: L'Ecole des Loisirs, 1994.
Van Allsburg, Chris. *Bad Day at Riverbend*. New York: Houghton Mifflin, 1995.
Van Ommen, Sylvia. *De Verrassing*. Rotterdam: Lemniscat, 2003.
Ventura, Antonio, and Elena Odriozola. *Cuando sale la luna*. Barcelona: Thule, 2006.
Willis, Jeanne, and Tony Ross. *Susan Laughs*. London: Andersen Press, 1999.

Films

Adaptation. Dir. Spike Jonze. Perf. Nicolas Cage, Meryl Streep, Chris Cooper, Cara Seymour, Brian Cox, Tilda Swinton, Ron Livingston, and Maggie Gyllenhaal. Sony Pictures, 2002.
Fight Club. Dir. David Fincher. Perf. Edward Norton, Brad Pitt, and Helena Bonham Carter. Art Linson Productions, 1999.
Friday the 13th. Dir. Sean S. Cunningham. Perf. Betsy Palmer, Adrienne King, and Harry Crosby. Georgetown Productions Inc, 1980.
Memento. Dir. Christopher Nolan. Perf. Guy Pearce, Carrie-Anne Moss, and Joe Pantoliano. Sony Pictures, 2000.

No Way Out. Dir. Roger Donaldson. Perf. Kevin Costner, Gene Hackman, and Sean Young. Orion Pictures Corporation, 1987.
Planet of the Apes. Dir. Franklin J. Schaffner. Perf. Charlton Heston, Roddy McDowall, Kim Hunter, Maurice Evans, James Daly, Linda Harrison, and Robert Gunner. APJAC Productions, 1968.
Psycho. Dir. Alfred Hitchcock. Perf. Anthony Perkins, Janet Leigh, Vera Miles, John Gavin and John McIntire. Shamley Productions, 1960.
The Others. Dir. Alejandro Amenábar. Perf. Nicole Kidman, Fionnula Flanagan, and Christopher Eccleston. Cruise/Wagner Productions, 2001.
The Sixth Sense. Dir. M. Night Shyamalan. Perf. Bruce Willis, Haley Joel Osment, and Toni Collette. Barry Mendel Productions, 1999.
The Usual Suspects. Dir. Bryan Singer. Perf. Stephen Baldwin, Gabriel Byrne, Kevin Spacey, Kevin Pollak, and Benicio Del Toro. PolyGram Filmed Entertainment, 1995.

Secondary Sources

Aristotle. "Poetics." *Identitytheory.com*. http://www.identitytheory.com/etexts/poetics.html (accessed 6/20/2007).
Bajour, Cecilia. "La artesanía del silencio." *Imaginaria* 226 (February 2008). http://www.imaginaria.com.ar/22/6/la-artesania-del-silencio.htm (accessed 2/28/2008).
Colomer, Teresa. "¿Cómo terminan los cuentos?" *Espacios para la Lectura* 1.2 (1996): 6–7.
Doonan, Jane. *Looking at Pictures in Picture Books*. Woodchester: Thimble Press, 1993.
Goodman, Kenneth S. "La lectura, la escritura y los textos escritos: Una perspectiva transaccional sociopsicolingüística." In *Los procesos de lectura y escritura 2* edited by María Elena Rodríguez. 11–68. Buenos Aires: Asociación Internacional de la lectura, 1996.
Haggerty, Geoff. Twist Endings. *McSweeneys.net*. August 11, 2006. http://www.mcsweeneys.net/links/lists/8GeoffHaggerty.html (accessed 5/22/2007).
Kermode, Frank. *The Sense of an Ending: Studies in the Theory of Fiction: With a New Epilogue*. Oxford: Oxford University Press, 2000.
Kress, Gunther, and Theo van Leeuwen. *Reading Images: The Grammar of Visual Design*. London: Routledge, 1996.
Kümmerling-Meibauer, Bettina. "Metalinguistic Awareness and the Child's Developing Concept of Irony: The Relationship between Pictures and Text in Ironic Picture Books." *The Lion and the Unicorn* 23 (1999): 157–183.
Nikolajeva, Maria, and Carole Scott. *How Picturebooks Work*. New York: Routledge, 2006.
Nodelman, Perry. *Words About Pictures: the Narrative Art of Picture Books*. Athens: University of Georgia Press, 1988.
Silva-Díaz, María Cecilia. "Libros que enseñan a leer: Álbumes metaficcionales y conocimiento literario." Diss. Universitat Autònoma de Barcelona, 2007.
Rosenblatt, Louise. *The Reader, the Text, the Poem: The Transactional Theory of the Literary Work*. London and Amsterdam: Feffer and Simons, 1978.
Turner, Nicholas. "Five Ways To End With A Twist." *Scriptfrenzy.org*. 2006. http://www.scriptfrenzy.org/node/413283 (accessed 5/19/2007).

Chapter Nine
The Narrative Power of Pictures
L'Orage (The Thunderstorm) by Anne Brouillard

Isabelle Nières-Chevrel

The first narrative picturebooks devoid of text appeared in France (coming from Italy) during the 1970s. The aim of these books was no longer listing—as we found in the baby concept books of the 1930s—but telling. Turning the page did not simply mean discovering the picture of a new object but creating a link between pictures, building a chronological sequence and deciphering the different steps of a story.

With this first generation of narrative picturebooks, the readability is ensured by the small amount of elements that could vary. There is a unity of space, frame, and point of view. The few characters—if any—are to be found on each page and they establish the continuity of space and the series of actions. The temporal sequence of events is chronological: it corresponds to the reading order, which is itself materialized by the turning of pages and the left-to-right reading. The narrative does not involve flashbacks nor breaks in the narrative ("In the meantime . . ."). These first books are often remarkable for the quality of their artistic innovations, and yet they present marked narrative constraints: the story is linear, the sequence of events is chronological and there is no variation in rhythm or in duration.

Is it possible to further explore the narrative possibilities of illustrations, even if it means that picturebooks become more complex and designed for older "readers"? A new generation of artists is attempting to explore further the possibilities pictures can offer when they are used as the only narrative medium of the book.

In this perspective, I would like to present the analysis of a picturebook by the Belgian artist Anne Brouillard entitled *L'Orage* (The Thunderstorm) and published in France in 1998 by Grandir Editions. It is a picturebook accompanied by no words and it is related to this artist's research on the narrative possibilities of pictures.

A thunderstorm is a spectacular meteorological event that lends itself to a setting to pictures. Anne Brouillard's picturebook describes a thunderstorm. Like any event, this thunderstorm develops in duration and thus the book acquires a narrative dimension. Not only is she abandoning the linear spaces of her two previous books *Voyage* (Travel, 1994), and *Promenade au bord de l'eau* (Stroll at the Water's Edge, 1996), Anne Brouillard creates a confusion in spatial landmarks in this book. She imagines a camera eye moving around in a three-dimensional space made of two distinct places (the inside of a house and an outside landscape) that finally reunite. She blurs the frontier between the inside and the outside as well as between the right and the wrong way round and she repeatedly plays with mirror effects. Reading the book requires the reader's full attention. He or she is confronted with riddles, has to elaborate hypotheses about the different connections between pictures and accept that not everything may be understood. This picturebook requires an active collaboration from the reader, or rather, the *viewer*.

The Thunderstorm, a Spectacular Narrative

In this book, text is reduced to a title. Therefore, the book is, in a way, the mere expanding of its title. A thunderstorm is an experience that is commonplace both to children and adults. Anne Brouillard depends on a knowledge that pre-exists her book. There is no need for words for the reader to identify the elements of a thunderstorm through a picture and to recognize their order of entry: he recognizes what he knows. Thunderstorms are meteorological events that possess a fixed temporal unfolding: forerunners, the brewing of the thunderstorm, the climax with thunder, lightning and cloudbursts, and finally the progressive return to a state of calm and to sunshine. We may thus say that thunderstorms are built like narratives. This meteorological narrative already possesses, in real life, its own rhythms and its own way of occupying space. We await something from thunderstorms, we feel the wind rising, we expect the first lightning to strike. The geranium pot, teetering unsteadily on the windowsill, mimics our expectancies and its fall mimics the effect of the rumbling of thunder. When the thunderstorm unfolds, the rain, the thunder and the lightning give the impression of invading the whole space. The picture easily renders this large scale with the use of the doublespread. The changes in rhythm are rendered by the blank margins as well as by the variations in the scale of the pictures. Since Anne Brouillard depends on a scenario that is already present in her reader's memory, she can build a picturebook accompanied by no words and whose development is infinitely more complex that those observed in 1970s' picturebooks.

Thunderstorms are spectacular events. They are therefore easy to render through pictures. We know that, from Giorgione to Constable and Turner, the motif of the thunderstorm is widely used in Western painting. Anne Brouillard takes delight in rendering its full visual richness: she shows gathering dark clouds, trees bending with the wind, lightings and cloudbursts. Nevertheless, *L'Orage* is more than a mere list of these predictable moments. This thunderstorm is truly an adventure into light. Everything in her book is in contradiction to the stable and neutral light of 1970s' picturebooks. (The growing darkness of the room alters the red shades of the coffee-maker.) The white light of the lightning is glaring and, as we may say, it "eats away" the forms. Finally, the transparent windows become mirrors.

A thunderstorm appeals not only to our sight but to all our senses. We feel the first gusts of wind and the first drops of rain; we hear the rumbling of thunder, we startle when the lightning strikes and when it is over, we smell the scents of the hot and wet earth. How can we grasp here touch, hearing, and smell, in other words all the senses that are, essentially, beyond the scope of a *direct* rendering through pictures? The solution Anne Brouillard chooses is to introduce three couples: two cows, two cats and two wanderers. These living creatures take on, in the diegetic space, all the sensitive perceptions felt during a thunderstorm. They are our representatives in the fiction; they are in charge of feeling beyond what we are bound to only see.

Anne Brouillard succeeds in reviving the thunderstorm experience for her reader. The sole time-reference in her book is the present time, the tense of the pictures. Pictures are indeed blind to the typical component of verbal communication that is the temporal axis (past, present, and future). The picturebook is made of successive "here and now" moments. It is as if we were witnessing the thunderstorm Anne Brouillard is creating for us. The visual narrator presents an unfolding thunderstorm without the medium of a verbal narrator. It is the sole narrator in control of the book.

Anne Brouillard combines this fundamental power of pictures—that is, to tell present time eternally—with the invention of a camera eye. She pictures our presence in the book in the disguise of a camera moving around in a three-dimensional space. The viewer enters a house through a half-open door and goes out of it through the window; he/she circulates at his/her free will.

In fact, the reading eye does not make its way from one room to the other but from one picture to the other. The absence of a verbal narrator means that only the visual narrator is responsible for the whole unfolding of the narrative. This visual narrator perfectly fulfils its controlling function: it plays on oppositions and symmetry, as well as leaps from the inside space of the house to the outside space of the wanderers. What is problematic is the reading of the ellipses. The visual narrator is indeed externally focalized, in Gérard Genette's words. It only grasps the outer aspect of beings and things. Thus, the reader has to interpret the characters' movements and to build hypothetical cause relationships between one picture and the next. The book actively seeks close attention and thoughtfulness from the viewer.

The Viewer's Collaboration

Anne Brouillard says that when her book first came into being, she had written snatches of text.

> *At first, I had written words accompanying this book. These were not final words but snatches. Yet, I had the feeling they might overshadow the pictures. In our culture, text takes precedence over pictures. When they are combined, we look at the picture as a whole, but not as a narration as a whole. I wished to tell everything in pictures. I wished we could read them as such.*[1]

Thus, her initial project was not a systematic exploration of the narrative power of pictures. She chose however not to resort to words and she realized she had to increase the number of pictures to ensure the narrative progression:

> *I had to [. . .] place more pictures, especially at the beginning of the book, in order to set places and characters. In the text version, there were leaps, particularly in the space representation.*[2]

Through this simple remark, she emphasizes the fact that she had to exploit the specific resources of pictures in order to build her narrative.

Anne Brouillard chose to use egg-painting. This technique intensifies colors and enhances lights rather than lines. Her picturebook is made of twenty pairs of pages. She combines pictures on simple page and on doublespreads. The viewer sometimes encounters groups of three or five smaller pictures set on a white background. This very diversity in the pictures scale builds up the rhythm of the book.

1.) The first picture is so hard to read that we may understand it as both a warning and an ultimate test. If we are able to read it, the rest of the book almost seems easy to read. Right from this first doublespread, Anne Brouillard blurs spatial landmarks. The picture is built as a triptych. In the middle, the viewer notices an oval mirror in which he/she can see the reflections of a patch of garden, a small red mill and the white pillar of a gate. We finally understand that the vertical and horizontal lines are the uprights of a transparent window frame that comes between the mirror and the outside landscape. Playing on reflections, Anne Brouillard creates confusion in space landmarks. The respective distances are abolished. Inside and outside unite on the same level surface. On the left and through a glass door, we can see a red living room. What we ultimately identify as a couple of cows grazing under trees could be a painting or another reflection in a mirror. The question is temporarily without answers. On the left, a French window is ajar. We notice a cat that is half-framed by the uprights of a window frame. Where are the occupiers of this house? They cannot be far away, since the piano is opened and the door is unlocked. The viewer is invited to look inside. And so we enter the house.

2.) Turning the pages of a picturebook is a temporal and spatial progress. The continuity of space is ensured by the re-using of elements that were present in the previous picture: namely, the piano, and the cat. We can see a window on the right. In the background, we make out the kitchen furniture with its drawers half-open. A red coffee-maker seems to be framed by the uprights of the window frame and thus takes over from the cat to show us into this second room.

Our eyes move over: matching the coffee-maker that is still framed, we notice a geranium pot in front of another window. A black cat is in front of us. Again, the cat is markedly framed by the uprights of the window frame. Anne Brouillard appeals to the identificatory function of colors: this cat is different from the one we saw in the living room. Yet, the *viewer* will never know if this other cat is *a* black cat or *the* household's black cat. This black cat draws his/her gaze toward the outside. Behind the cat, the viewer can notice another patch of garden and a gate that is clearly distinct from the first one.

3.) Our camera eye meets the cat. We are now outside the house. Its gaze takes over from its body to direct our own gaze upwards, toward a sky loaded with clouds that we discover on the right page. The treetops bend with the wind.

Figure 9.1   Illustration from Anne Brouillard: *L'Orage*. Nîmes: Editions Grandir, 1998.

4.) The viewer is still looking at the sky. The spatial continuity is ensured on the left by the bending treetops. He/she can conclude that the upper side of this large house belongs to the house he/she looked round earlier. In the bottom left-hand corner, beside the wall, he/she can notice a silvery form that is striated with blue lines: is it a glass roof? A veranda?

5.) The re-using of one or two elements has thus led our progress from one picture to the other. When the viewer comes to think he/she has understood how the book works, he/she is confronted by a riddle. In the background, we see a church, two white houses, and a narrow red house. The red color of the buildings and the clouds are the sole elements suggesting the continuity of the story. In the foreground, Anne Brouillard introduces a couple of cows, two people and a building that could well be a small chapel. Did the cows we saw on the first page move? Was a mirror hanging in the red living room? The color of the cows does not help our deciphering; nothing looks more blatantly like a cow than another cow. The entrance of the two teenagers leads the viewer to think that they are the heroes of a story that is about to start.

6.) The following picture immediately cancels out this option. The return to the big red house gives the previous doublespread the role of a mysterious aside. Anne Brouillard adds up all the fragments she has thus presented, and reunites them on this doublespread: the dark sky, the bending treetops, the house, and the black cat. This global representation finally sets all the elements in relation to one another. The viewer eventually identifies a veranda on the left and can deduce where the living room and the kitchen are situated in the house, since he/she had only seen them from the inside so far. From this doublespread on, Anne Brouillard will appeal to her reader's memory, which must re-use the information already gathered.

The black cat moves. Did it feel a drop of rain? It seems to move toward the half open window on the sill of which we can notice a bowl. It could eventually be the beginning of the cat's story.

7.) The viewer is back inside. The spatial continuity is ensured on the left page by the treetops we can see through the window. The half-open window may be announcing the cat's entrance. We can now clearly identify the two rooms and their respective location. We recognize the geranium pot. On the right picture, a change in the angle in the living room enables us to discover an armchair and a mirror that reflects the uprights of a window frame and a form that looks like a tree shaken by the wind. The reader has to turn the page to understand that these two pages establish the characters of the coming scene.

8.) The viewer discovers a sudden change in the layout. He/she hesitates considering the reading order of these two pairs of close-ups. Are they to be read from the top downwards or from left to right? There is no doubt about the answer: they are to be read both ways. From left to right, (to start with) we discover, on the left, the movement that prepares for the drama, and, on the right, we witness the cat's nap; then we witness the (subsequent) crash on the floor and the sudden awakening of the cat. From the top downwards, we are told, on the left page, that a sudden burst of wind has opened the left-hand window that consequently has hit the pot. The plate and the pot have fallen down and broken. On the right page, the cat that is sleeping in the adjacent room is suddenly awakened. The horizontal white margin is the axis of time ("first, then"); the vertical white margin is the axis of space. The central folding imitates the wall separating the kitchen from the living room. Here is a typical example of the power of pictures to represent simultaneity, while a text could essentially only present it with two successive utterances.

9.) The viewer is back outside with the cat. This leads him/her to think that the detour via the geranium pot and the awakening of the red cat are part of the black cat's story. The window is no longer kept shut by the geranium pot; the way in is possible. Reading the right-page picture requires a lot of attention. Is the cat still outside and thus looking inside or is it inside and thus looking back? The re-using of the branch whose bend is inverted by the reflection in the window is the key to understand that the cat is now inside, looking back outside.

The linking with the following picture is made through the cat's eyes. What the visual narrator shows us is reflected on the windows and in the cat's eyes. The cat looks scared.

10.) Here is another break in the narrative. We abandon the black cat's story and see a landscape we have already seen. The frame is slightly narrowed and the chromatic scale is darkened. The thunderstorm is raging furiously; cows and human beings are sheltering. The reader may wonder if the wanderers' story is starting for real.

11.) The answer is a no. This movement back to the place where the teenagers are wandering functions as a temporal marker, a sort of visual "in the meantime." While the wanderers were sheltering, the cat has arrived on the living room's doorstep. On the right-hand page picture, the close-up on the left window indicates a narrative pause. Is this the end of the black cat's story?

12.) Four vignettes illustrate another rapid action. The white light of the lightning suggests a successive reading of this composition, from the top downwards and from left to right. The slight increase in height and width of pictures 2 and 3 conveys the impression of the invasion of space. On the right-hand page pictures, the cat's position under the chair can be interpreted as a sign of fear. What is the cause of its movement away: the lightning or the black cat's settling?

13.) This new layout is not easy to interpret. It is probably an artistic translation of the increasingly rapid succession of lightning flashes: another flash of white light in the kitchen and in a fragment of landscape, streaks of lightning above the two houses in the wanderers' space and above the red house. The pictures are linked together and progressively invade the whole space. For the first time here, Anne Brouillard establishes a link between the two spaces—the wanderers' space and the house—on the same doublespread.

14.) Anne Brouillard extends the artistic closeness of the two spaces. Yet the entirely new layout creates a triangular relationship. One of the wanderers looks out of the little chapel's door at the character from the previous page that is sheltered at home. This visual link may have arisen from the teenagers' desire to be back home too. This hypothesis enables the understanding of the re-using, in the bottom right-hand corner, of the gate seen on the first picture in the book. For the first time, the relationship between the pictures seems to be a "mental" relation, the setting of thoughts to pictures.

15.) This composition made of five vignettes confuses the inside space of the house and the wanderers' space since our gaze is directed from the inside to the outside step by step. We are indirectly told that the thunderstorm is over and that the sun is out once again through its reflection in the mirrors created by the rain itself. In the second vignette's extreme close-up the last drops are still blurring the surface of the bowl. Then the mirror becomes smooth and we make out treetops bending with the wind. This inversion in upper and lower is very clear on the right page. The black reflections on the upper vignette seem to belong to black trees whose trunks and first branches can be seen in the lower vignette. We discover with great surprise that the bending tops of the green trees are also reflecting in the mirror of this pool of water. The spaces of the garden and of the wanderers were in fact close by.

16.) The return to a state of calm puts an end to the fragmentation of the pictures. The red cat is looking at the bowl on the windowsill, as the viewer was. The red cat directs the viewer's gaze outside then toward the treetops and the cloudless sky, just like the black cat did at the beginning of the book.

17.) This doublespread emphasizes the return to sunshine. Anne Brouillard encompasses the two spaces in one doublespread. The house and the landscape that were once separated can now be situated in relation to each another.

18.) The sun is now shining throughout inside and outside spaces. In the living room, the cats have changed seats.

19.) The sun is glowing. The cows have left their shelter under the trees. The two teenagers are back on their stroll and are probably going back home. The figures of the cows are reminiscent of what the reader saw in the opening picture of the book. With its yellow tint provoked by the sun, the last page will confirm the idea that a mirror—and not a painting—is indeed hanging in the red living room.[3]

20.) The book's last picture is the counterpart of the first. The wanderers' figures are eventually reflected in the oval of the mirror. The three couples are now united and each has its place in the triptych: End of the thunderstorm, end of the stroll and end of the book. The angle is not entirely frontal anymore; it is slightly orientated toward the right. The sun lights up the sill of the open window. The door is open for the young wanderers to come in.

I would like to make three short comments as a conclusion:

The Thunderstorm draws on all the potential of visual literacy. Anne Brouillard combines both the narrative and depicting powers of pictures in this book. The succession of pictures, their layout and the variation in their scale build the unfolding and the transformation in space and time that are the main features of any narration. Pictures enable Anne Brouillard to represent the successive components of a thunderstorm and her artistic choices give the pictures a mimetic status. Pictures have a "make-believe" power over the reader/viewer; they create an illusion of reality that revives memories of thunderstorms.

The absence of words is not a simple feat of artistry. It is totally relevant and in keeping with the topic of the book. Thunderstorms are events that appeal to all our senses but they do not necessarily require explanations through words.

The final question is: Why did Anne Brouillard chose to build her book around two distinct—and at first disconnected—spaces? I assume that there could be an inclusive relationship between these two spaces. The house may have been just thoughts in the wanderers' head "What is happening in the house while we are away? We have left the door open. We have left a window open in the kitchen too. What are the cats doing? Are they afraid?" When the wanderers come back, they can find only one tangible sign of what happened while they were away: the geranium pot has fallen down on the floor and the pot is broken; probably because of the wind. The multiplication of plays with mirrors in Anne Brouillard's *L'Orage* probably puts us on the right track. Her picturebook focuses—at the same time—on reflections on the status of pictures and on the naive belief we may have in them. After *L'Orage*, Anne Brouillard continued to publish picturebooks devoid of text (*Le Pêcheur et l'oie* [The Fisherman and the Goose], 2006), but she would never realize again such an ambitious one.

Notes

1. Sophie Van der Linden (2006, 81).
2. Ibid.
3. However, Anne Brouillard told me recently that, in her mind, it was a painting, not a mirror.

Bibliography

Primary sources

Brouillard, Anne. *Voyage*. Nimes: Editions Grandir, 1994.
Brouillard, Anne. *Promenade au bord de l'eau*. Paris: Editions du Sorbier, 1996.

Brouillard, Anne. *L'Orage*. Nîmes: Editions Grandir, 1998.
Brouillard, Anne. *Le Pêcheur et l'oie*. Paris: Seuil Jeunesse 2006.

Secondary sources

Genette, Gérard. *Figures III*. Paris: Seuil, 1972.
Hamon, Philippe. *Du Descriptif* [*Introduction à l'analyse du descriptif*, 1981]. Paris: Hachette, 1993.
Nières-Chevrel, Isabelle. "Le narrateur visuel et le narrateur verbal dans l'album pour enfants." *La Revue des livres pour enfants* 214 (December 2003): 69–81.
Van der Linden, Sophie. *Lire l'album*. Le Puy-en-Velay: L'Atelier du poisson soluble, 2006.
Van der Linden, Sophie. "Interview d'Anne Brouillard." *Hors cadre[s]* 1 (October 2007): 14–15.

Chapter Ten
Picturebooks and Trojan Horses
The Nordic Picturebook as a Site for Artistic Experiment during the 1950s

Elina Druker

The 1940s and 1950s was a dynamic period for the Nordic picturebook. A new generation of picturebook artists were reacting against the conventions that preceded them. The traditional narrative and aesthetic form of children's literature was experienced as inadequate in the attempt to describe the modern world that the child was part of; children's literature was regarded to be in need of a new language, new forms and "modern" images.

To illustrate this dynamic era, I will analyse the picturebook *Historien om någon* (The Story about Somebody, 1951) by the Swedish author Åke Löfgren and the Danish-Swedish artist Egon Møller-Nielsen. This innovative picturebook is constructed as a game of hide-and-seek, taking place in a seemingly deserted, empty house. Each spread of the book presents a room, linked to other rooms in a sequence and the book covers function as the outer walls of the building. In this chapter, I will use *Historien om någon* to discuss the conceptual and spatial investigation of the picturebook medium. I will specifically consider the use of the analogy between book and building, arguing that this method can be seen as a part of a larger artistic context, both within book illustration historically and within the avant garde artists' books. Wendy Steiner remarks in *The Colors of Rhetoric. Problems in the Relation Between Modern Literature and Painting* (1982), that the book is an enclosed world in a similar manner as the building, cut off from that of nature and the outside world (144). The book covers function as a framing device that isolates the work from the real world. My focus lies on how the book's visual presence, its objectness, as well as its conceptual dimension, are investigated, and

140 • Elina Druker

furthermore, how this aesthetic approach relates to a contemporary artistic and cultural context.

In Møller-Nielsen's and Löfgren's *Historien om någon* the method to construct the book as a building is established already on the book cover, depicting a key hole with a pair of eyes peeking through the hole. Somebody is hiding behind the door: a game of hide-and-seek is initiated. As we open the book, we also open the front door to the house where the story takes place. The cover literally functions as external wall or frame for the book. A narrator is inviting us into the apartment: "Somebody has sneaked inside through the street door and in through the door opening . . . [—] Who could it be? Where could he be now? Let's see who is hiding in the next room!" On the next spread, we enter the living room. A piece of knitting lies on the floor, the thread of woollen yarn runs through the room and disappears through the next door on the right—somebody seems to be playing with the ball of yarn, which is missing. We then follow the red yarn through the book, passing a series of rooms: the kitchen, a pantry, a hallway, a staircase and a bedroom, in our search of the hidden somebody.

The narrator seems to be familiar with this home, he mentions, for example, that somebody has eaten up the fish that *he* intended to have for dinner. Constantly turning towards the reader, the narrator uses phrases such as "Let's open the door . . ." "Shall *we* see who is hiding inside?" or "Do *you* think that there is somebody there?" *Historien om någon* follows the structure of a treasure hunt or a detective story where the act of searching is central—the

Figure 10.1 Illustration from Åke Löfgren and Egon Møller-Nielsen: *Historien om någon*. Stockholm: Kooperativa Förbundets förlag, 1951.

reader's role is activated. The concept of the detective story was initially suggested by Møller-Nielsen, who had written the words "a detective novel" with a pencil on the title page of the original illustrations.

On every spread a clue is presented: a milk jar that has fallen and spilled its contents in a kitchen cupboard, a flower pot that has been pushed down and smashed against the floor or a goldfish that has fallen out of a fish bowl (the narrator urges us to put it back into the bowl again). The relationship between words and pictures is dynamic. The narrator gives us clues and suggestions, pointing out certain details throughout the story. These small details are of importance in our search for the mysterious somebody, and they are presented on every doublespread, functioning as page-turners that invite the reader to turn the page. When it comes to the pictorial methods, techniques from different media are used. Close-ups or a slight change of perspective in certain scenes foreground significant details, giving the reader hints about whom or what the mysterious somebody might be. However, apart from the final scene where the mysterious somebody is revealed (a small kitten)—the house is vacant. This is the most striking feature of *Historien om någon*—there is no main character. In fact, the house is completely empty. Something has already taken place in these vacant rooms, but we can only guess what and why. Instead, it is the reader who takes the place of the main character, navigating through the rooms, searching for the hidden somebody.

Spatial innovation is a prominent feature of this picturebook. Attention is brought to the book as a concept. The game of searching that is initiated by the narrator in the first scene and the compositional and dynamic changes in perspective and focus, propose the picturebook as a site of play and fantasy where the role of the reader is imperative. The continuous movement from one scene to the next is established in both the verbal and the visual narration. Each time a page is turned, a new room is exposed. Thus, the structure of the house is connected to the physical qualities of the book. Johanna Drucker indicates in her study *The Century of Artists' Books* (1994/2004), that focus on the margins and edges point at the construction of the book: "[. . .] use of the edge of the page to manipulate the tension between continuity and discontinuity is so fundamental to the book form that it shows up in many works. In every book a decision has to be made about how to either emphasize, ignore, or overcome the fact that the openings are discrete units, separate spaces, each from the next and yet a part of a continuous whole" (175–176). In Møller-Nielsen's picturebook every spread consists of a separate spatial unit, connected to the next opening through doors or staircases. The margins of the page as well as the covers of the book are used to form the interior and exterior walls of this house—the book's physicality is fundamental to its meaning.

The red yarn running through the rooms, although motionless, appears dynamic and mobile in contrast to the still and static compositions in the interior scenes. The interior of the apartment is presented in a realistic manner with traditional furniture and familiar everyday objects characteristic of the time. Some slightly deviant elements have been added: contemporary, modernist paintings are hung on the walls. Page-turners in this story are both visual—the red thread being the most obvious one as we follow its way from one page to another—as well as verbal as the narrator's voice urges us further. Because of its decorative and organic manner the yarn seems to allude to something more abstract than just a woollen yarn. The same woollen yarn is depicted already on the book cover, where the word "somebody" (någon) in the book title is formed with the yarn. The red yarn stands for the game of seeking, for a story being told, for fantasy and imagination. The spatial-temporal construction of a picturebook consists of a literary element—words—and a visual element—a sequence of pictures. It is the combination of words and images in their capacity to express both temporal and spatial qualities that creates an illusion of movement and spatiality. A spatial-temporal quality is furthermore implied through the material form of the picturebook, for example through the act of turning of pages. Drucker remarks that "the act of turning or opening of a page is inherently visual as well as temporal and spatial" (175). In *Historien om någon* the turning of pages functions as a part of a nearly performance-like reading act, setting a certain pace and leaving short gaps in the story. The separate images work together, bound into a fixed sequence. Sometimes a sentence is left unfinished and continues on the next spread: "But the thread is running further through the hallway and . . . [turning of page] . . . up the stairs to the second floor." A short pause takes place as we turn the page, a short gap is created and the narration is halted momentarily which increases the tension. The story depends upon the turning of pages and how one picture follows another. A tempo and a rhythm is formed and through the structure of scenes that follow each other the reader is lead closer and closer to the solution of the mystery. In Møller-Nielsen's story attention is continuously called to the physicality of the page and to the structural elements of the book.

The implications of artificiality, although subtle, are prominent throughout the story. The self-disclosing narrator's voice signals to the reader that a certain kind of attitude is required. This kind of self-reflective focus on the work of art is also expressed through the focus on the book as a bodily object. The analogy between book and building brings to the fore the elements of the image, including its borders and frames. Attention is called to the material qualities of the work. As the art historian Victor Stoichita demonstrates in his study *The Self-Aware Image. An Insight into Early Modern Meta-Painting* (1997), artwork with self-reflective qualities often stresses the status and boundaries of the painting. In *Historien om någon* fiction signals its own fictionality in different ways. The abstract paintings hanging on the living room wall are a kind of self-reflective detail. They are, of course, *images* of paintings imbedded inside a larger image, the illustration in the book. A variation of the self-reflective motif is even found in the last scene, where we reach the end of the story and enter the final room in the attic. The room is crowded with seemingly random things: bags, shoes, a broken chair, an old tea pot, buckets and bottles, a bicycle wheel and tools. There are also an empty stretcher for painting canvas and a brush hanging on the left-hand wall. This small detail, the empty stretcher bars framing in the artist's brush, can be seen as a meta-artistic commentary, thematizing the act and material of painting.

The book form is considered as a conceptual and even performative space. In *Historien om någon* the house is presented with the front wall removed, a kind of a cross-section image of a building—a stage-like construction where the edge of the sheet resembles the edge of a stage. The expression "fourth wall" stems from the notion of an imaginary wall, that is, the absence of a fourth wall in front of a theatre stage. The similar concept is applied in painting. Stoichita demonstrates that representations of interiors generally illustrate the room with the fourth wall removed. This missing component is replaced by the surface of the pictorial image (44). In a way, the convention of a "fourth wall" in *Historien om någon* is broken by the narrator addressing the reader.

And yet, despite the stage-like visual construction, we are not simply looking from the "outside" toward the "inside." The sequential structure of the book, in contrast to a painting, means that a series of interiors are connected inside the book covers. We are not only looking in, but also being guided *through* a series of rooms. The ongoing movement from one interior to another in Møller-Nielsen's picturebook house is clearly confined within its frames that are the covers of the book. The doors in *Historien om någon* connect the rooms and, on most openings, offer a glimpse of the next scene. It is also significant that the doors between the rooms have been opened, thus allowing the reader to "enter" the next room. The doors function as passages between the sequences of rooms presented. The windows, on the other hand, are opaque, hindering us from seeing out, and closing out the outside world. In interior painting, doors and windows are traditionally used in different ways. Victor Stoichita shows in his study that while the window opens the interior up to the outside, implying being indoors looking out, the door structurally functions as a transportation means through two areas (44). Although specifically discussing Western painting with self-reflective features, his remark is relevant here too. Stoichita continues: "In paintings that contain door frames, window frames, or niches, the spectator is invited to see the image through the eyes of the artist/ communicator. [—] the boundaries of the image are elicited" (56).

Both the book and the building require an "entrance" and a closure—quite often depicted as a back door in picturebooks, as in Tove Jansson's *Hur gick det sen? Boken om Mumin, Mymlan och lilla My*, (What Happened Then? The Book about Moomin, Mymble and Little My, 1952). In this book, too, a keyhole is presented, formed as an actual, tiny hole on the book cover. The key to the moomin-house is hanging beside the door, as if welcoming the reader to return to the book/house. Even in the contemporary Danish picturebook *Huset* (The House, 1947) by Grete Janus and Mogens Hertz, the analogy between book and building is used consistently. The covers of this large picturebook form the outer walls of the house with windows, a front door and a roof. When opened, the inside of the book presents a series of doors leading to different apartments, all formed as miniature books within the book, thus presenting several stories within the main frame. The structure of the book as building is constructed as a "Chinese box" or a "mise en abyme", in which an image contains a smaller copy of itself. In this case a larger structure—the house as spatial unit—is used to frame a smaller one—the interior rooms. This way the smaller narratives are both included in and at the same time separate from the framing story. The Danish picturebook *Huset* can be seen as a part of the tradition with mechanical books, an old visual practice with flaps, revolving parts or other movable pieces, often folded out to create a three dimensional construction.

Although the book's physical boundaries are accentuated in a similar fashion in *Historien om någon*, with emphasis on the materiality of the medium, the connection to mechanical books is not quite as evident. Instead, I argue that Møller-Nielsen's method to construct the house as a closed three-dimensional spatial unit with book covers as walls and each opening presenting an interior, can be seen in relation to Møller-Nielsen's training as a sculptor and architect. He forms the book as if he was constructing a building or shaping a sculpture. The analogy between the house and the building is, certainly, not a new invention in art. As David Bland shows in *A History of Book Illustration: The Illuminated Manuscript and the Printed Book* (1969) title pages have often presented an engraved architectural motive as triumphal arches or ornamental doorways. Using the format and margins of the page as walls for a building, an entrance or a room, are visual conventions used already in medieval painting and book illustration (144). This kind of emphasis on beginnings and endings was, as Bland points out, perhaps most apparent in baroque book design, where the analogy was used frequently (144). Illustrations associate the physical structure of the book with another kind of space, the building.

The material aspects of the page and the book are examined by Møller-Nielsen already in his wordless picturebook *Historien om...* (The Story about... 1947) where actual holes cut in the pages have a similar function. Møller-Nielsen treats the book almost as an architectural space, exploring space and volumes, two-dimensional and three-dimensional shapes, the concept of page and book.

Åke Löfgren's and Egon-Möller Nielsen's *Historien om någon* is representative for an aesthetic turn during the 1940s and 1950s. It is a period within the Nordic picturebook aesthetics when a new generation of children's literature authors and illustrators emerge. Egon Møller-Nielsen was an architect and sculptor, educated at the Royal Academy for Arts in Copenhagen, and worked as a trainee at famous architectural offices like Alvar Aalto in Helsinki and Gunnar Asplund in Stockholm during the 1930s. When the Second World War broke out he moved to Sweden and soon became part of the Swedish modernist movement during the 1940s and 1950s. Although mainly working with painting and sculpture, he received a great deal of attention for his monumental sculptures produced during the 1940s and 1950s, placed in public places. When Møller-Nielsen created his first picturebook in 1947, he approached the medium in a similar manner as he did with his sculptures—investigating the material and spatial form of the medium.

The way Egon Møller-Nielsen applies this visual convention in his picturebook proposes the book as a site for playing. Both Møller-Nielsen's monumental sculptures and his picturebooks invite involvement. His sculptures with primary geometric forms, produced in concrete or granite, were placed in parks and playgrounds and had two purposes: they were works of art but could also be used by children as playground equipment.

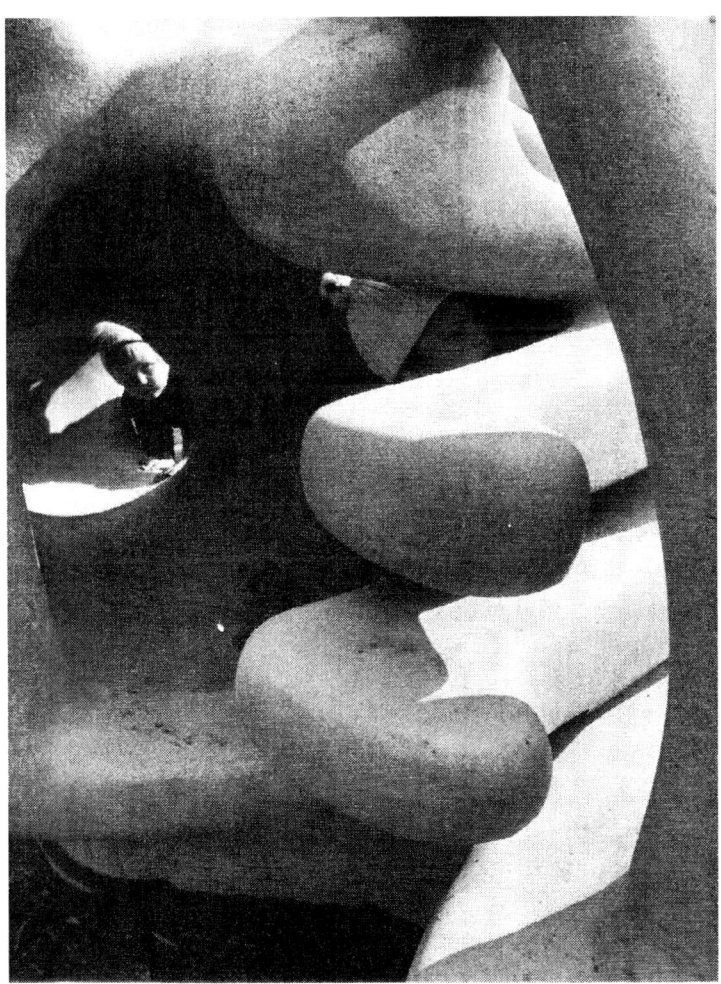

Figure 10.2 Sculpture "Tufsen" (1948) by Egon Møller-Nielsen at Park Humlegården, Stockholm.

Children could climb these massive sculptures, slide on them, or crawl through carved openings. The artist called his playground sculptures for "machines for playing," a paraphrase of the architect Le Corbusier's formula *une machine à habiter* (1923). Corbusier's idea of the house as "a machine for living" emphasizes functionality and construction, aspiring to represent the modern machine age in both structure and form. As many of the modernist sculptors, Møller-Nielsen stripped the sculpture from its ornaments and focused on the three-dimensional exploration of space and volumes. But if his sculptures can be described as "machines for playing," can this formula be applied to his picturebooks?

Conceptualizing the picturebook and focusing on its material qualities raise several critical and theoretical questions. The way the picturebook is investigated as an object as well as the self-reflective elements in *Historien om någon* is parallel to many so called artists' books, books which are intended as artworks. As Tom Guest points out in his article "An Introduction to Books by Artists" (1981) artists' books are produced by artists and are distinct from other kinds of art publishing, in that they are not tied to the conventions of literature, criticism, or arts (7). As Johanna Drucker indicates there are a number of artists who began to explore the book as artists' medium in the late 1940s and early 1950s (12). Drucker shows that the artists' books have been part of various significant modern art movements, from the early twentieth-century avant-garde, Dadaism and surrealism to the present. Although neither Drucker nor Guest include picturebooks for children in their discussion of the medium, artists' books as a field—only partially related to the field of mainstream art and yet connected to it—offers several conceptual and aesthetic parallels to the picturebook medium. I suggest, that even the picturebook as an artistic and literary field, is both related to and at the same time secluded from the field of art and literature, using the conventions of literature and art but often not restricted by them to the same extent as mainstream art and literature. The flexibility and the possible variations of the book form offer an alternative area for artistic experiment. The interest for the picturebook among the young Nordic artists and authors prior and after the Second World War can be seen as a part of an inter-artistic tendency, exploring the limits between different forms of art and searching for alternative zones of activity.

By naming the sculptures "machines for playing," the modernist sculptor Møller-Nielsen was able to disguise the drastically modern piece of art that might have caused controversy, as potential playground equipment. His monuments in public places functioned as a Trojan horse. The metaphor was used by Møller-Nielsen's colleague, the Hungarian surrealist painter Endre Nemes. Nemes claimed that the monumental sculptures in the playground in fact were "Trojan horses"—a strategy to smuggle controversial, modern art to various locations throughout the city. Interestingly, the size of the openings and dimensions of the steps on the playground sculptures are surprisingly small in relation to the monumental form and scale. The sculptures were clearly formed primarily for children. And yet, although intended to be used by children (and also formed accordingly), the playground sculptures introduced radically new modes of artistic expression in public room. Thus, the playground, and children playing with the sculptures, becomes a method to introduce modern art in public places. The child—and even more so, children *playing*—had a symbolic position in the Swedish post-war society and culture. The child obtained an important metaphoric significance as an image of the uncorrupted, vital, and innocent. It is a romantic notion of the child as a metaphor for the future and progress. The child, youth, and youthfulness were idealized.

A parallel worthy of noting is the contemporary Danish picturebook artist Egon Mathiesen. He wanted to introduce children to modern art through picturebooks and illustrated children's literature. The view of the picturebook as a place for artistic expression is shared by both artists. "I see the pictures as a painter does" Mathiesen stated in his article "The Artist and the Picture Book" in *The Horn Book Magazine* (1966). He emphasized the importance of inter-artistic ambitions and proposes an artistic approach to picturebooks, "free from dogma, from standardized meanings and connotations" suggesting the picturebook as a means to introduce not only modern aesthetics but also a way to establish "modern humanism" (96). Møller-Nielsen's ambition with his sculptures was similar; to make modern art accessible for children but even more so, to introduce modern art *through* children. The children were the hidden warriors inside the Trojan horses.

What kind of position did the picturebook have during this period? Other prominent picturebook artists with a similar approach can be mentioned. The author and illustrator Tove Jansson, for instance, also worked with painting, graphic design, political cartoons, and stage design. Stig Lindberg, one of the most prolific designers in Scandinavia and a frontal figure in the Swedish post war picturebook modernism, created together with Lennart Hellsing some of the most innovative picturebooks in Sweden during the 1950s. Even Lindberg worked with multitude of materials, artistic media and techniques that included painting, ceramic art and textile, and industrial design and illustrations. In the case of artists like Egon Møller-Nielsen, Stig Lindberg, Tove Jansson or Egon Mathiesen—to mention a few of the most prominent names—the picturebook became an alternative art form to the mainstream mediums of art and literature. The picturebook medium could offer an alternative for artistic innovation and exploration in a search of new images, forms, and materials.

The way Møller-Nielsen's picturebook *Historien om någon* is constructed proposes the book as a site of artistic experiment. The book can be seen as a part of the ambition to modernize and raise the level of children's literature during the 1940s and 1950s in Sweden. Also, the turning to picturebooks coincides with the reinvented role of the artist in the young generation of artists after the Second World War. Many of the Nordic modernists during the

1940s believed that artistic activity should lead to practical and public applications, such as sculptures and murals in public places, which would benefit the whole society. Even the picturebook can be seen as a part of this tendency: children had a fundamental part in the national ideology in the Swedish postwar society and culture. Children became a metaphor for progress and development—they became representatives of a better future, and thus received a significant ideological and symbolic position in the society. Children's culture and education became significant, and was discussed and debated publicly. Offering the children correctly formed toys, clothes, films, playgrounds, and books, was thought to shape their development as individuals. This tendency is also reflected in the picturebook production: the number of new children's books published during the 1940s and 1950s was high and the artistic and technical standard of production was noticeably improved.

In *Historien om någon*, a traditional narrative pattern is used in an innovative manner. The picturebook as a physical object with its material qualities as its format, covers, the turning of pages, even details as the placing of the middle gutter, is used to stage a detective story in miniature. The reader is required to fill in the blank spots and questions and, in this way, has an active part in creating the story. This kind of challenging and activating of the reader is characteristic for the children's literature of this period, reflecting the changing conception of the child and the child reader. For Nordic artists like Egon Møller-Nielsen, Tove Jansson or Egon Mathiesen, the picturebook becomes a site for artistic experiment. The picturebook was not to the same extent restricted by the conventions and criticism of the mainstream literature and arts and yet, the book form, similar to the artist' books, offered a medium for conceptual and aesthetic exploration. Choosing the picturebook—or in the case of Egon Møller-Nielsen—the playground as a place for aesthetic experimentation, can also be seen as a part of the tendency within Nordic Modernism where the artist aspired to make arts a part of the society. Emphasizing the connection between function and construction is characteristic for both Møller-Nielsen's playground sculptures and his picturebooks. Through children as mediators, both the sculptures and the books function as Trojan horses, introducing modernist aesthetics and artistic innovation.

Bibliography

Primary Sources

Jansson, Tove. *Hur gick det sen? Boken om Mumin, Mymlan och lilla My.* Helsinki: Schildts, 1952.
Janus, Grete, and Mogens Hertz. *Huset.* Copenhagen: Hirschsprung, 1947.
Löfgren, Åke, and Egon Møller-Nielsen. *Historien om någon.* Stockholm: Kooperativa Förbundets förlag, 1951.
Møller-Nielsen, Egon. *Historien om . . .* Stockholm: Kooperativa Förbundets förlag, 1947.
Møller-Nielsen, Egon. *Historien om någon.* Original illustrations to the manuscript. 1951.

Secondary Sources

Bland, David. *A History of Book Illustration. The Illuminated Manuscript and the Printed Book.* London: Faber and Faber, 1969 [first edition of 1958].

Drucker, Johanna. *The Century of Artists' Books.* New York: Granary Books, 2004 [first edition of 1995].

Guest, Tom. "An Introduction to Books by Artists." In *Books by Artists.* Toronto: Art Metropole, 1981.

Marcus, George H. *Le Corbusier. Inside the Machine for Living.* New York: Monacelli Press, 2000.

Mathiesen, Egon. "The Artist and the Picture Book." *The Horn Book Magazine* 42 (1966): 1.

Moore, Barbara and Jon Hendricks. "The Page as Alternative Space. 1950 to 1969". In *Artists' Books. A Critical Anthology and Sourcebook* edited by Joan Lyons. 87–95. Rochester, NY: Visual Studies Workshop Press, 1985.

Nemes, Endre. *Egon Møller-Nielsen.* Edited by Tore Ahlsén, Conny Andersson, Kerstin Møller-Nielsen, David Westman and Edvin Öhrström. Stockholm: Konstakademin, 1963.

Steiner, Wendy. *The Colors of Rhetoric. Problems in the Relation Between Modern Literature and Painting.* Chicago and London: University of Chicago Press, 1982.

Stoichita, Victor. *The Self-Aware Image. An Insight into Early Modern Meta-Painting.* Translated by Anne-Marie Glasheen. Cambridge: Cambridge University Press, 1997.

Waugh, Patricia. *Metafiction: The Theory and Practice of Self-Conscious Fiction.* London and New York: Routledge, 1988.

Chapter Eleven
A Strawberry? Or the Planet?
Children's Aesthetic Response to the Picturebook *Strawberries* by Susumu Shingu, Moving Art Sculptor

Tomoko Masaki

A Strawberry?

When children looked at the front cover of the picturebook *Strawberries*, a boy cried, "strange! strange!"; another boy cried, "too big!, too huge!"; and yet another boy cried, "doesn't look delicious"; a girl shook her head saying nothing, but seemed to express the feeling, "I don't want to eat it"; another girl said, "why is it so red all over the cover?, I want a strawberry to be only red"; a boy said, "scared, perhaps because of the black shadowy lines on the strawberry"; and a girl said quietly, "I like it."

I shared the picturebook *Strawberries* created by Susumu Shingu, a Japanese moving art sculptor, primarily with a reading group of 7- to 9-year-old children, and also with other reading groups of different ages. In this chapter I want to discuss how children develop a deeper insight and interpretation of a picturebook through a reading from cover to cover. In order to talk about a child-reader's act of reading, I will apply Wolfgang Iser's theory of aesthetic response to the children's initial response to *Strawberries*. The words that I mentioned previously were the children's response to the front cover (Fig 11.1).

Susumu Shingu, Moving Art Sculptor

Before analyzing the picturebook *Strawberries*, the artist Susumu Shingu should be introduced. Susumu Shingu is an artist who is known world-wide

Figure 11.1 Book cover from Susumi Shingu: *Strawberries*. Tokyo: Bunka Publishing Bureau, 1975.

for creating moving sculptures which utilize the natural energies of wind and water. His monumental works can be seen not only in Japan, but also in cities such as New York, Boston, Milan, Genoa, etc. He has also organized two traveling outdoor exhibitions on a global scale. The Windcircus exhibitions were held throughout 1987–1989 in Bremen, Germany; Barcelona, Spain; Florence, Italy; Lahti, Finland; at The World Trade Center in New York; in Chicago, Boston, and Los Angeles, in the United States; Paris, France; and in Sanda, Japan, where he has his atelier. The Wind Caravan project (http://www.wind-caravan.org) was held in 2000 and 2001 starting at traditional rice paddies in Sanda, Japan; at an uninhabited island called Motukorea in New Zealand; at the frozen Lake Inari, Finland; at the rocky village Tamdaght, Morocco; at the green steppe Undur Dov, Mongolia; and at the white dunes of Cumbuco, Brazil. All his wind or water functioning works have been seen in cities all over the world. People, passing by his works, may have stopped to watch the moving and whirling of the wings of his works. Rudolf Arnheim describes the reaction of Harvard University students who watched a tree-like structure exhibited in the hall of the Carpenter Center for the Visual Arts.

> [T]he spectacle of the tumbling cans cast a spell on the busy art students. They stopped their runs to and from the studios, and squatting on the floor like monks in meditation, they watched for half hours the tiny waterfalls discharging at unforeseeable moments and places. A similar fascination holds the glance of pedestrians, drivers, and onlookers as in the midst of an urban commotion they find their eyes captured by the unperturbable rounds of cosmic model high up on its stand, reminding them at least for a while that the old forces moving the world remain also the new ones. (8)

This quotation refers to the nature of Shingu's art. When we meet his works, we will stop to see what it will be or do, and we will sit or squat on grass, stones, or roads to prepare to wait for something fantastic to happen, often for a while, when his sculpture catches the wind or water. Presently it may move, twirling, or whirling. The way of moving is not showy or astonishing or overwhelming at all. It may move gently according to the power of wind and water. The image of beholders watching Shingu's works reminds me of sitting in the tatami room in front of the garden of old Japanese temples. Quietness occupies the atmosphere, while emptiness occupies my body. Pierre Restany wrote about Shingu's work: "Susumu Shingu invokes the dance of the wind. I feel at home there, in the heart of emptiness" (15). Emptiness is one of the key words in understanding Shingu's works. I will refer to it later.

Shingu talked about his own works in the interview with Joseph Giovannini: "there's always a power outside of my sculpture. The object itself without that power has no meaning. When connected with that power, the sculpture will become alive" (288). Shingu's modest words, that his object has no meaning without the power of nature, can be interpreted that his works will be perfected when they meet the natural power of wind or water. His works stand still on the ground, though their figures are beautiful themselves, especially with the sky in the background. However, once they catch the power of the wind, they start moving and whirling as if they are alive. Shingu's words about the relationship between his artistic works and natural powers explain how the former functions by the latter. The relationship of one affecting the other can be seen a parallel to the relationship between an artistic work and the beholder (the reader). The work may stand alone and independent. However, once it is watched and emotionally accepted by a beholder, it starts living within the beholder. Picturebooks exist on a desk. However, once they are read and watched by readers, they start their own life within the reader. Readers start making their own stories from the works.

Wolfgang Iser mentions, "the literary work has two poles, which we might call the artistic and the aesthetic: the artistic pole is the author's text and the aesthetic is the realization accomplished by the reader" (21). Here is a picturebook titled *Strawberries* created by Susumu Shingu with words, pictures, and design, and a reading group of six children of 7- to 9-years-old. We (the children and I) gathered around the table and sat on soft cushions in a tatami-mat room. I read aloud the picturebook to them. We have been enjoying sharing picturebooks for months and they love to view picturebooks.

Reading the Picturebook *Strawberries* with 7- to 9-year-old Children

The front cover of *Strawberries*, a shape of approximately 25cm square, is covered all over in red. The flat bright redness catches the reader's eye. In the middle, a very big strawberry drawn in black contour fills the cover from the top to the bottom. Title letters are written in white. Children know strawberries well. Strawberries are small, pretty, and delicious, but here is a huge, gigantic strawberry. Being too big in scale and too red in color, it looks strange, not delicious, and it looks unreal. As soon as they had a look at the front cover, they expressed those reactions I introduced in the beginning. This strong front cover, however, appeals to children to look at the pages inside. I started reading aloud to them as usual from the title, "Strawberries."

Turning the red front cover, we find the white end-papers. Being white all over, the end-papers made readers forget the red front cover and the huge strawberry for a second. The next doublespread shows the author-artist's preface and the title page, with red letters in the white background.

The first doublespread shows only flat pale grey which covers the whole two pages. The sentence reads: "The strawberries have all gone away, but in the dusk their sweet fragrance still drifts from the field." No strawberries appear anywhere, but their fragrance seems to be drifting here, from the inside book into the outside here.

The second doublespread is white with shining green leaves in the middle. The sentence is: "The life of the strawberries is held in the glossy green leaves." The third is also white, with red vines bouncing from leaves. The two red lines of vines are horizontal and downward, crossing over the white ground. The sentence is: "Each bounce of the red vines gives birth to a child." The fourth is covered with dark greenish grey, and there are bunches of leaves in rows. The sentence is: "The children line up in the field."

The fifth doublespread is grey with white snow-dots all over the two pages, showing a white earth at the bottom. The sentence is: "Tucked under the snow, they sleep peacefully." The sixth is dark blue with white star-dots. When I read the sentence, "On freezing nights they see a multitude of stars," a boy says, "I think strawberries can't see stars, because strawberries are covered with snow." When he used the word "strawberries" it sounds as though he includes himself because he seemed to consider he became tiny strawberries under snow. That is why he could not look up the dark blue sky.

The seventh doublespread changes into bright daytime. Yellow clouds are flowing and flying in the blue sky, as if they are approaching to us in order to state "the spring has come." The field covered with grass is spread at the bottom. The sentence is: "The wind brings light." A boy said, "Look! Strawberry fields are green now." Another boy said, "Look! Clouds like doughnuts! Mister Donut has this sort."

A bright yellow color covers the eighth doublespread. Several shining big green leaves are spreading stalks into the corners of the pages. The sentence written in green letters reads: "A golden shower—a gift from the sun." A boy said, "I think this yellow color represents the light of the sun." Since the yellow color is so bright and shiny, we feel as if we are bathing in golden spring sunlight.

The ninth doublespread is white. A bee is visiting two white flowers with yellow hearts. The sentence is: "The bees come calling when the flowers bloom." The tenth is white. A sapling now bears two tiny star-like strawberries. The sentence is: "The petals fall, leaving in their tiny green stars." A boy said, "They are buds." They are actually fruits, but look like pretty buds. They also look like stars.

The eleventh doublespread is white. The two white strawberries are hanging from the top of the page. The sentence reads: "The stars turn into white strawberries." A boy said, "They look delicious." So I said, "They are still white." The boy answered, "Yes, I heard white strawberries are delicious. Strawberries growing without the sunshine are white. The red color is due to the sun." Then another boy asked, "What is the taste of white strawberries? White strawberries do not contain water, do they?" The former boy answered, "Without water they don't grow. I would like to eat white strawberries." Another boy said, "We may be able to try white ones." "Where?" I asked. This boy thought and said, "In Nose. I went to Nose to try to grow and harvest rice with mother and sister. I can ask Mother whether we can eat white strawberries there." Nose is in the northern countryside of Osaka and the town provides city families with paddy fields to let children experience farming. ("Nose" is pronounced "no-say," not "nose" as with the English word meaning a part of the face.)

The twelfth doublespread is covered with red as the front cover. In the middle, in the horizontal manner, there are sentences written in golden yellow: "They watch the glow of a brilliant sunset, enchanted by the red blaze." All the children silently watched the red scene with no strawberries. The thirtieth doublespread is the most colorful in the book: green leaves, white flowers each with a yellow center, tiny yellow fruits, and red strawberries hiding under leaves. The sentence is: "The strawberry patch bursts with color and sweet fragrance." Children seemed to breathe a sigh of relief. Then the boy who eagerly wanted to eat white strawberries said, "Strawberries have become red. But I want to eat white ones."

In the fourteenth doublespread (Fig. 11.2), a strawberry is diagonally visualized in four stages of its growing process from a tiny green fruit to a red big one. The three natural energies—wind, rain, and the sun—help the strawberry grow big, red, and sweet. Three words are written in Chinese characters: "Wind, Rain, and the Sun." The boy who had visited Nose stared at arrow marks which indicate the strawberry becoming sweet and becoming red,

156 · Tomoko Masaki

Figure 11.2 Illustration from Susumi Shingu: *Strawberries*. Tokyo: Bunka Publishing Bureau, 1975.

saying, "White strawberries are not delicious at all." The White Strawberry boy dwelled on, "White strawberries are called 'Snow Strawberries.'"

The fifteenth doublespread shows an enormously big red strawberry in the white ground as big as the one in the front cover. The difference between this in these pages and that on the front cover is that the strawberry has tiny yellow dots on its surface. Each child did not say anything like the words they said in the beginning when they talked about the front cover. When I read: "Every strawberry has a north and a south pole," the Nose boy was astonished, opened his mouth, brought his hand to his mouth and slowly grinned at me. I continued to read: "and golden rivets tacked down in between." The Nose boy asked, "Rivets are seeds, aren't they?" The white strawberry boy answered, "Seeds, yes, seeds."

The sixteenth doublespread reveals the big sectional picture of a strawberry, an inside picture cut lengthways in its middle. Its central part is as white as snow. I read: "The sun never touches the cold, white world in the center of the red fruit." The children did not respond to these words, but stared at the picture. The Nose boy said, "The other day the TV showed a close-up of the inside of a strawberry. The center was not white but orange." The White Strawberry boy said, "But the leaves were as green as these here," and he added "I want to eat a white strawberry." The Nose boy consoled the boy, "We can go to Nose. Nose is not far." But the boy said, "I think white strawberries grow in Ishikawa Prefecture." I asked, "Why do you think so?" He answered, "Just I think so." To go to Ishikawa Prefecture, we have to ride on an express train for more than two hours.

In the seventeenth doublespread, the two pages remain almost white. At the bottom, the top part of a big, big strawberry appears. The sentence says: "A strawberry is a boundless landscape." The Nose boy questioned, "What does it mean?" The white strawberry boy said, "The yellow dots on the strawberry seem like flowers that have been removed."

The eighteenth doublespread shows that the strawberry is floating and flying through the dark blue universe and a round white star is depicted in a smaller scale and higher than the strawberry. This doublespread contains no sentence. I showed the picture of the universe silently. The Nose boy said, "They are the moon and the strawberry. The strawberry is disguised as a planet." The White Strawberry boy said, "The strawberry is like the sun."

The last doublespread is the same as the first grey one. When I closed the picturebook, the Nose boy described the artist of this picturebook by saying, "Mr. Shingu is good at representing pictures."

Reading Picturebooks in Groups

I have been administering my own private library, Aoyamadai-Bunko, in Osaka, since 1973 and sharing picturebooks, poems, and storybooks with babies, school children, and adults. I shared *Strawberries* with children in two different groups: children in the lower grades, 7-to-10-years-old and children in the upper grades, 11-to-12-years-old.

The group I introduced previously is the group of lower graders. The Nose boy is in the third grade and the other five children are in the first grade. One of the three boys is restless and runs around. He is not accustomed to sitting, watching, and listening, but he wants to join the reading group. I think someday he will be able to share picturebooks with us. At the end, I asked him, "Which picture or page do you like? Are there any pages you like?" Immediately he answered, "The first page." He meant the artist's preface page, the opposite page to the title page before the first doublespread. On this page Shingu writes to readers: "I love strawberries. They are born from the great world of nature, yet are so small that one berry barely makes a mouthful. Sweet, beautiful, and hardy—they have character. In every country I have ever been, I have seen people enjoying strawberries." The artist's words on this page are written in five languages: Japanese, English, French, German, and Italian, with no pictures. I asked the boy, "Only letters here, with no pictures. Why do you like this page, if I may ask?" He answered, "Japanese and English, and English, a lot of English letters. It's cool!" He could only recognize the languages other than Japanese as "English." I said, "Yes, Shingu's words are written in Japanese, English, French, German, and Italian." Then the other two boys tried to read English, though they have never learned English. So I read the artist's words in English.

I asked the other five children which pages they liked. The Nose boy and the White Strawberry boy mentioned the same doublespread, the scene of Wind/Rain/Sunshine. The three girls, all in the first grade, gave me each of their favorite scenes: the strawberry field full of colors (13th doublespread), the blue pages with twinkling stars on freezing nights (6th doublespread), and the grey scene of falling snow (5th doublespread).

Reading *Strawberries* with Children of the Upper Grade

The group of the upper grade consists of five children (four girls and one boy) in the fourth to sixth grade. Their most interesting attitude which is different from the children in the lower grade is that they are particularly interested in language. According to the Japanese school system, children start to learn another language, normally English, at junior high schools. (The Ministry of Education and Science has started to emphasize the early introduction of English in primary schools.) Therefore these children have not learned English in ordinary public schools. *Strawberries* carries five languages in each doublespread from the front cover to the last doublespread. Children asked and talked with each other. "Why does this picturebook carry these four languages as well as Japanese?" "We can read Japanese, and we can know the meanings of sentences, but we can't read the other languages." "What is the use of these languages?" Then a girl said, "I think the artist wanted *Strawberries* to be read by many people in different languages." Then the other girl asked, "Then, why doesn't he use other languages like Korean Hangul?" Last year one of my Korean friends visited this library several times and introduced Korean picturebooks to the children. Her way of speaking in the Hangul language was so dynamic that we were all fascinated by Hangul.

I asked the artist Susumu Shingu about his use of languages after these reading sessions. He answered that *Strawberries* was first published in 1975, and the idea using Hangul and Chinese did not hit him. But now he thinks it proper to adapt the book to these Asian languages. *Strawberries* were published in Korea in 2001 and in Taiwan in 2005, but not yet in any European countries.

Reading *Strawberries* with English Children of the Fourth Grade

While I stayed in England for six years from 1994 to 2000, I was invited to introduce Japanese picturebooks to children in schools, museums, or local community halls. It gave me happy chances to share picturebooks with children brought up in a different culture from mine. I always included *Strawberries* among the two dozens or so Japanese picturebooks. *Strawberries* was a particularly useful picturebook for me in three ways: English children know and like strawberries as well as Japanese children; *Strawberries* carries the English language as well as Japanese and the other three languages, so that I do not need to translate from Japanese to English. Besides these points, the representation of pictures on each of the pages is very artistic: the colors, structure, and design are simple, beautiful, and sophisticated. The work conveys the idea of "life" given from nature.

When I introduced *Strawberries* to children in England, I first read the book aloud in English and later in Japanese, because I wanted English children to listen to the sounds of the Japanese language. Each language in the world has its own particular sound, rhythm, and intonation, whose characteristics present its own culture. The Japanese language is apt to add vowels for every pronunciation, so that speech may sound slower and softer. To me every language is beautiful. I enjoyed sharing *Strawberries* with English children very much. The most impressive scene to them was the picture of Wind/Rain/Sunshine. I said to them, "Please look at this character 'Rain.'" English children of the fourth grade were very much surprised to find that the Chinese character "rain" was really made up of four raindrops. It was their first occasion to encounter the ideogram. Then, I asked, "Do you like strawberries?" All the boys and girls answered, "Yes." I asked another question, "Do you know that a strawberry would have a north pole and a south pole?" They shook their heads. I introduced the magnificent picture of the big strawberry. They were astonished that a strawberry would have both a north and a south pole.

Child-Readers' Aesthetic and Cognitive Response to *Strawberries*

Wolfgang Iser's theory of aesthetic response can be applied to the child-readers with whom I shared *Strawberries*. He analyzed literary works, but his term "literary work" can be replaced with "picturebooks." The term "literary texts" in "literary texts take on their reality by being read" can be replaced with "visual texts."

Any text prepared by creators (authors and artists) offers a perspective view of the world to readers, according to Iser (35). Readers react to perspectives represented by artists in different ways according to their experiences. The discourses mentioned previously reveal different aesthetic and cognitive aspects of children individually and in grades. Younger children react and interact more freely to each scene and sometimes they reveal their own fantastic ideas triggered by texts both visual and verbal. A perspective has the structure of theme and horizon. Iser wrote:

> *The structure of theme and horizon constitutes the vital link between text and reader, because it actively involves the reader in the process of synthetizing an assembly of constantly shifting viewpoints, which not only modify one another but also influence past and future synthesis.*
>
> *The continual interaction of perspective throws new light on all positions linguistically manifested in the text, for each position is set in a fresh context, with the result that the reader's attention is drawn to aspects hitherto not apparent. (97)*

When it comes to the nature of picturebooks, this quotation is useful in comprehending it. (When we discuss here about picturebooks, we can change the word "linguistically" into "visually.") The structure of theme and horizon can clearly explain children's responses. The front cover shows an extraordinary big strawberry as the "theme." The size of the strawberry, however, was too big for children to accept as an ordinary fruit, so they rejected the artist's idea, as it was "strange," "doesn't look delicious," "I don't want to eat it," and "scared." The strawberry they are familiar with is small, red, and sweet. This front cover's strawberry was far from the idea of what they can accept as a strawberry. Besides the theme of a strawberry, children cannot find the horizon here, because the red color spreads over all the surface of the cover including the strawberry. Here the red strawberry as the theme looks like it is dissolving into the red surroundings of the horizon. This must be the artist's intention. But the naïve child-readers could not bear this idea, and they had to protect themselves from this big scary strawberry. However, they were still attracted by this picture, which actually invited them into the world of the picturebook.

Here I would like to modify Iser's usage of the theme and the horizon in order to adjust to the nature of picturebooks. According to the "theme" I can use the term as he does: the theme as the subject or the central object. Regarding the "horizon," he conceives it as "making up of all those segments which had supplied the themes of previous phases of reading." So "the theme always stands before the horizon of the other perspective segments in which he had previously been situated" (97). Iser speaks about novels. When it comes to picturebooks, the visual perspective in one doublespread can be clearly presented in front of readers. Here, if we can use the "horizon" as the visual ground which may cover themes (subjects or objects) which have previously been situated (appeared), we can more easily and psychologically interpret the artist's and the reader's aesthetic attitudes.

The first doublespread shows only the grey horizon with no theme. Child-readers had seen the strange, gigantic strawberry on the front cover a second before. However, here they saw the grey monochromatic scene without even a slight hint of the strawberry, their image of the strange strawberry had been wiped away, though that image unconsciously remained. The artist prepares three more doublespreads with this kind of horizon in the book: the grey, snowy scene (5th doublespread), the blue freezing night (6th doublespread), and the red brilliant sunset (12th doublespread). The children have read sentences such as "the life of the strawberries." "Each bounce of the red vines gives birth to a child," and "The children line up in the new field," before the "grey", "blue," and "red" scenes appear. Child-readers, with words like "life," "birth," "child," and "children" in their memories, feel as if they are strawberries themselves. Particularly when they do not see visualized strawberries as objective themes on doublespreads, children can view themselves as strawberries in the story.

In the fifth, suggested by the word "tucked under the snow," they would be psychologically curled up under the snow, peacefully. From under the bottom of the page (in the earth or on the ground), they are looking up at snow falling from the sky. When a boy said "strawberries can't see stars because strawberries are covered with snow," he might have psychologically felt the freezing coldness around him as if he were a strawberry. When children watched the red sunset silently, they also watched "the glow of a brilliant sunset" as strawberries. Thus pictures of horizon without themes (objects) can function to invite readers into the scenes.

On the other hand, there are pages with objects: leaves, flowers, tiny fruits, white strawberries, strawberry fields with red strawberries. Watching the process of growing strawberries, or becoming strawberries themselves through the picturebook, readers constantly shift their viewpoints, are sometimes reminded of the former scenes, often foresee upcoming scenes, and try to combine all the images they get. The reader's act is to synthetize what he/she finds in the book.

As Gombrich mentions: "[I]t is the guess of the beholders that tests the melody of forms and colours for coherent meaning, crystallizing it into shape when a consistent interpretation has been found" (204), readers of picturebooks try to seek to find coherent meaning to stitch forms and colors through doublespreads. Children always try to guess using their more primitive and more naïve nature to bridge from page to page and from scene to scene. They seem to feel the theme as if they can actually feel the real surroundings with their physical body. So that children more easily enter the horizon of doublespread pictures to grasp the true meaning from the depth of the work.

When children again met a strawberry (15th doublespread) as big as the one on the front cover, they never said, "too big," "I don't want to eat it," "scared," though this time the strawberry is shown with a white background. Now they know this strawberry as the theme: for it has looked up at snow falling, at stars on freezing nights, and beautiful golden sunsets: it has absorbed wind, rain and sunshine; it has been given life from natural energy. So that is why it has grown so big. The big size does not show the outer scale, but the inner enormous energy. When I showed the big strawberry and read aloud to children, "Every strawberry has a north and south pole," a boy showed a sudden astonished expression, and in a few seconds he grinned at me. The nine-year-old boy totally understood the artist's idea and agreed with him. He knows that the flowing strawberry is a planet as well as a strawberry. He knows that he, in the picturebook, was once a strawberry, and now he can be a planet. As a strawberry changes through the picturebook from a tiny yellow star, to a white strawberry, then a red strawberry, and finally to a planet floating in the universe, a child-reader metamorphoses from a strawberry to a planet.

I have shared books with children for years. They have sometimes given me unexpected ways to get new insights into the meaning of books. As for Shingu's *Strawberries*, their way to feel, interpret, and understand the work gave me their aesthetic and cognitive aspects. At first they refused to engage with the book, but attracted by the artist's strategy to use the structure of theme and horizon, they entered into the book. Iser writes about the possibility of communication among readers: "Each actualization represents a selective realization of the implied reader, whose own structure provides a frame of reference within which individual responses to a text can be communicated to others" (65). Though Iser may be thinking of readers of James Joyce or Virginia Woolf, both primary school children and adults can communicate with each other and happily and profoundly share picturebooks.

Characteristics of Susumu Shingu's Moving Art and Picturebook Art

Shingu created a great many moving sculptures but only eight picturebooks: *Strawberries*, 1975; *Spider*, 1979; *Whale Shark*, 1991; *Kippis's Earth Journey*, 1994; *Little Pond*, 1999; *Wind Planet*, 2004; *When You Turn on the Faucet*, 2004; and *Little Bird*, 2007; all published in Japan. A few picturebooks were published in other languages: *Strawberries* in Korea, 2001; and in Taiwan, 2005; *Spider* and *Little Bird* in France, 2006. I want to consider the characteristics of Shingu's moving art and picturebook art.

Susumu Shingu was born in Osaka in 1937. After graduating from the Tokyo University of Fine Arts, specializing in oil painting, he spent six years in Italy. He talks about the beginnings of his moving art in the interview with Giovannini: "One day I took some pieces outside to photograph, and I hung them from a tree branch. They started to move. It bothered me at first because I wanted to take a picture, but watching them move I saw that if I used certain shapes or mechanisms more suitable to wind, their motions have a more interesting feel of motion" (287).

The phrase "watching them move" is key to interpreting his works. Shingu's works are moved by the natural energies of wind or water, which are not made by human beings. We cannot tell when they move. What we can do is to wait, when they move. When readers look at *Strawberries*, they feel something within begin to stir. His moving works of art start moving when they catch the proper wind, the grown-up strawberry, blessed with proper wind, rain, and sunshine, starts to move through the universe. The architect Renzo Piano, who asked Shingu to create a work for the ceiling of Kansai International Airport, Osaka, writes about Shingu, "Wind is invisible, yet Shingu makes it perceptible. Water is fleeting energy, and Shingu gives it shape" (17). The act of moving makes wind and water become visible.

Shingu's works seem to be whirling eternally up in the sky. After watching his works for a while, beholders start to conceive that we are in a vast universe. Our busy, fragmented surroundings disappear and we are floating in a limitless time and space. The substantial existence of beholders (readers) is dissolving into the universe, regaining eternal life.

Shingu mentioned, "The object itself without that power has no meaning," as I have quoted before. He wants to say his work is not independent, but is perfected with natural power. His work has the ability to assimilate into the universe, while it is unique, individual, and powerful. In *Strawberries*, the strawberry looks to dissolve into the horizon, it represents powerfully its existence. Iser mentions, "Textual structure and structured act are related in much the same way as intention and fulfillment" (36). Shingu structures his work (moving art or a picturebook) with the intention of making beholders (readers) involved with his work, by interpreting it and fulfilling its meaning.

As I specified before, Iser mentioned that the work has two poles: the artistic pole and aesthetic pole. The former is created by the artist and the latter is realized by the reader. However, Shingu is, himself, not only a creator but also a reader. I can say he is at first a reader of nature and he becomes an artist by realizing (creating) what he has aesthetically felt.

In the interview, Giovannini asks Shingu, "You've talked about the sculpture existing in an environment in which you exist, and that you make sculpture partially to understand the way you live. Can you explain that a little more fully?" Shingu answers, "Personally, I want to try to understand how we are part of nature through making my sculpture. So in making sculpture I'm making a machine to help me observe nature in a personal way. Also, it's important to understand that this is a shared observation." (288).

His works are twirling and whirling with the natural energies of wind and water: for example, *Sky Image*, Cultural Center of Suita, Osaka, Japan, 1985; *Gift of the Wind*, Porter Square MBTA Station, Cambridge, Massachusetts, United States, 1985; *Wings Breath*, Olympic Park, Seoul, Korea, 1989; Water Tree, Aono Dam Park, Sanda, Hyogo, Japan, 1992; *Boundless Sky*, Kansai International Airport, Japan, 1994; *Dialog with the Sun*, Queens Criminal Court, New York, 1995; *Duet of Water*, Montecatini Terme, Italy, 1998; *Resonance of Life*, Hakone Open-Air Museum, Japan, 1999; *Song of the Sun*, Juscelino Kubitschek Branch, San Paulo, Brazil, 2001. All his works in the world have been shared so that people can enjoy their movement. His picturebooks have been shared as this spirit too, so that people can enjoy a sense of movement from page to page as their insight develops from cover to cover.

Strawberries for Susumu Shingu, Creator-Reader of Nature

When I watch the chronological list of his moving art, I detect a change around 1975, when *Strawberries* was published. His early works seem to stand out among their surroundings: vivid colors, sharp lines, and bold shapes. They have more weight than later works, as if they would like to emphasize their existence. His later works, made up with fine, light materials, show more flexibility, more elasticity, and more freedom to dissolve into surroundings (air or horizon). In the process of creating his first picturebook *Strawberries*, he seems to have observed nature not from outside, but from inside.

Strawberries might act for him as a change to his own structure of theme and horizon, realizing himself as the theme, a strawberry flowing into the universe, or dissolving into the universe, he might visualize himself assimilating with the universe (horizon). Assimilation with horizon brings an emptiness and absence of self and a oneness with nature inside the body, which may have weakened the competitive urge of an up-and-coming artist. He could be himself.

Arnheim mentions about Shingu's work: "Shingu's work expresses an almost religious gratitude to those lifegiving powers" (8). Child-readers got the point of *Strawberries* by successful communication through the structure of theme and horizon which Shingu had prepared and had experienced.

Appendix

Picturebooks by Susumi Shingu
Strawberries. Tokyo: Bunka Publishing Bureau, 1975.
Spider. Tokyo: Bunka Publishing Bureau, 1979.
Whale Shark. Tokyo: Fuso Publishing, 1991.
Kippis's Earth Journey. Tokyo: Fukuinkan Shoten Publishers, 1994.
Little Pond. Tokyo: Fukuinkan Shoten Publishers, 1999.
Wind Planet. Tokyo: Fukuinkan Shoten Publishers, 2004.
When You Turn on the Faucet. Tokyo: Fukuinkan Shoten Publishers, 2004.
Little Birds. Tokyo: Bunka Publishing Bureau, 2007.

Bibliography

Primary Source

Shingu, Susumi. *Strawberries*. Tokyo: Bunka Publishing Bureau, 1975.

Secondary Sources

Arnheim, Rudolf. "The Moving Art of Susumu Shingu." In *Shingu: Rhythm of Nature* edited by Susumu Shingu. 8–9 Osaka: Brain Center, 1991.
Gombrich, E. H. *Art & Illusion: A study in the psychology of pictorial representation*. London: Phaidon, 1960.
Iser, Wolfgang. *The Act of Reading: A Theory of Aesthetic Response*. Baltimore and London: The Johns Hopkins University Press, 1978.
Piano, Renzo. "Working with Shingu." In *Shingu: Message from Nature* edited by Owen Dugan. 17. New York, London and Paris: Abbeville Press Publishers, 1997.
Restany, Pierre. "The Nature and Forms of Emptiness." In *Shingu: Message from Nature* edited by Owen Dugan. 14–15. New York, London and Paris: Abbeville Press Publishers, 1997.
Shingu, Susumi. "Interview with Joseph Giovannini." In *Shingu: Message from Nature* edited by Owen Dugan. 286–289. New York, London, and Paris: Abbeville Press Publishers, 1997.

Chapter Twelve
Off-Screen
The Importance of Blank Space

Fernando Zaparaín

Picturebooks are comprised, initially with text and images as *represented sequential enunciation*. These, however, are achieved using *graphic ellipsis*: this refers to that related to enunciation, which representation avoids, due to the selective nature of the *frame* and the discontinuity between images required for serialization. *Off-screen* is a spatial ellipsis which excludes a scenic portion (characters, decoration, sound or atmosphere) which is significant for the story (e.g., Gómez 2003). Strictly speaking, any unframed reality would remain *off-screen* with regard to the selected one; however, in this case the concealment of the known or knowable that can have a relationship with the story is the only aspect of interest. As such, it would be more appropriate to speak of a process of *metonymy* with regard to the representation of the whole with one part, since in *off-screen* the blank space in itself is not used but rather how it relates to what has been selected. In addition to verifying the succinctness of means obvious throughout the selection, an attempt will be made to define *off-screen*, to ascertain how it is established and to determine under what conditions it has greater narrative effect.

Blank Space and Connotation. Definition of Off-Screen

The capacity of the blank space to add tension to and form the plastic object was theorized by Heidegger during the small conference in 1969 entitled *Die Kunst und der Raum* (Heidegger 1970). It was there that the Aristotelian concept of *space* as *place* was taken up again, generated by the relationship between shapes (an issue already experienced by cubism), compared to platonic previous space and then Cartesian space in which things are located (e.g., Van de Ven 1981). It was emphasized that *space* means *creating space*, opening a clearing in the forest in order to live, generating a vacuum where relationships take place. It was stressed that it is the absence[1] which, paradoxically, allows that something is possible there, which realizes what is missing and what is not, of the tensions between things just as a bridge evokes the other riverbank even if we do not cross over to it. These reflections can be applied to the *off-screen* inherent in visual narration because this *scenic absence* generates expectations and, as a partial representation, invites diegetic progress, just like the girl in Dyan Sheldon's and Gary Blythe's *The Whale's Song* (1991) promises infinite horizons of adventure when she gazes beyond the page.

On the other hand, blank space and absence are conveyed in the image by their very existence.[2] As revealed by Barthes in his seminal study *La chambre claire* (1980),[3] image is quite precise in its *denotation* of reality by functioning as its *analogue*. However, at the same time, the image is partial and imprecise because it can be interpreted in various ways (*polysemy*) or because there may be many signs for reflecting the same reality (*metaphor*). As such, in order to guarantee the narration, the sequence of images is not sufficient and a text is required, at least implicitly, which annotates the interpretation. As a result, picturebooks work within this limit between *polysemy*, which makes the image suggestive, and *connotation* which the image receives from the context into which it is inserted and from the text it accompanies. *Ellipsis*, and with it *off-screen*, are intended to reduce information to a maximum to leave the reader with space however without depriving him of the minimum information required to make the story work. Absences, by emphasising expectation, push the story to the forefront.

Cut. Establishing Off-Screen

The processes of visual selection and the subsequent narrative exploded view require the reality to be segmented. Given that we cannot cover the continuity of what is real, with the *ellipsis* of the *representation* we choose the minimum number of fragments which allow reconstructing a story however without the meaning of the story being lost. In our mental discourse there is a need to proceed in parts, a division prior to the physical cut which is typical of the medium (Virilio 1998). In picturebooks, the establishment of a *frame* or window is the founding act through which the representation chooses the significant portions and confronts them with those rejected. It consists of a *cut* with its subsequent *montage*, either when creating the page with the frame (*internal montage*) or when sequencing various pages (*external montage*) (Sánchez-Biosca). This immediately generates the *shot* of the selected portion that in turn leaves the rest *off-screen*. This action, initially spatial and paradoxical, goes beyond mere scenic segregation and achieves subjective, temporal and narrative effects as is clearly shown in a page of Anthony Brownes *Voices in the Park* (1998) the frame of which includes Charles who looks beyond the left-hand margin where a future friend is suggested and who is now only recognisable from some pieces of clothing. Many pages later this friend, Sunshine, will continue *off-screen*, however, her presence will become clear because we will see the inverse angle of the previous scene with her eyes.

Frame and Phantasmatic Cube. Off-Screen Modalities

The *frame* segregates and generates a *virtual* space, which does not only include what is shown however what is suggested as well (Rowe 1978). Through a spatial *ellipsis*, *off-screen* allows building settings which do not exist without actually implementing them physically (Espuelas 1998). The important spatial contribution of the *frame* or window is that by dividing, it reunites four realities dialectically: the understood *object*, the hidden *object*, the *subject* perceiving it, and the *mechanism* employed to enclose the world (to *rationalize it*). As such, an artificial system superimposes the real one until analysing it and repurposing it subjectively. There is a transition from mere observation to the narrative. The visual experience generates the so-called *phantasmatic cube* (Burch 1985), which is a focal pyramid originating from the observer, with six sides to which a seventh could be added: the sound in *off* (Vila 1997). The different narrative points of view existing in this scenic exploded view are summarized in the *general perceptive scopic diagram* here enclosed.

The most *objective* area is the *shot* that is included in the selection. The *external off-screens* are created by comparison, i.e., areas that have not entered inside the frame however about which we are informed and which would appear if the framing were varied sufficiently. The *objective external off-screen*, is comprised of the elements nearest to the *shot* itself, or the parts of it which do not fit in the window. Moreover, since we are aware that there is an observer; his non visible world presents itself in the *subjective off-screen*. If we move further back from the observer, the *mise en abyme* appears, associated with the omniscient narrator who can observe the observer and what he is looking at in order to perform a *making off* and reveal the complete production mechanism. However, even in the *shot* itself there may be areas which are not visible which we will refer to as *internal off-screen*, suggested by the *square within the square* (windows, doors, books or mirrors) or hidden by other objects in the *shot* depending on their *depth*.

This entire mechanism is, for example, conveyed well in *Las Meninas* of Velázquez. The *shot* is the room; however some areas remain in the *external objective off-screen* such as the walls which we partially see. The mirror reflects the *subjective off-screen*, which is the area of the kings in which we should also appear. The windows, doors and squares conceal other possible horizons, thus creating an *internal off-screen*. Moreover, everything is subjected to *mise en abyme* through the inclusion of the painter himself and the canvas frame.

In picturebooks, in addition to the *off-screen* inside the *frame*, another *interstitial* off-screen must be considered due to the *sequence*. It is the blank paper and the turn of the page which separates two consecutive images.

All of the aforementioned can be summarized into the following classification:

frame	external off-screen	between shot and off-screen	objective	what is not seen of the observed
			subjective	what is not seen of the observer
			abyss	what is not seen of the system
	internal off-screen	within the shot		what is not seen of the shot
	sonorous off-screen			what is not seen but is heard/read
sequence	interstitial off-screen	between shot and shot		the shots which are not seen

Once the various modalities of the *off-screen* are narrated we can examine how they are used in the particular language of the picturebooks.

External Objective Off-Screen

It is what is not seen of the observed either because the scene does not refer to it, or because it is momentarily off-scene or because it leaves one part outside the scene. Firstly, it responds to succinctness in the representation that saves giving a total definition of the setting and shows it only with some of its parts. However, more frequently it tries to emphasize a relevant aspect of the story within the general frame. This is the case of close-ups that concentrate on facial expression and do not show the complete figure. When something disappears momentarily from the shot or is only announced with one part, it is possible to push towards a new illustration that will satisfy the expectation created. However the mere absence of something is not enough to makes us aspire to it. If the *objective off-screen* is to be efficient, its absence must be foreseeable and evident for which it will have to be announced beforehand with signs and establishing shots with a portion which is sufficient to completing the whole, such as the seven tails of the *Seven Blind Mice* (1992) by Ed Young.

External Subjective Off-Screen

What is not seen of the observer? Invariably, the viewer is shown by the very selection of a scene as soon as it is observed (Metz 1979). The person watching, due to the physical limitation of the scopic semi-sphere (Gaudreault 1995), cannot be included in his own visual field, however presents itself when opting for a line of sight and also by showing traces of him such as the edge of spectacles or a drawing hand. As we see in *La petite marionette* (1994) by Gabrielle Vincent, the reader can identify himself directly with the observer-narrator or move to the surprising visual location of a doll that comes to life. In all cases his gaze is directed to assign him with a subjective and diegetic value (Nodelman 1988). This subtle presence of the gaze is one of the main instruments of the cliffhanger because it turns the viewer into one of the actors. Since the viewer's world is not visible by definition, it is normally shown with successive changes of point of view which make perceptive movement evident and suggest different positions with regard to the story which go from asepsis of an establishing shot up to the implication of seeing through the eyes of the subjective shot.

External Omniscient Off-Screen (Mise en Abyme)

It is what is not seen of the productive system that the observer has around him. Strictly speaking, it is the shift backwards from the *subjective off-screen*, raising the position of the observer and even of the scene, until contemplating the actual apparatus of expression. In this way information is conveyed regarding *representation* and the *mechanism* at the same time. This ensures that the representation includes the devices used to achieve it. The *scene* appears alongside *the obscene* (what is around the *scene*). The points of view are multiplied and the reality is conveyed at the same time, of its formal expression and of the fiction process used to form it and analyse it. The *mise en abyme* usually appears at the end of the visual experience like a trick which returns the viewer to his segregated condition and makes him heave a sigh of relief bringing to mind that it has all only been fiction. It has the character of metalanguage or reflection on the medium itself, typical of the current moment of certain maturity, in which the new authors see themselves obliged to quote increasingly more established classics.

In the *late modern* picturebooks the back pages and flyleaves are privileged areas for discussing the book itself, for remembering some of its best moments or for showing the *other side* of a particular drawing. This is what happens in Lauren Child's *The Princess and the Pea* (2005), a picturebook that always shows its elaboration by using micro-scenes and which in the end shows its authors working in small premises. The framing changes are a

170 · Fernando Zaparaín

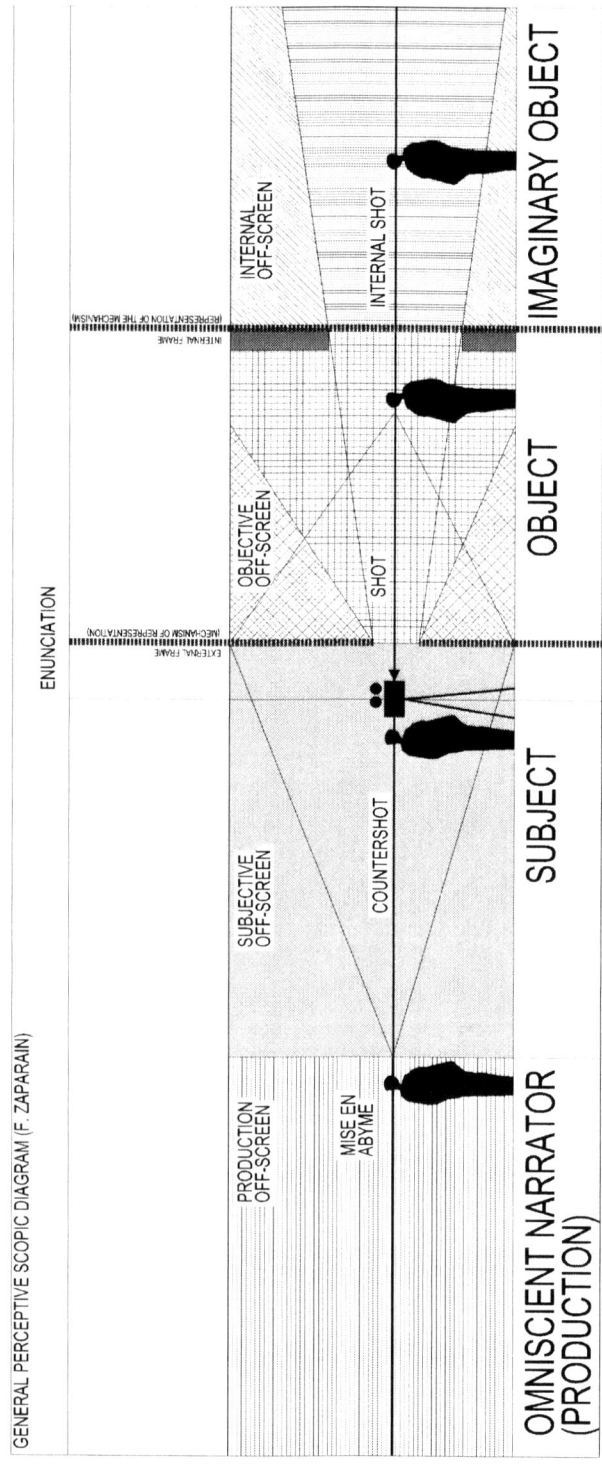

Figure 12.1 Table "General Perceptic Diagram" by Fernando Zaparaín

privileged system for expressing the *mise en abyme* since they reveal new *shots* that were previously hidden. Within these movements the *zoom* backwards is very expressive because it holds the axis of the gaze however increasing its amplitude until covering the scene and the observer, something which can be seen in the picturebooks by Banyai, *Zoom* (1995), *Re-Zoom* (1995) and more recently *The Other Side* (2005). All of these have this mechanism as a theme and each page is converted into the *mise en abyme* of the previous one. A final example of a successive *mise en abyme* would be the masterly vignette by Hergé in *L'Affaire Tournesol* (1956), in which we are aware of the hired assassin who controls how another spy watches his victims.

Internal Off-Screen

This is what is not seen of the shot, a surprising absence because the privileged eye of the observer accepts not seeing beyond the scene however does not expect things to be hidden from him in the scene. This modality introduces the tension of a gap in the space itself in addition to what already exists with regard to the outside world. In this way, it is possible to multiply a scene into various scenes without having to turn the page. A way of producing it is the use of *depth* (Wölfflin 1952) with which the elements from the scene are superimposed hierarchically within the focal pyramid. Some hide others and adjust their presence like the rabbit in *The Tale of Peter Rabbit* (1902) by Beatrix Potter which is suggested inside a watering can while Mr McGregor is seen in the background. The *picture inside the picture* (Gorlin 1982, 51) is a rhetoric modality which, through the representation of windows, doors or mirrors, reinforces the general frame with another internal one (Perec 1989). Peter Sís in *Madlenka* (2001) uses a hole in the page to introduce the next one. There are also elements that normally, by appearing within the scene, evoke non-visible worlds. This occurs with steps, boxes or chimneys, however above all with books, letters, maps and drawings which announce another possible story within the one we are experiencing. In this sense, the way in which Hergé[4] incorporates the story of Sir Francis Haddock by having the head of the current Captain Haddock poking through the painting is unique.[5]

Sonorous Off-Screen (Sound in Off)

In a picturebook, even although no sound is reproduced, its place of origin can be expressed and spaces beyond the page can be defined. This is what happens in the second part of *The Pied Piper of Hamelin* in the version illustrated at the end of the nineteenth century by Kate Greenaway. During such an early period, the illustrator chose a sonorous off-screen to graphically add tension to the revenge of the piper who attracts the village children from faraway with his music. The children start to move from the left to the right and in the last scenes form a procession which rises above the margins and crosses various pages until joining the piper. The figures are propped up towards the right; they dance and make gestures to capture the notes that are coming from outside the page thus making the reader continue to find the source of the sound. There is no drawn spatial frame. Not even the ground has been represented, it is only guessed at due to the shadows that are projected by the protagonists over the blank paper. In this purified context, and beyond the frame, it is the sound that governs the movements and is made real in our imagination, without the need to have been represented. This example is very rich in content because what is not drawn is capable of moving the narration and providing it with a context. It is perfect for expressing what we can define as *phenomenologic space* (Merleau-Ponty 1975) made of sensations and not of geometric or graphic lines.

Interstitial Off-Screen (Between Shot and Shot)

The off-screens analysed up until now are common to all scenic representations, including painting, as a singular image. However the new kinetic media of expression are formed over various sequenced images although not continuous, separated by a *caesura*, or *interstitial off-screen* which has different physical characteristics in each case. Cinema appears to be continuous, however in reality supports itself on the phenomenon of retinal persistence to link two fixed images with slight variations and, to a greater extent, uses the *phi effect* (Aumont 1992) through which each viewer fills the existing gap between two different attitudes of a character which are fixed in two successive images (Arnheim 1952). Comics use, above all, *the blank space* between vignettes and picturebooks take advantage of the *page-turner* which implies a cut between spaces and situations. Given the choice, this would be the most specific *off-screen* of those considered up until now for our study since it originates as a compulsory consequence of the narrative character.

This can be understood by observing the transition between two pages of Maurice Sendak's *Where the Wild Things Are* (1963). Both represent the same room of Max dressed as a wolf at the start of the story.[6] It could be thought that there is continuity given that the spatial frame remains however, subtly, with the change of page; the room starts to change into a forest. The white edge disappears as we enter further into the world of fantasy until completely disappearing. The physical jump between two images is used to transmit the advance of an interior state of the protagonist, who without moving from his room moves further into an imaginary world. The technique is highly purified given that traditional systems are avoided in order to tell the transition from reality to imagination with changes of color or edges in the shape of a cloud. It is here that the scenic frame is transmuted and the character is kept inside it however advancing with the book. When turning the page, not only are two different moments described but also two different mental states.

Montage. Functional Conditions of Off-Screen

For the purposes of picturebooks, *off-screen*, although it also economizes resources, is truly rich when it propels the story forward. If something is concealed too much the story disappears, and if it is shown very obviously it is not attractive enough. As such, in the language of visual sequencing the change from one scene to another will be strengthened with the momentary concealment of portions of reality and the promise of accessing them further ahead. It also has to be gauged very well at what moment information is extracted and when it is revealed.

First of all, this narrative dynamism is guaranteed when respecting specific functional conditions originating from our psychology of perception (Montes 1989) that can be summarized in the *general law of perception by expectations*. The human gaze is not automatic but intelligent and selective (Marina 1992). It searches for that which it is interested in according to a preliminary frame of expectations (Gombrich 1961). It meets the sensitive world, loaded with its own programme: it anticipates, prevents, recognizes, interprets, and uses well-known information. In short, we can venture to say that *off-screen* does not function alone and requires a *shot expectation* in order to be efficient.

In addition to respecting the general laws of perception, the *cut* performed with the frame or the sequence must be resolved with a subsequent *montage*. This recomposition is based on the actual laws of visual exploded view, shared by the creator who cuts and the viewer who stitches. The following are some examples:

Law of etc. (Gombrich 1961): In all representation, it is sufficient to mention an initial number of elements so that the viewer is able to complete the whole. This occurs in the book *Jeanne d'Arc* (Boutet de Monvel 1896), whose battles are suggested with partial views of some weapons and combatants in the background.

Laws of continuity (Balló 2000): through which it is easier to associate an image with subsequent images. For example: keeping the coherence of the elements of *atrezzo*, changing the visual axis according to the direction of movement, closing all the initiated argumental arches, gaining support in the sense of reading and page turning. This is something which we can verify by comparing the first drawing of Jane Yolen's and John Schoenherr's *Owl Moon* (1987) with which the book comes to a close. The first drawing, following Ford in *The Searchers*, shows someone framed by the open door and prepared to go out into the snow-covered landscape where the night-time adventure will take place. The last page shows the reverse camera of the initial situation. From outside, this same protagonist returns in her father's arms towards the door from which she left, which is now a rectangle of light in the night. The important fact is that the scene keeps its initial coherence in spite of many things having occurred. The snow is the same, the bluish night tone remains; the hat, scarf and the boots are the same. The protagonist is now among the bare trees which before could be seen in the distance. The house from which she left reappears in the distance. Even the change in perspective is justified because if on the first page we were leaving the house, it would seem very logical that at the end we return in the opposite direction. Even the point of view is kept.

Laws of symbolic association. The relationship between the things we see and those which are hidden from us can be more subtle and substitute a reality with a symbol (metaphor) already established or specifically created for this work as occurs in *Gewitternacht* (2000) by Michèle Lemieux, where the empty bed creates an internal off-screen to hide the protagonist and to evoke the attempt to lead him to his death when he arrives.

Laws of partial substitution. These are agreements through which a reality is recognized from the moment a part of it is seen (*metonymy*). As such, there is suspense because the appearance of the terrible or mysterious events is delayed. The *print* is emphasized in the visual language among those graphic instruments. It is understood as the sign of the presence of something hidden that is recognized by its shadow, its reflection, its sound or its remains. In Mark Weatherby's *My Dinosaur* (1997) the nighttime arrival of the enormous pet is announced by the projection of a silhouette against the wall. A masterly vignette in *Tintin au Tibet*[7] reflects the stormy relationship of Haddock with the Yeti however without the latter appearing. An even more difficult feat is that various hours in the life of the Yeti remain frozen against the white support. By following his footprints, we can participate in finding the bottle lost by the captain. Some footprints further ahead we can see the effect of alcohol in the shape of drunkenness and a fall, followed by fleeing unsteadily towards the distant mountain. On the left-hand side of the vignette Haddock is shouting; on the right-hand side his enemy, who has left, is present without having to be represented. From one corner to the other of the drawing, several kilometres of Himalaya are transferred for us to a small frame by the brilliance of an expert. In between, the white immensity of the non-drawing of the snow, which like all blank space invites reading between the lines, guarantees narrative tension and ensures that a picturebook has as many interpretations as the absences which we are able to detect in it.

Notes

1. See Bonitzer (1972) for a thorough analysis of this topic.
2. "*Filmique ou non, l'image est toujours incomplète puisqu'elle n'est jamais que la représentation* particulière *d'un fragment* particulier *du monde*" (Mitry 1990, 93).

3. These ideas also occur in Barthes (2001).
4. See Asouline (1997).
5. Hergé. *Le Secret de la Licorne*. p. 25
6. For a thorough analysis of this picturebook, see Nikolajeva and Scott (2001).
7. Hergé. *Tintin au Tibet*. p. 26.

Bibliography

Primary Sources

Banyai, Istvan. *Zoom*. New York: Viking, 1995.
Banyai, Istvan. *Re-Zoom*. New York: Viking, 1995.
Banyai, Istvan. *El otro lado*. México: FCE, 2005 (*The Other Side*, 2005).
Borland, Polly, and Lauren Child. *La princesa y el guisante*. Barcelona: Serres, 2005 (*The Princess and the Pea*, 2005).
Browne, Anthony. *Voices in the Park*. New York: DK Publishing, 1998.
Browning, Robert, and Kate Greenaway. *The Pied Piper of Hamelin*. New York and Toronto: Knopf, 1993.
Boutet de Monvel, Louis-Maurice. *Jeanne d'Arc*. Paris: Gautier-Languereau, 1990.
Hergé. *Le Secret de la Licorne*. Paris: Casterman, 1943.
Hergé. *L'Affaire Tournesol*. Paris: Casterman, 1956.
Hergé. *Tintin au Tibet*. Paris: Casterman, 1960.
Lemieux, Michèle. *Noche de tormenta*. Salamanca: Lóguez, 2005 (*Gewitternacht*, 2000).
Potter, Beatrix. *Perico el conejo travieso*. Barcelona: Beascoa, 2004 (*The Tale of Peter Rabbit*, 1902).
Sendak, Maurice. *Where the Wild Things Are*. New York: Harper and Row, 1981.
Sheldon, Dyan, and Gary Blythe: *The Whales' Song*. New York: Penguin Books, 1991.
Sis, Peter. *Madlenka*. Barcelona: Lumen, 2001.
Vincent, Gabrielle. *La petite marionette*. Paris: Casterman, 1994.
Weatherby, Mark Alan. *Mi Dinosaurio*. Madrid: Kókinos, 2002 (*My Dinosaur*, 1997).
Yolen, Jane, and John Schoenherr. *Owl Moon*. New York: Philomel Books, 1987.
Young, Ed. *Seven Blind Mice*. New York: Penguin Books, 1992.

Secondary Sources

Arnheim, Rudolf, *Art and Visual Perception*. Berkeley: University of California Press, 1974.
Asouline, Pierre. *Hergé*. Barcelona: Destino, 1997.
Aumont, Jacques. *La imagen*. Barcelona: Gedisa, 1992.
Barthes, Roland. *La chambre claire. Note sur la photographie*. Paris: Cahiers du Cinéma / Gallimard /Seuil, 1980.
Balló, Jordi. *Imágenes del silencio*. Barcelona: Anagrama, 2000.
Barthes, Roland. *La cámara lúcida. Nota sobre la fotografía*. Barcelona: Paidós, 1999.
Barthes, Roland. *La Torre Eiffel. Textos sobre la imagen*. Barcelona: Paidós, 2001.
Bonitzer, Pascal. "Hors-champ (un espace en défault)." *Cahiers du cinéma* 234–235 (1972): 125–140.
Burch, Noël. *Praxis del cine*. Madrid: Fundamentos, 1985.
Espuelas, Fernando. "El claro en el bosque. Reflexiones sobre el vacío en arquitectura." *Arquitectos* 147 (1998): 40–43.
Gaudreault, A., and F. Jost. *El relato cinematográfico*. Barcelona: Paidós, 1995.
Gombrich, Ernst. *Illusion and Art*. New York: Pantheon, 1961.
Gómez Tarín, Francisco Javier. *Lo ausente como discurso. Elipsis y fuera de campo en el texto cinematográfico* (PhD thesis). Valencia: Servicio de Publicaciones Universidad de Valencia, 2003.

Gorlin, Alexander. "Ghost in the Machine: Surrealism in the Work of Le Corbusier". *Perspecta* 18 (1982): 51.
Heidegger, Martin. "El Arte y el Espacio". *Eco* 122 (1970): 113–120.
Merleau-Ponty, Maurice. *La fenomenología de la percepción*. Barcelona: Península, 1975.
Marina, José Antonio. *Teoría de la Inteligencia creadora*. Barcelona: Anagrama, 1992.
Metz, Christian. *Psicoanálisis y cine. El significante imaginario*. Barcelona: Gustavo Gili, 1979.
Mitry, Jean. *La semiología en tela de juicio*. Madrid: Akal, 1990.
Montes, Carlos. *El cómic; potencialidades del lenguaje gráfico e ilusión de realidad*. Valladolid: ICE, 1989
Nikolajeva, Maria, and Carole Scott. *How Picturebooks Work*. New York: Garland, 2001.
Nodelman, Perry. *Words about Pictures*. Athens: University of Georgia Press, 1988.
Perec, Georges. *El gabinete de un aficionado*. Barcelona: Anagrama, 1989.
Rowe, Colin. "Transparencia, literal y fenomenal." In *Manierismo y arquitectura moderna y otros ensayos* edited by Gustavo Gili. 140–151. Barcelona: Gustavo Gili, 1978.
Sánchez-Biosca, Vicente. *El montaje cinematográfico*. Barcelona: Paidós, 1996.
Van de Ven, Cornelis. *El espacio en arquitectura*. Madrid: Cátedra, 1981.
Vila, Santiago. *La escenografía. Cine y arquitectura*. Madrid: Cátedra, 1997.
Virilio, Paul. "La Arquitectura improbable." *El Croquis* 91 (1998): 9.
Wölfflin, Heinrich. *Conceptos fundamentales en la Historia del Art*. Madrid: Espasa-Calpe, 1952.

Part III
Making Sense Out of Picturebooks

Chapter Thirteen
Being a Guide into Picturebook Literacy
Challenges of Cognition and Connotation

Ingeborg Mjør

Reading aloud of picturebooks can be an important contribution to children's development of literacy, especially *visual* literacy[1]. Reading aloud, when it is *motivated*, can be seen as a guide into literacy, and into cultures' different ways of relating to fictions.

In *The Implied Reader* (1974) Wolfgang Iser has described how reading is a mental and active process, where readers continuously process the informations from the text. When we read "[w]e look forward, we look back, we decide, we change our decisions, we form expectations, we are shocked by their nonfulfilment, we question, we muse, we accept, we reject; this is the dynamic process of recreation" (Iser 1974:223). This role of a reader has its parallel in the dialogue related to texts that motivated parents (or other grown ups) invite small children to join actively, by ensuring attention, asking questions and appreciating responses, in ways Anat Ninio and Jerome Bruner have described (Ninio and Bruner 1978). Parents, when guiding their children in meaningmaking processes, seem to be concerned about presenting the text as relevant to the child, about relating it to his or hers own life experiences. They pay much attention to the activation of the child's own knowledge. An assumption is that parents analyse the relationship between the child as "real reader" and the implied reader of the text; the text's own image of its presupposed audience. Torben Weinreich describes the implied reader as a set of competences and interests that the real reader is expected to have, an example is the ability to recognize relevant intertextuality (Weinreich 2001). During reading aloud, it might happen that parents analyse the relationship between real and implied reader not to be in balance, and so they try to overcome this lack of balance through different strategies.

Cognition and *connotation* are important parts of the role of the implied reader, and crucial for the development of literacy. I here use the term literacy in relation to understanding and interpretation, and to how reading creates subjective involvment in fiction.

Meaning as a Cognitive Concept

Cognitive psychology deals with how human experience and knowledge is organised and stored in mental schemata. These structures ensure that we can remember and activate knowledge when we need it. Cognitive anthropology works from the perspective of schemata theory, for example within research on media use, and I find these perspectives as relevant supplements to reception theory, when concerned about how children can experience fiction and picturebooks as meaningful.

The psychologist Jean Matter Mandler claims that meaning is dependent on structure: "People either discover structure inherent in the world, or impose structure upon it" (Mandler 1984:19). She claims a very close connection between organizing information and memorizing information, "to organize is to memorize, and to memorize is to organize" (ibid.:8). And the concept of schemata is "the basic building block of cognition", since schematas reflect our experiences and form our expectations (ibid.:2). They enable us to understand and respond functionally to situations and phenomenons. Bradd Shore, a media researcher who works within a cognitive approach, uses the term cultural or mental *model* in stead of schemata. We are dependent on our "models-in-the-mind" to relate to "models-in-the-world", for example texts or picturebooks. When our brains can match external patterns with those already stored in memory, we experience *meaning*. Meaning is both "a kind of *discovery* of the world and a kind of *recognition* of what we already have in mind", in relation to situations, activities, persons, emotions, etc (Shore 1998:11). There are probably no limits for how models can be organized in different typologies, both when it comes to structure and functions, I will use *classifications, scripts, scenes, stories,* and also *emotion* and *gender models*. It is important that schemata should not be regarded as mechanical concepts, they are flexible and often overlapping concepts that we use in meaningmaking processes, and include aspects of emotions, the body and the unconscious.

Classification are about typologies, for example that animals are organized in different species, sub-species and families. In regard to the understanding of literature and film, I will underline *stereotypes* as a vital dimension of classification, they affect how we relate to information, especially our first reactions. A *script* organises sequences of everyday actions; to get up in the morning, to go to a restaurant, to be a guest. In different situations, we know how to behave and in which order. *Scenes* organize our topological experiences from places. We know what inventory we can expect to find in a park, we know how tables and chairs must be organized to cohere with restaurant-schemata. The *story* schemata is a narrative schemata, a mental structure based on our expectations of how stories are formed, reflecting the regularity of our narrative experiences (Mandler 1984). Mark Turner claims that narrative is our basic cognitive and rational instrument, based on our daily physiological experiences and needs, the need to master our immediate surroundings, for example in a crowded street. Narrative form is based on temporality and causality, and enables us to see into the future, to form rational expectations, to make plans and to explain experiences (Turner 1996). There are also cultural models that teach us how to feel and how to express our feelings. Emotions have for example specific names and are represented by body postures and facial expressions. We relate to models all the time, most of the time unconsciously. We get aware of models when we find we haven't got one and feel we need one, an example is when we feel uncertain whether a person is a man or a woman. We relate to gender through models.

The children in my data are approaching the age of 2 years, and through real life and fiction they have established various mental schematas and models. And these experiences are the basic resource for the reader when approaching a text in a book or a film. Mandler puts it this way: "How could we understand a given story if we had no knowledge about what is likely to happen in a specific domain?" (Mandler1984:20). Susan Neuman claims that the schemata theory until now is the most fruitful contribution to our understanding of what it means to be an active reader or watcher of television (Neuman 1995).

Connotation

The study of meaning often deals with distinctions between denotation and connotation. Denotation refers to the specific signification of a given sign, for example the word 'white', which denotes the one quality that all different kind of white things have in common, whether they are foam, snow or paper. Denotation is often explained as *reference* or *core* meaning. But white also *connotes* abstract concepts of whiteness (e.g. purity), and then we speak of *additional* meaning, *second* meaning or *emotive* meaning. This is the meaning that derives from the associations activated by a certain sign. Traditionally denotation were seen as shared and collective meanings, while connotations were seen as individual and variable.

Until Roland Barthes, connotation was first and foremost a linguistic issue, he started discussing connotation in relation to visual image, especially photography (Barthes 1977a). A contribution from Barthes is also his statement that connotations not primarily are individual, but culturally shared meanings. Barthes calls these connotations *myths*, broad concepts of ideology. In *Mythologies* (1957) he discusses italianess, frenchness, militariness, and so on, as such myths. An evidence of the collective character of connotations is that they function extremely well in the globalized mass culture, for example in advertising.

Connotation comes along through culturally shared associations, and through specific connotators in a text. Theo van Leeuwen defines a connotator as a specific pointer, placed in a text because the producer has "an interest in trying to get a particular message across to a particular audience" (van Leeuwen 2002:95). The producer has a social agenda, and tries to guide the audience in intended directions. Barthes points out especially important connotation procedures, one of *content*, and one of *form* (Barthes 1977b). When it comes to content, Barthes points at *poses* and *objects* as very important connotators. There exists a historical grammar or an unwritten "dictionary of poses which is known to everyone who is at all exposed to the mass media" (van Leeuwen 2005:38–39). During reading aloud, parents introduce this dictionary to their children, by explicitly explaining by words, voice and body how they shall understand different poses. Children will gradually learn the conventional meanings of the different poses, for example dizziness, pleasure related to food, melancholia or self confidence. And children first understand the conventions we label clichés or stereotypes, because they are so frequent in popular culture. Next to poses, Barthes points at objects as inducers of ideas; the book, the cross, the hijab, and so on.

When it comes to form, Barthes points out what he calls *photogenia*, the various types of visual style and techniques, e.g "lighting, exposure and printing" (Barthes 1977b:23). Means like this influence how we experience what a picture actually communicates.

Where do Meanings Come From?

Gunther Kress and Theo van Leeuwen analyse how semiotic *innovation* comes along, and explain this through "semiotic import" (Kress and van Leeuwen 2001). Meanings are transported to new areas or discourses, so that the new areas achieve some of the meanings from the origin. The Beatles achieved this when they started to use Indian folk music in their own pop music, and then benefitted on different positive meanings from Indian culture. A question we often need to answer is where meanings, or connotations, come from, how the meaning potential of the semiotic resources can be explained and described. And *origin*, for example India, represents a source that can explain meaning. This is the principle of intertexuality and tradition, established meanings travel and bring their history with them. Kress and van Leeuwen use the term *provenance* about origin.

A Picturebook for Toddlers and Challenges of Interpretation

This article investigate how mental schemata, models and connotation are part of the competences required when we read picturebooks. Interpretations are dependent on individual experience, children need to relate words and pictures to their own life experiences, stored in memory. Then fiction can be experienced as being *about* something, and at its best: about something that creates involvement. Sometimes there is a lack of balance between a picturebook and the child's ability to play the role of the implied reader. Such imbalances represent challenges for the guides into meaningmaking, the adult readers. I will show some examples of how this can be identified.

The Swedish picturebook *Apan fin* (1999) might be translated to *The pretty monkey*. It is a minimalistic story that follows the concept of home, away, and home again during a day. We see a little girl leave her mother, go out to play, meet a dog, get frightened, hide in a tree, jump down, get wet, go home, get comfort and milk. Finally she goes to sleep. Three problems of cognition, connotation and semiotics can be identified in the parents' readings of this book.

1) A Problem Regarding the Plot

The implied reader of this book is a reader who understands the dramatical essence of the plot; *the threat the girl feels from the dog*. It is a *bad* dog, and the monkey is *afraid*. A bad dog is analogue to a *bad guy*, we should expect bad intentions. On the third spread of *Apan fin* the monkey girl leaves home, optimistically facing the wide world in the direction of the turning page and the next spread. She is placed almost on the bottom line of the spread, in the right corner. This principle of visual composition is called a pageturner, it urges the reader to continue. The encounter between dog and girl is then presented in two proceeding spreads:

The "Bad dog"- spread (Hunden dum) displays a big dog entering from the right, and in picturebook dramaturgy the right represents the unknown and possible threat. The dog approaches the girl, she however is *not* pictured here. But she turns up again on the next spread (Apan rädd), facing the right. Now she is afraid, mind her body. The implied reader of this book synthezises

Figure 13.1 Illustration from Anna-Clara Tidholm: *Apan fin*. Stockholm: Alfabeta, 1999.

APAN
RÄDD

Figure 13.2 Illustration from Anna-Clara Tidholm: *Apan fin*. Stockholm: Alfabeta, 1999.

these spreads into one motif, the monkey and the dog are approaching a face-to-face-situation. The role of the implied reader is also to identify and accept the discomfortable psychology in the meeting, but will all *real* readers play the role of the implied reader? The double spreads show only one figure at a time, one has to keep the girl in mind while only seeing the dog, and the dog while only seeing the girl. It seems that the parents analyze this as challenging to the children. They seem to give up linking the spreads together, and they spend very little time on them. None of the parents communicate an actually dangerous dog or a frightened girl—that is, they do not put much effort in modelling emotions that the children can recognize. And we can wonder why, other times during reading they put very much effort in emotions. My assumption is that they experience a dilemma concerning the children's cognitive capacities, but also a dilemma concerning representation: How can they *represent* fear, through words and voice, without *imposing* fear on the child reader? These dilemmas change a dramatic story into an undramatic story about a day in the life.

The children and their parents also face a problem of *script* schemata. The children of course know what it means to meet someone. They know face-to-face scenes. But the advanced syntax of the spreads makes it complicated for the children to activate both the relevant script for how meetings unfold, and to see spreads as one scene. This gives them a problem with the meaning of the plot. A well established narrative schemata could help a reader to make the relevant link between girl and dog, so that one easily recognize that 'the meaning here is that the girl went along, *then* the bad dog came and *that is why* she got frightened'. This would include both linearity and causality, key dimensions of narrative. But such a mental task might be complicated for these children, and I think the parents have some sense of this. How could they help the childrens' understanding of what Iser would call a blank in the text, and more specifically, along the syntagmatic axis of the text (Iser 1978, Maagerø and Tønnessen 2001)? It is almost impossible to watch two spreads at the same time.

A Problem Concerning Classification and Connotation: The Bad Dog

The dog in this book has been called the first *bad* dog in Swedish childrens literature[2]. If this is right, and it might well be, this is an important dimension according to an analysis of how small children are able to understand this actual dog.

The small children in my study know dogs, they have met dogs. But they probably have none or few experiences with so called bad dogs. Where they live, dogs seldom run around alone. Dogs are pets, they are charming, soft, funny, and toddlers most often meet them when being pushed safely along in a stroller. They develop positive and emotional relations to dogs. In the tapes it is obvious that some children respond with joy when this dog appears on the page. As mentioned, none of the adults seem to succeed in communicating the meaning of the bad dog. Most of them don't even try, and one mother also said, afterwards, that she didn't want to do anything that could give her child negative feelings for dogs. So parents undercommunicate the "bad dog". Some nearly wisper and quickly turn the page, some change the written text: "A *big* dog came!" A big dog probably matches the childrens' experiences better than a bad dog. We see how parents adapt the book to the child, not the other way around, probably because of a certain assumption; the childrens' experience is essential to their understanding, and parents do have an intimate and rather precise knowledge of these experiences.

In reading this book, parents face a problem of experience, and it affects classification and connotation. This dog is chosen from a wide range of possible dog representations. It lacks an important feature that is salient to the dogs otherwise represented in toddlers books, films or toys: friendliness or charm. I have experienced that adult students laugh at the dog, and call him stupid, or ugly. When parents prefer to call him big, it might be because they feel that the relation between the word bad and the actual picture is problematic. There might be a problem of aptness, or motivation, in the relation between the word "bad" and this particular picture.

This picture denotes the core meaning *dog*, but many of us read it as a *certain* kind of dog, we add connotations. This dog can be a *mongrel*, because of some signs that constitute "shabbiness", lack of race, unkept fur, and lack of delicateness. These are important connotators for the adult audience, we respond to a dog stereotype. We might also see him as masculine, and then remember that once upon a time there was another little girl dressed in red, away from home ... Small children, on the other side, recognize the denotative meaning—a few of them seem to add a positive, emotional meaning, they smile when he occurs. If they are not familiar with negative meanings of dogs, it is more difficult for them to adjust to the implied reader of this book. Parents and children face a problem of classification and stereotyping. At this age, the children are able to recognize a dog, but not to understand a specific type of dog. And the difference between recognition and understanding is crucial. They lack experience when it comes to "dog variation", and I think the parents have some sense of this. The problem of the bad dog is a blank along the paradigmatic axis of the text, the one that relates to experience and content (Iser 1978, Tønnessen 1998).

A Problem of Gender

Even if the monkey obviously is dressed in a skirt and such denotes femininity, several of the parents, both men and women, talk about her as a *he* (Mjør 2007). They say "Look, he is jumping in bed!", "Now he is going out to play", etc. Ulla Rhedin refers to a three year old girl who insisted upon the monkey being a boy, even though she was confronted with the skirt: "- But it is a boy anyway—I just see it!" (Rhedin 1994:73). A father admitted to me that he also had spoken of the monkey as a boy.—"But you saw the skirt?", I asked him, and he answered: "- Yes, in a way, but I felt it didn't matter, anyway, he was jumping in bed, and to me that is a boyish thing to do ..." Remember Barthes and the poses, poses also are gendered and function as cultural and mental models.

The little monkey girl obviously suffers from a gender problem. The skirt is not the only connotator of feminity, though. This monkey is also tied to several discourses frequent in stories with girl protagonists. There is the title, it implies femininity, we seldom read books about boys whose main characteristic is prettiness. She also has an intimate relation to her mother, and she responds whith anxiety when facing the dog, and with defeat when getting wet. We have all seen male protagonists handling situations like this more actively. And, as mentioned, there is a link to the story of Red Riding Hood. But these feminine discourses do not help, parents still see her as a boy.

There are several semiotic explanations to the girl's gender problems. There is a problem of *title*: The protagonist is not given a first name, she is only "monkey". A girl's name, used in the title, would follow the main rule of books like this, a girl's name would make it more difficult to speak of a he. This makes Bartes' principle of *anchorage* in the interplay between words and images relevant. Anchorage is when the verbal text guides us in how to understand a picture, when words narrow down the potential meaning of a picture, when words give precise information where a picture can not be that precise; for example by naming (Barthes 1977a). The lack of a first name makes the anchoring too weak in this book, and this is part of the problem.

But the monkey should also be investigated as a cultural and a mental model. "I think we usually think of monkeys as boys", one mother said, in a discussion about the gender issue, and she is probably right. There is a strong cultural tradition that combines monkeys and masculinity, King Kong and Tarzan are two examples. The famous books and films about Curious George are also important, George is the male adventurous trickster (Curious George is created by H.A Rey and Margret Rey). Parents know him well. In Norway there is also Julius, a chimp living in the zoological garden in Kristiansand, a place nearly no Norwegian family can escape, because of a popular pirate park. Julius is heavily exposed, through television, books and songs, the nation has followed him all the way from babyhood, through bachelorhood, and today he is a retired grandfather. In Norway the word monkey also is used to characterize football fans, most of them male, and "the hill of the monkeys" is their place at the stadium.

The concept of provenance or origin was mentioned as an important source that explain how we create meaning. It seems that culture's use of the monkey in different discourses has created a provenance that has masculinity as its most salient dimension. This provenance plays an important part on how we understand monkeys, also when they show up in skirts.

Male and Female Models: The Signs of Girlishness

The author first presented this book to her publisher with a *boy* protagonist. She then was confronted with the strong need for more girl protagonists in childrens' literature. She did not at all mind to change hero to heroine, and it is of course disappointing that this heroine has difficulties with her femininity. These problems are also connected to a lack of explicit feminine attributes, feminine connotators.

The signs of femininity are no longer red, green and yellow, that was long ago. They are now pink, and violet, and decorative details are crucial. The ultimate girlishness today is represented by the Barbie doll and the Disney princesses. The monkey mother in *Apan fin* is more into today's fashion, she has the right colours, the blouse is decorated, she has got hair and hairband. The daughter has no hair, and a girl without hair is indeed provocative. A four year old girl explained the gender problem competently to me, her opinion was that the girl looked a *bit* like a boy, and mentioned the lack of hair. "Girls *have* hair, you know". Then she focused on the jacket with collar and buttons: "And this jacket, you know, it looks a bit like a shirt". She explained a shirt as something boys wear when they go to birthday parties, and proposed a pink dress and eye lashes to make the monkey more girllike.

In this book, feminine and masculine models seem to compete, and it seems that the masculine connotators are the stronger. The monkey as a *model-in-the world* has difficulties in matching femininity as a *model-in-the mind*. To break the masculine tradition and provenance of the monkey, a girl protagonist needs more help than a yellow skirt to secure her existence as a girl. Maybe hair and a girl's name? Maybe eye lashes? Lashes seem to be one of the earliest signs of femininity children notice, we can see them in girls' early self-portraits, and we can see them in animated films, where the female animal has lashes, the male not.

Gender ambuigity isn't necessarily important to very young readers, none of the parents mentioned this as a problem for the children. *Apan fin* has indeed one interesting protagonist that makes the book worth reading, again and again. The gender problem in the book is a greater challenge for the adults than for the children, because adults are more familiar with the semiotics of gender.

This article has tried to show some challenges adult readers can face when they take on the task of guiding children into the role as an implied reader of a picturebook. Books that seem simple can represent challenges of understanding. Adult readers first interpret the text themselves, then they analyze how the child will be able to find it meaningful. Paradoxes sometimes appear, and children have to work things out through several readings and dialogues about words and pictures. Most of them find these processes interesting and pleasant, and work things out, with a little help from friends.

Notes

1. My study analyses video tapes where parents have recorded reading sessions in their private homes, when reading for their own toddlers, children about 18 months old.
2. http://www.barnfamiljen.com/templates/article.asp?id=3427

References

Barthes, R. *Mythologies*. Paris: Editions du Seuil, 1957.
Barthes, R. "The Rhetoric of the Image" (first published 1964). In *Image Music Text* by Roland Barthes and Stephen Heath. 32–51. London: Fontana Press, 1977a.
Barthes, R. "The Photographic Message" (first published 1961). In *Image Music Text* by Roland Barthes and Stephen Heath. 15–31. London: Fontana Press, 1977b.
Iser, Wolfgang. *The Implied Reader*. Baltimore: John Hopkins University Press, 1974
———. *The Act of Reading. A Theory of Aesthetic Response*. Baltimore: Johns Hopkins University Press, 1978.
Kress, Gunther and Theo van Leeuwen. *Multimodal Discourse. The Modes and Media of Contemporary Communication*. London: Arnold, 2001.
Leeuwen, Theo van. "Semiotics and Iconography". In *Handbook of Visual Analysis* edited by Theo van Leeuwen and Carey Jewitt. 92–118. London: Sage, 2002.
Leeuwen, Theo van. *Introducing Social Semiotics*. London: Routledge, 2005.
Mandler, Jean Matter. *Stories, Scripts, and Scenes. Apects of Schema Theory*. Hillsdale, N.J.: Elbaum Ass, 1984.
Mjør, Ingeborg. "Berre eit skjørt? Genusproblem i bildeboka *Apan fin*". In *Årboka litteratur for barn og unge* edited by Per Olav Kaldestad and Karin Beate Vold. 60–70. Oslo: Samlaget/NBI, 2007.
Maagerø, Eva and Elise Seip Tønnessen. "Wolfgang Iser". In *Samtaler om tekst, språk og kultur*. 67–93. Oslo: LNU/Cappelen Akademisk Forlag, 2001.

Neuman, Susan. *Literacy in the Television Age. The Myth of TV Effect.* Norwood, N.J: Ablex, 1995
Ninio, Anat and Jerome Bruner. "The Achievement and Antecedents of Labelling". In *Journal of Child Language* 5. 1–15. Cambridge [u.a.], 1978.
Rhedin, Ulla. "Småbarnsboken och det lilla barnet". In *Bilderbokens hemligheter.* 47–79. Stockholm: Alfabeta, 1994.
Shore, Brad. "Models Theory as a Framework for Media Studies". In *Cultural Cognition. New Perspectives in Audience Theory* edited by Birgitta Höijer and Anita Werner. 7–40. Göteborg University: Nordicom, 1998.
Tønnesssen, Elise Seip."Understanding a Story. A Social Semiotic Approach to the Development of Interpretation". In *Cultural Cognition. New Perspectives in Audience Theory* edited by Birgitta Höijer and Anita Werner. 119–135. Göteborg University: Nordicom, 1998.
Turner, Mark. *The Literary Mind,* Oxford University Press, 1996.
Weinreich, Torben. "Den fortællende læser—bidrag til udviklingen af en teori om mødet mellem tekst og læser". In *Nedslag i børnelitteraturforskningen 2.* 115–148. Copenhagen: Roskilde Universitetsforlag, 2001.

Chapter Fourteen
First-Person Narratives in Picturebooks
An Inquiry into the Acquisition of Picturebook Competence

Eva Gressnich and Jörg Meibauer

Introduction

Although the meaning and function of the personal pronoun *I* are not easily acquired, young children are confronted with picturebooks containing first-person narratives at an early age. Thus, not only the question arises how it is possible for children to understand those narratives, but also the question how they relate them to the respective pictures. In our chapter, we will focus on both questions. Our background is linguistics, particularly the study of child language. We believe that the acquisition of literary competence, conceived of as the ability to understand or to produce literature, is intimately connected with language acquisition. If we are right, it is necessary to reflect on the interaction of both.

Because children, at least in Western cultures, are exposed to literature at an early age, language acquisition and literature acquisition correlate in complex ways (Meibauer 2006). Thus, the growing phonological abilities of children interact with the detection of rhyme, as displayed in nursery rhymes. With the beginning of vocabulary acquisition at twelve months, children engage in pointing to and labeling pictures of simple objects without any accompanying text, thereby acquiring several skills that are fundamental for further language acquisition, visual and literary literacy (Kümmerling-Meibauer and Meibauer 2005). While children's knowledge of their language increases further in the multi-word stage, more and more text is integrated into picturebooks made for this age-group, thus reflecting the children's mastery of the sentence and a bigger vocabulary. By the age of four years, several abilities that enhance the acquisition of children's literature emerge. First, children's development of metalinguistic awareness (understood as the ability to reflect upon language) and a *Theory of Mind* (understood as the ability to reflect on beliefs and attitudes of others) form the cognitive basis of an elementary understanding of irony and metaphor, which is so important for literature in general (Winner 1988). Second, with the emergence of children's own narratives, the insight into narrative structures as contained in more complex picturebooks grows. While the elementary mastery of a first language is supposed to be complete by the start of school, it is in the first years of primary education, when children learn to read and write, that the foundations for an advanced understanding of children's literature are laid. More complex syntactic structures and textual patterns are acquired, and the vocabulary is further expanded. The ability to reflect upon narrative structures widens, and knowledge of other media increases. As a result, children gather more and more experience with literary genres (Shine and Roser 1999).

In our chapter, we will go into a specific aspect of the acquisition of picturebook competence, namely the mastery of first-person narratives. Obviously, the understanding of picturebooks displaying first-person narratives presupposes some initial understanding of how the personal pronoun *I* functions. But this step, as we will show, is by no means an easy task for the child. In addition, it may be asked whether first-person narratives presented to children have any influence on the course of their language acquisition. To picturebook researchers, it is evident that pictures are somehow related to the referents of a narrative. But the question how a child can ever uncover those complex relations is seldom discussed. In our contribution, we will go into some of these questions against the background of Perry Nodelman's seminal paper, pointing out further aspects of first-person narratives in picturebooks.

The Acquisition of *I* and *you*

Within linguistics, the use of personal pronouns such as *I* and *you* is analysed under the heading of deixis (or indexicality); the basic insight being that deictic expressions possess a double nature. On the one hand, the personal pronoun *I* denotes the speaker, and this is a semantic fact. On the other hand, the actual referent of *I*, in a specific discourse situation, can only be identified if that discourse situation is available to the hearer. Therefore, deixis is considered as a pragmatic phenomenon, too (Levinson 2004). Thus, deictic expressions (or indexicals) are elements of a language that have only little semantic content, their meaning being highly dependent on the context of utterance (Fillmore 1997). For instance, understanding the sentence *Bring me the book on the right now* and interpreting the words *me*, *right*, and *now* require knowing who is saying the sentence, where that person is, and when it is being said. Although deictic elements are not acquired easily, some of them belong to the earliest words a child acquires (Clark and Sengul 1977; Wales 1986). For example, German children know the word *da* ("there") before the vocabulary spurt starts, i.e., before eighteen months of age. *Da* is a very general expression that is used by the child to point at all objects (including persons) that are of interest to her.

Pointing and labeling are also important processes that accompany joint attention to picturebooks. For example, an adult points to a thing depicted and the child's task is to present the correct label, or, vice versa, the child points to a certain depicted thing and the adult presents the conventional word for it (Jones 1996; Ninio and Bruner 1978).

The young child refers to persons with proper names that are also part of her small lexicon. For example, Simone, at the age of twenty-two months, refers to herself with *Mone* and to her mother with *Mama*:[1]

(1) Mone auch heia
 "Simone sleep too"
(2) Mama raus
 "mama out"

Note that child directed speech often reflects this preference for proper names, even when the child has already acquired some deictic expressions.

To grasp the meaning of the personal pronoun *I* is by no means easy.[2] This is demonstrated by Paul Bloom who considers the learning situation of the child in the following:

> *Consider a child, Margaret, who is learning the pronoun* I. *Suppose she talks only with her mother. Margaret might reasonably draw the conclusion that* I *is her mother's name. Her mother uses this word only to refer to herself, after all, and the word has the same syntax as* Margaret *or* Mommy. *It would help rescue Margaret from this semantic dead-end if she hears another person use* I. *(124)*[3]

Moreover, there are other learning problems. First, because Margaret hears the word *I* used to refer to everyone but Margaret (Margaret is always called either *Margaret* or *you*), the child could conclude that this word can refer to everyone but her. But this generalization is never made by children, maybe, because they view themselves as persons engaged in conversations that have the right "to be an *I* sometimes" from early on, as John Macnamara points out (43).

Bloom considers that a further learning problem arises with the acquisition of the personal pronoun *you*. The question is—since the child is addressed as *you*—why she does not infer that *you* is her name?: "After all, the way Margaret learned her name is *Margaret* was presumably by hearing herself, and nobody else, called *Margaret*. So why doesn't the same reasoning apply when she hears herself called *you*?" (124). One solution to this puzzle could be that the child observes the principle of contrast (Clark 1993), a pragmatic principle that consists in assuming that two words never mean the same (or that there is no synonymy in language). Only later Margaret will learn that *you*, *Margaret*, *Maggie*, *Peggy*, and *Peg* may refer to the same individual.

Yuriko Oshima-Takane argues that the acquisition of pronouns is a case where the child does not learn word meanings by listening to child directed speech, but where the child overhears the talk of others. It is exactly here, where she hears that other people are called *you*, and from this she is able to infer that it is not her name. Bloom points out that this is a quite radical proposal, because "this would require that children can cope with utterances that are faster, longer, and more complex than those typically directed at them" (125).

Note, however, that overheard speech of adults may not be the only input that is available for children. For example, in picturebooks, others are addressed with *you*, too, and picturebooks constitute an input that is more fine-tuned to the children's needs. Thus, text from picturebooks may be repeated, and there are, in principle, adult explanations available.

If it is not so easy to learn the meanings of *I* versus *you*, it can be predicted that there will be reversal errors. And in fact, some children go through phases of using *you* as a label for themselves, and *I* as a label for their adult addressee (Tomasello, 202–203).

(3) Adult: Shall I pick you$_i$ up?
    Child: Pick you$_i$ up. (= Pick me$_i$ up)

How this phenomenon is to be explained, is far from clear. Michael Tomasello discusses several approaches (200–208), among them pragmatic confusion (poor social-cognitive skills), imitation or mimicry (the child echoes or anticipates the adult's utterance, see (3)), and frequency of input (*you* is much more frequent in use than *I*). Bloom points out that autistic children make this kind of mistake very often, autism going together with a reduced ability to follow the discourse of others (125).

With thirty-six months of age, most children have acquired the distinction between *I* and *you*. They understand that *I* refers to the speaker, so that reference to individuals may change in the context of utterance. With the acquisition of first-person deixis, the egocentrism of the child, i.e., her tendency to consider herself as the deictic centre, vanishes.[4] We conclude that in the third year of life, most children know that *I* is a context-referential word that may refer to themselves as well as to others.

First-person Narratives in Picturebooks

Let us now turn to the use of first-person narratives in picturebooks. When deictic expressions are used in literature, they do not point at aspects of an actual immediate context of utterance, but at aspects of an imaginary fictional space ("Deixis am Phantasma," to use the term by Karl Bühler). The personal pronoun *I* used in a narrative text refers to the narrator of the story. Clearly, it requires complex cognitive processes to identify the referent of *I* in a reading situation, because the reader has to determine the referent within the context of the story.

Let us first point out that children are confronted with first-person narratives in picturebooks at an early age. As a matter of fact, first-person statements occur already in books for the young reader. Gunther Kress and Theo van Leeuwen discuss a picture from the early picturebook *Baby's First Book* (21).[5] The text accompanying the picture of a water-filled bathtub with a toy duck swimming on the surface says: "Every night I have my bath before I go to bed." The short text in this spread is definitely not a story, just a statement, but the sentence contains the indexical *I*. Now imagine a reading situation with a child and her father. From the point of view of the child, the pronoun *I* could refer to the following persons or entities:

(4)   a. the one who is speaking (the father)
      b. the one who is spoken to (the child)
      c. the toy duck
      d. the "narrator"
      e. the author/illustrator

Hypothesis (4a) would be a good hypothesis, because the father is the one who is speaking to the child. To exclude this hypothesis the child must possess some pragmatic knowledge about the reading situation. For example, that the utterance in the text, understood as a statement of the father, makes no sense in this situation, but has to be related to information connected to the context of the book.

Hypothesis (4b) is excluded when the child knows that *I* does not exclusively refer to her, but has the potential to refer to infinitely many speakers.

Hypothesis (4c) is a good example for certain ambiguities that might arise. In fact, because toys are animated in many children's books, and could be conceived as a "living" character, this hypothesis is not as weird as it appears at first sight (Kuznets 1994).

Whether and when the child has any ideas with regard to (4d) and (4e), is up to now far from clear. As long as a child reader is not yet familiar with first-person narratives, there is no need for her to develop a concept of the narrator. Since the narrator in third-person narratives remains in the background and does not refer to herself, the child does not have to be aware of some kind of narrative instance within these stories. She does not have to identify the person telling the story as different from the person reading the story to her. Thus, when hearing the pronoun *I* within a narrative text for the first time in a joint reading situation, the child will probably relate the *I* to the person reading the story. However, incongruencies will occur, and the child will notice that the narrative utterances understood as statements of the person reading to her do not make any sense. How and when she eventually manages to determine the correct reference is far from clear. Own experiences with hearing stories from others as well as with the production of own stories are certainly relevant in this context (Bamberg 1987; Berman and Slobin 1994; Boueke et al. 1995).

It follows then that the child needs some strategies that could help her to determine the correct reference. For example, the child could use an elementary pattern of pragmatic inference in order to derive the implicature that it is not the father that is referred to by *I* in the preceding text. An implicature is conceived as context-dependent meaning that is not entailed by "what is said," but inferred on the basis of contextual and background knowledge (Grice 1989; Meibauer 2006).

(5) A pragmatic inferencing pattern
Step 1: While looking at the book, the father says: "Every night I have my bath before I go to bed."
Step 2: *I* could refer to the father.
Step 3: If *I* refers to the father, the father is telling me that every night he has his bath before he goes to bed.
Step 4: But this statement is hardly relevant in the context of book reading.
Step 5: The father is cooperative; he is not kidding me, etc.
Step 6: Therefore I assume that it must be someone besides the father that *I* refers to.
Step 7: The father has done nothing to stop me thinking that he is not the referent of *I*.
Step 8: Therefore he intends me to think that he is not the referent of *I*.
Step 9: And so he has implicated that he is not the referent of *I*.

To which extent children around three years of age, are actually using such a Gricean inferencing pattern, is far from clear. But it is reasonable to assume that such patterns play a role in language acquisition anyway,[6] and furthermore, it is reasonable to assume that joint picturebook reading provides a special learning situation where the kind of reasoning that is relevant for the acquisition of deictic expressions such as *I* and *you* is important. In sum, then, there is evidence for the assumption that joint attention to picturebooks will have influence on the acquisition of deixis.

Let us now point out another crucial aspect of first-person picturebooks. In his seminal paper, Perry Nodelman observed that the verbal narrative in a picturebook may be in the first person, while the accompanying pictures "rarely convey the effect of an autodiegetic first-person narration in which the same person is both the teller of the story and a key figure within it" (2). Maria Nikolajeva and Carole Scott add that "while identification with the "I" of the verbal text in itself presents a problem for young children, the contradictory perspective of the visual text is rather confusing" (125). Let us call this dilemma Nodelman's Observation and characterize it as in (6):

(6) Nodelman's Observation
In picturebooks, there is often a mismatch between first-person narratives and pictures that do not imply the narrator's point of view.

As an example for this mismatch, take a look at Tomi Ungerer's picturebook *Otto. Autobiographie eines Teddybären* (Otto. Biography of a Teddy Bear, 1999). Throughout the book, the first-person narrator, a teddy bear named Otto, is shown in almost every picture, but the viewer does *not* take the teddy bear's point of view to follow the scenes depicted.

Note that Nodelman correlates the discrepancy between text and pictures with the concept of identification. He states that the mismatch between text and pictures is a convention in picturebook art—an attribute that Nikolajeva and Scott also attest to film (125)—and that the child has to acquire certain competences in order to understand this convention. At first sight, the mismatch between "a text that demands empathy and pictures that imply the objectivity of distance would seem to demand far too much of young readers" (3), and probably complicate the child's identification with the *I* of the story. However, Nodelman comes to the conclusion that these picturebooks and "the objective distance implied by their pictures is a source of strength rather than a disruptive weakness" (22), when he reconsiders the general identification process of readers:

> But to read well is always to read with a sense of the doubleness of literature, which requires us to become involved in, even to identify with, its characters and situations but also to stand back and understand those characters and situations with some objectivity. In the clear-cut doubleness of their words and pictures, picture books like these can offer inexperienced readers an introduction to one of the most basic and most rewarding of literary competences. (30)

While Nodelman's assumptions appear to be convincing, we think that the idea of children "identifying" with characters or with the narrator of a story has to be taken *cum grano salis*, because the concept of identification, beyond its intuitive appeal, is not well-studied, and certainly will turn out as a quite complex process from a cognitive point of view. Thus, we will neglect this aspect in the rest of our chapter.

Growing complexity

From an acquisitional point of view it may be asked, how the child deals with the apparent mismatch between text and pictures in first-person picturebooks.

One might argue that the mismatch is hard to grasp for children, but whether this assumption is right, or whether this mismatch poses, quite on the contrary, no problems for the child, is something we do not really know, because empirical research is lacking in this area.

However, we predict that the convention of relating first-person narratives to "objective" pictures (i.e., pictures with a bystander's perspective) is acquired more easily than the use of first-person narratives combined with subjective perspectives in pictures. The reason for our hypothesis is that we believe that the pictures in picturebooks provide a context, within which the child reader can or rather has to interpret the information given by the text.[7] Thus, pictures have the purpose to help the child create mental images about the plot of the book. Just like the objective picture naturally depicts characters and objects that are different from the narrator, it also contains the referent of the *I* who tells the story, as long as the narrator is a central character within the plot. Therefore, it supports the child in imagining the fictional narrator. A child will probably search the picture for the referent of *I*, before she will eventually conclude that the first-person narrator is *not* depicted, as it turns out indeed with those pictures exclusively displaying subjective perspectives.

Based on this consideration and the hypothesis that first-person narratives, because of the complex reference of *I*, are in general hard to grasp for children of a certain age, we suggest the following typology of picturebooks. It implies growing complexity depending on the combination of a certain type of narration with a certain type of visual point of view. We illustrate each type with one or more typical spreads. Let us first consider the lowest level of complexity.

(a) Third-person narrative, picture implies an objective (bystander's) perspective

Several spreads in Jean de Brunhoff's picturebook *Babar* (1934) fall into this category. Consider, for instance, the picture of Babar telling his friends in the city about his life in the forest. The picture contains an objective (bystander's) perspective and is linked to a third-person narrative. It is reasonable to assume that this pattern is the standard case, at least when one considers how frequent picturebooks of this type are.[8] The characters of the story are referred to with proper names or with third-person pronouns, and in case they are depicted in the picture, the scenery is shown as if it was perceived from the perspective of a bystander.

However, we also find different perspectives in third-person picturebooks, as we will show with the next category.

(b) Third-person narrative, picture shows a back view of a character or picture implies a "subjective camera" perspective

At the end of Anthony Browne's picturebook *The Visitors Who Came to Stay* (1984), there is a picture of Katy and her father looking at Sean and Mary's house. The viewer almost shares the protagonists' point of view, as the picture depicts the back of their upper bodies with the viewer positioned right behind them. We guess that this specific form of depiction makes the subjectivity of the perspective more clearly to the young reader. In this case, the child should take an intrinsic perspective, i.e., a scenario is seen from the point of view of another person or thing. How such an intrinsic perspective is acquired or whether it is learned as a convention, is, as far as we know, not clear and calls for further research. One purpose of the use of this point of view within the conventions of pictures appears to be the creation of an impression of moving forward.

Very unusual is the use of so-called "subjective camera" perspectives in third-person picturebooks. The term "subjective camera"-perspective is used with regard to film and featured by Nikolajeva and Scott as a case, in which "the point of view of the protagonist/narrator and that of the reader/viewer coincide" (125). As mentioned before, we assume that this perspective is not as easily grasped by children as the bystander's perspective is. Only a few third-person picturebooks display this visual point of view. In Anthony Browne's *Willy the Wizard* (1995), there is a picture showing a close-up of Willy's football boots. Because the accompanying text says "Willy stared at them with wonder," we assume that we are sharing the protagonist's point of view in the picture.

Let us come to first-person picturebooks and, thus, to a higher degree of complexity.

(c) First-person narrative, picture implies an objective (bystander's) perspective

Note that this is the case to which Nodelman's paper attests "oddity," because here we find a mismatch between the first-person narrative and the visual bystander's perspective. This combination is to be found in numerous first-person picturebooks.

Consider Ellen Raskin's *Nothing Ever Happens on My Block* (1966). This book is a so-called ironic picturebook (Kümmerling-Meibauer 1999) in that the text offers different information from the pictures in a very specific way. In the text, the first-person narrator Chester tells the reader how nothing happens on his block. In the pictures, however, we take an objective perspective seeing the boy from a distance, and also seeing a lot of exciting things happening around him. Interpreting the subjective information given by the text within the context of the objective pictures, enables us to understand the whole story, in particular that Chester is not able or maybe unwilling to notice the world around him.

The second spread in Anthony Browne's *Into the Forest* (2004) offers another example, though *not* implying an ironic relationship between words and pictures. While the story is told from the protagonist's point of view, the picture depicts the first-person narrator, a young boy, sitting with his mother at the kitchen table. However, as the following two categories show, Anthony Browne uses a variety of perspectives in this particular book (as well as in many of his other works).

(d) First-person narrative, picture shows a back view of the narrator or picture implies a "subjective camera" perspective

Rarely, but actually more often than in third-person picturebooks, "subjective camera" perspectives or close-to "subjective camera" perspectives are used in first-person picturebooks. In Browne's *Into the Forest*, the two pictures of the boy arriving at his Grandma's house contain a back view of the child narrator's body. Thus, as in the example from the picturebook *The Visitors Who Came to Stay*, we almost share the narrator's point of view as we are positioned behind him.

Ann Jonas's first-person picturebook *Now We Can Go* (1986) offers several examples of genuine "subjective camera" perspectives. From the second to the penultimate spread, the viewer's and the narrator's visual point of view coincide. Each spread depicts a toy box and a bag seen from above, but certainly not the child narrator who continuously seems to be putting items from the box into the bag. A similar perspective is used in Anthony Browne's picturebook *Voices in the Park* (1998). In the section that applies the mother's point of view in the text, the picture illustrating the scene in which she discovers her son talking to a girl implies a "subjective camera" perspective.

(e) Unusual visual perspectives in first-person picturebooks

Finally, there are some examples of unusual and highly complex perspectives in first-person narratives. In fact, they belong to category (d), but, because of their additional complexity, which is based on some special features, we treat them as a separate category.

In *I Met a Dinosaur* (1998) by Jan Wahl and Chris Sheban, a girl reports on her meetings with dinosaurs. While these dinosaurs are shown in the pictures, the reader concludes that they are not real for the adults. It appears as if they are only real for the child. This subjective perspective of the child is emphasized by the first-person narrative. There is one picture of the girl shown from a back-view-of-the-narrator perspective, in which she is driving down the scarped hill into the valley while she is greeting the dinosaur who is confidentially looking at her. Most likely the different and complex axes of motion in this picture are not easy to interpret for children.

Another spread from Anthony Browne's *Into the Forest* (2004) is an example for "subjective camera" perspective. In the picture of the mother spreading her arms toward and looking at her son, we see the scene with the narrator's eyes. Thus, the additional complexity arises from the fact that in this picture, the mother seems to be glancing out of the picture. The difficulty increases, when we compare this example to pictures in Ann Jonas's *Holes and Peeks* (1984). Here, several spreads do not depict a story character different from the narrator looking at the first-person narrator, but the first-person narrator herself glancing out of the picture. That means that the child reader has to differentiate between two possible cases in which a depicted person seems to be glancing out of the picture.

Now it is tempting to argue that differences in the degree of complexity correlate with the child's developmental stages. For example, that a third-person narrative combined with a bystander's perspective is sort of a standard scenario that is earlier and more easily grasped, and that the examples in category (e) are the most demanding scenarios in that they presuppose more abilities to derive adequate interpretive assumptions. Because there is a lack of empirical studies in this regard, we emphasize that our typology is only suggestive in this respect. Finally, note the very important aspect that within one picturebook, complexity arises in particular because of the many shifts of visual perspective from page to page.

Nodelman's Observation, as we called it, certainly is very important with regard to a general theory of the status of pictures as displayed in picturebooks. As we have stressed, we suggest that the primary job of the pictures is to provide a context for the text, and thus we do *not* believe that they constitute some kind of autonomous "visual narrative" or "visual text" in and by themselves (Arizpe and Styles 2003). After all, even the content of textless picturebooks calls for narration, so that the widespread assumption of the concept of "visual text" is by no means self-explaining. Instead, we think that the verbal narrative and the visual perspective are two principally independent modes of representation; if so, there is no *a priori* need for the "matching" of both, but the need, of course, to calculate their interaction, a task both for the author and for the reader.

Conclusions

What we have shown is that the interaction between language acquisition and the acquisition of literary competence is far more complex than usually acknowledged. The connection between both areas of research has been studied by focusing on the use of the personal pronoun *I* as a referential device pointing to the narrator in first-person picturebooks and children's emerging strategies of dealing with this process. Clearly, it must be difficult for a young child to assign the correct reference on the one hand, and to relate the narrative text to the corresponding pictures on the other hand, but, eventually, most children manage this task. Our typology of different combinations of verbal and visual point of views suggests varying degrees of complexity as well as a possible order of acquisition. Most of the points touched upon in the course of our chapter call for further empirical research. Lots of first-person picturebooks appear to exist, even for the young reader, so this field of research remains a relevant as well as a promising one.

Notes

1. Examples taken from Miller (1979: 14, 55).
2. For a general treatment of *I*, see Brinck (1997).
3. By "the same syntax," Bloom certainly means the parts of speech status as noun/pronoun. With respect to agreement, the syntax is of course different (Gunther Kress, p.c.).
4. Miller observes that egocentric children "express 'centered linguistic material' [. . .] in an implicit fashion whenever these elements refer to the deictic center and its role in the communicative act" (210). For example, if Simone wants out of her cart, it suffices to utter *raus* ("out"), but when she wants to get into her cart, she says *karre rein* ("in cart").
5. For this book type in general, see Kümmerling-Meibauer and Meibauer (2005).
6. See Clark (1993) on lexical acquisition; see Winner (1988) on the acquisition of irony and metaphor, which are classical cases of conversational implicature.
7. The need for observing the pictorial information is obvious with ironic picturebooks, e.g., Ellen Raskin's *Nothing Ever Happens on My Block* (1996); see also Kümmerling-Meibauer (1999).
8. Exact data is not available, so this assumption has to be corroborated.

Bibliography

Primary Sources

Browne, Anthony. *Willy the Wizard*. London: Random House, 1995.
Browne, Anthony. *Voices in the Park*. London: Random House, 1998.
Browne, Anthony. *Into the Forest*. London: Walker Books, 2004.
de Brunhoff, Jean. *Die Geschichte von Babar, dem kleinen Elefanten*. Translated from French by Claudia Schmölders. Zürich: Diogenes, 1976 (*L'Histoire de Babar*, 1931).
Jonas, Ann. *Holes and Peeks*. New York: Greenwillow Books, 1984.
Jonas, Ann. *Now We Can Go*. New York: Greenwillow Books, 1986.
McAfee, Annalena, and Anthony Browne. *The Visitors Who Came to Stay*. London: Hamilton, 1984.
Raskin, Ellen. *Nothing Ever Happens on My Block*. New York: Atheneum, 1966.
Ungerer, Tomi. *Otto. Autobiographie eines Teddybären*. Zürich: Diogenes, 1999.
Wahl, Jan, and Chris Sheban. *I Met a Dinosaur*. Mankato, Minn.: Creative Editions, 1997.

Secondary Sources

Arizpe, Evelyn, and Morag Styles. "The Nature of Picturebooks: Theories about Visual Texts and Readers." In *Children Reading Pictures. Interpreting Visual Texts* edited by Evelyn Arizpe and Morag Styles. 19–38. London and New York: RoutledgeFalmer, 2003.
Bamberg, Michael G. *The Acquisition of Narratives. Learning to Use Language*. Berlin and New York: de Gruyter, 1987.
Berman, Ruth A., and Dan I. Slobin. *Relating Events in Narrative: A Cross-linguistic Developmental Study*. Mahwah, NJ: Lawrence Erlbaum Associates, 1994.

Boueke, Dietrich et al. *Wie Kinder erzählen. Untersuchungen zur Erzähltheorie und zur Entwicklung narrativer Fähigkeiten*. München: Fink, 1995.
Bloom, Paul. *How Children Learn the Meaning of Words*. Cambridge, MA and London: MIT Press, 2000.
Brinck, Ingar. *The Indexical "I". The First Person in Thought and Language*. Dordrecht: Kluwer, 1997.
Clark, Eve V. *The Lexicon in Acquisition*. Cambridge: Cambridge University Press, 1993.
Clark, Eve V., and C. J. Sengul. "Strategies in the Acquisition of Deixis." *Journal of Child Language* 5 (1977): 457–475.
Fillmore, Charles. *Lectures on Deixis*. Stanford: CSLI Publications, 1997 (CSLI Lecture Notes; 65).
Grice, Paul. *Studies in the Way of Words*. Cambridge, MA and London: Harvard University Press, 1989.
Jones, Rhian. *Emerging Patterns of Literacy. A Multidisciplinary Perspective*. New York and London: Routledge, 1996.
Kress, Gunter, and Theo van Leeuwen. *Reading Images. The Grammar of Visual Design*. New York and London: Routledge, 1996.
Kümmerling-Meibauer, Bettina. "Metalinguistic Awareness and the Child's Developing Concept of Irony: The Relationship between Pictures and Text in Ironic Picturebooks." *The Lion and the Unicorn* 23 (1999): 157–183.
Kümmerling-Meibauer, Bettina, and Jörg Meibauer. "First Pictures, Early Concepts: Early Concept Books." *The Lion and the Unicorn* 29 (2005): 324–347.
Kuznets, Lois Rostow. *When Toys Come Alive. Narratives of Animation, Metamorphosis, and Development*. New Haven and London: Yale University Press, 1994.
Levinson, Stephen C. "Deixis." In *The Handbook of Pragmatics* edited by Laurence R. Horn and Gregory Ward. 97–121. Oxford: Blackwell, 2004.
Macnamara, John. *Names for Things. A Study of Human Learning*. Cambridge, MA and London: MIT Press, 1982.
Meibauer, Jörg. "Language Acquisition and Children's Literature." In *The Oxford Encyclopedia of Children's Literature* edited by Jack Zipes. Vol. 2. 400–401. Oxford: Oxford University Press, 2006.
Meibauer, Jörg. "Implicature." In *Encyclopedia of Language and Linguistics* edited by Keith Brown. 2nd edition. Vol. 5. 568–580. Oxford: Elsevier, 2006.
Miller, Max. *The Logic of Language Development in Early Childhood*. Heidelberg and New York: Springer, 1979.
Nikolajeva, Maria, and Carole Scott. *How Picturebooks Work*. New York and London: Garland, 2001.
Ninio, Anat, and Jerome Bruner. "The Achievement and Antecedents of Labeling." *Journal of Child Language* 5 (1978): 1–15.
Nodelman, Perry. "The Eye and the I: Identification and First-Person Narratives in Picturebooks." *Children's Literature* 19 (1991): 1–30.
Oshima-Takane, Yuriko. "The Learning of First and Second Person Pronouns in English." In *Language, Logic, and Concept: Essays in Memory of John Macnamara* edited by Ray Jackendoff, Paul Bloom and Karen Wynn. 373–409. Cambridge, MA and London: MIT Press, 1999.
Shine, Stephanie, and Nancy L. Roser. "The Role of Genre in Preschoolers' Response to Picture Books." *Research in the Teaching of English* 34.2 (1999): 197–254.
Tomasello, Michael. *Constructing a Language. A Usage-Based Theory of Language Acquisition*. Cambridge, MA and London: Harvard University Press, 2003.
Wales, Roger. "Deixis." In *Language Acquisition. Studies in First Language Development* edited by Paul Fletcher and Michael Garman. 401–428. Cambridge: Cambridge University Press, 1986.
Winner, Ellen. *The Point of Words: Children's Understanding of Metaphor and Irony*. Cambridge, MA and London: Harvard University Press, 1988.

Chapter Fifteen
Remembering the Past in Words and Pictures
How Autobiographical Stories Become Picturebooks

Bettina Kümmerling-Meibauer

Definitions of autobiography have never proved to be definitive, but they are instructive in reflecting characteristic assumptions about what may well be considered the main aspects of this literary genre. One of the best-known definitions was formulated by Philippe Lejeune in the 1970s in his famous essay "The Autobiographical Pact": "Retrospective prose narrative written by a real person concerning his own existence, where the focus is his individual life, in particular the story of his personality" (4). Lejeune also stresses the existence of an identity between author and narrator on the one hand, and narrator and protagonist on the other. Through this, Lejeune reveals the commitment by theorists of autobiography to the referentiality of the autobiographical text, demonstrating the conceptual impasse they are faced with. As cognitive and memory studies have shown, autobiographical memory belongs to the realm of "higher-order consciousness." It involves the ability to construct a socially based selfhood, to model the world in terms of past and future, and to be directly aware that every recollection is a kind of perception, and every context will alter the nature of what is recalled.[1] This description infers the ability to step back from the immediacy of a situation and reflect upon past events. Moreover, in order to understand the specific features of autobiographical memories, the acquisition of Theory of Mind, i.e., the ability to distinguish one's own experiences from other people's experiences, is essential.

My concerns are both literary and cognitive, for the selves displayed in autobiographical texts are doubly constructed, not only in the act of writing and illustrating a life story, but also in a lifelong process of identity formation in which the writing/illustrating usually occurs at a comparatively late stage.

This chapter focuses on four picturebooks consisting of autobiographical stories written and illustrated by the authors: *War Boy* (1989) by Michael Foreman, *Self-Portrait* (1981) by Trina Schart Hyman, *Lumberjack* (1974) by William Kurelek, and *Tibet through the Red Box* (1998) by Peter Sís. The authors are all established artists who were already well known for their picturebooks and paintings before they created these autobiographical works.

The focus and reasons for creating autobiographical picturebooks vary from author to author. Trina Schart Hyman's book is the only one covering a whole lifespan, from Hyman's birth in 1939 up to 1981, when the book was published. The three other picturebooks under discussion focus on different periods in the lives of the author-illustrators. In Foreman's *War Boy* it is the Second World War, starting in April 1941 when the first-person narrator was three-years-old and a bomb damaged his bedroom, and ending with the victory celebrations after the capitulation of Germany in 1945. Kurelek's *Lumberjack* describes two lengthy stays by the author in a Canadian lumberjack camp in 1946 and 1951, when he was a young man aged nineteen and twenty-four. *Tibet through the Red Box*, by Peter Sís, covers the period from 1954 to 1955 when he was five-years-old. His father was on a secret mission in Tibet and the boy had to celebrate his birthday and Christmas without him.

Each author had a different reason for writing and illustrating his/her autobiographical picturebook. Hyman was asked by the publisher Harper & Row to contribute to its new series of autobiographical picturebooks by distinguished people.[2] Kurelek wanted to record for posterity a traditional line of work that he knew well, which had passed into history by the 1970s. Foreman's childhood in the British countryside in Pakefield was dominated by the Second World War, and the author could never forget this experience. However, the main reason for creating his picturebook was the death of his beloved mother, to whom he dedicated the book. It was she who saved him from the bombing attacks and helped him to survive.[3] The motivation for Sís' pictorial autobiography was a letter the author received from his father in 1994, in which the latter bequeathed to him the mysterious red box on his desk. The letter inspired Sís to return from New York to Prague, his birthplace, to take delivery of the box, which contained his father's secret diaries of his travels in Tibet.

All four picturebooks involve texts by first-person narrators recounting events in which they play a central role. The author is therefore both narrator and protagonist of the story. Moreover, in autobiographical picturebooks the narrator appears both in the text and in the pictures. The physical presence of the characters in autobiographical picturebooks is one typical feature that distinguishes this type of book from autobiographical texts without illustrations. I shall therefore begin by asking what these autobiographical picturebooks can teach us about the ways in which individuals in a particular culture experience their sense of self. Using interrelated pictures and text, the author-illustrator narrates his autobiography employing two different media: he writes his life story, and illustrates it. Whereas the text is based on mental images evoked by the author's description of locations, characters and moods, the pictures provide visual information, transforming the mental images into real illustrations. This enables the reader/viewer to share the author's recollections of past events and inner feelings, as well as the memorized visual images.

In this context it is interesting to note the different narrative and pictorial strategies the artists employ to emphasize the truth of their stories and pictures. Their autobiographical accounts are based on diaries, photos, newspaper reports, conversations about the past with parents, other relatives, and close friends, and sketches and letters, all of which support the authenticity of the picturebook's narrative. However, only two of the four authors under discussion, Sís and Foreman, include this material in the published work. Sís integrates passages into his picturebook from his father's diary consisting of excerpts in tiny handwriting and elaborate drawings, while Foreman uses a collage-type technique incorporating press cuttings, handwritten letters, pictures from scrapbooks, advertising leaflets, technical drawings of airplanes and weapons, and political pamphlets. Hyman and Kurelek make no use of documentation.

Whatever the case, the reference to autobiographical memory is underlined by the complex, multi-layered structure of the text. This complexity is emphasized by different literary strategies: paratextual passages, as demonstrated by Foreman, Hyman, Kurelek and Sís, who wrote forewords and epilogues to their picturebooks; metatextual reflections on the reliability of one's own memory in Hyman's *Self-Portrait*, and a combination of frame story and three internal stories in Sís' *Tibet through the Red Box*.

Sís conceives of identity as relational, and the autobiographical text he writes is also relational, for he believes that his father's story holds the key to his own. In this respect the autobiographical narration is doubled: the story of the father is accompanied by the story of the first-person narrator assembling his own life-story. Sís creates a hybrid form, neither pure autobiography nor biography but a mixture of both, and history as well. This book defies the boundaries we seek to establish between genres, for it is an autobiographical text that offers not only the autobiography of the first-person narrator, but also the biography and autobiography of his father. The autobiographical act is duplicated because the story of the father is accompanied by the story of the first-person narrator gathering this history. To help the reader/viewer distinguish between the various diegetic levels and narrative frames, different print types are used for the different stories (block letters for the frame story, italics for the childhood memories, and handwriting for the diary). The sophisticated structure of the narrative is enhanced by the complex illustrations. Each chapter of Sís' picturebook is given a different color scheme: his father's office and the three spaces his father has to conquer on the way to the Dalai Lama are alternately colored in red, green, or blue.[4] In the last chapter, when the first-person narrator has finished reading the diary and his father finally has an audience with the Postal (i.e., the Dalai Lama), who turns out to be a young child, everything is colored black; only the contours of people and objects stand out. This color code is determined by Tibetan folklore and Buddhism: red stands for fire, green for earth, blue for water, and black (as equivalent to white) for both air and infiniteness.[5]

The narratives are accordingly characterized by an overlapping of perspectives and voices: the narrator's perspective, the anonymous voices of the incorporated newspaper clippings, letters and leaflets, and in Sís' case, the voice of his father in the diaries.

These narratives are complemented by complex illustrations distinguished by a variety of styles. The number of illustrations varies, ranging from twenty-six in Kurelek's work to seventy-seven in Foreman's picturebook, while the picturebooks by Sís and Hyman contain forty-one and fifty-three illustrations respectively. Hyman's book includes watercolor pictures reminiscent of her illustrations for fairy tales—she has even depicted herself as Little Red Riding Hood. Kurelek's illustrations, painted in oil or mixed media on canvas, show the influence of his landscape paintings. By contrast, Foreman and Sís alternate between colored pictures painted with watercolors, black and white drawings, and sepia illustrations that give the impression of yellowed old photos. Foreman even includes an oil painting depicting a laundry. Irrespective of their different styles and painting techniques, the illustrators create atmospheric drawings and paintings that enhance the lyrical effect of the texts. The artists employ an interesting process in drawing more or less detailed illustrations based on photos, such as Sís' black and white pictures showing the young boy with his mother at the beach, at Christmas or at his birthday party. To evoke his missing father, Sís cut his father's figure out of the illustrations, so that the viewer sees only an empty white shape with his father's silhouette.

The perspective in these picturebooks varies from panoramic views to close-ups. The panoramic perspective conveys an impression of the locations, i.e., landscapes, buildings, streets or cities, while the close-up illustrations usually show individual figures or single items of importance to the narrator, like the red box in Peter Sís' picturebook, or the woodcutters' tools in Kurelek's book. Other illustrations center on a group of people, parts of a room or exterior scenes, offering an intermediary perspective between panoramic view and close-up. Furthermore, the perspective alternates between high and low, giving either a bird's eye or worm's eye view of the people and their surroundings. The close-up pictures are mainly at eye level with the viewer, offering a closer look at the figures or objects.

Picturebooks differ from illustrated books in having a specific combination of text and pictures that mainly consists of both media mutually and inseparably complementing each other. This means that two aspects should

Remembering the Past in Words and Pictures • 209

Figure 15.1 Illustration from Peter Sís: *Tibet Through the Red Box*. New York: Farrar, Straus & Giroux, 1998.

be considered in analyzing these autobiographical picturebooks. Why did the artists choose to create this form of book instead of writing an autobiography or childhood memoir without illustrations? And what is the point of view mirrored in the text and the pictures?

On careful reading of the picturebooks we realize that it is impossible to separate the text from the illustrations. In most cases, the text refers to the pictures by naming the figures depicted or describing the settings or events illustrated. Sometimes the authors even call the reader's/viewer's attention to details that might otherwise be ignored. But the authors also provide information that is not shown in the illustrations. In Kurelek's *Lumberjack* for example, it is the text alone which tells us that the narrator is reading Shakespeare instead of joining in the other people's games, or that many of the camp dwellers are immigrants, especially from Ukraine[6] and the Baltic States.

In general, the illustrations serve two functions: they convey the moods and atmosphere already evoked in the text by visualizing them, and they help the (child) viewer to get a deeper insight into the historical and social background of these autobiographical stories, which often describe individual experiences and historical events from the past.

In this sense, the *I* of the narrative functions as an auto-ethnographer; it acts as the insider who explains to the uninitiated the customs and way of life of a bygone era or unknown community. The artists provide authentic reports based on their autobiographical memory, and at the same time their detailed description is a contribution to the broader concept of cultural memory. The authors of these four picturebooks are preserving the memories of a social group like the lumberjacks, wartime experiences in the British countryside during World War II, the impressions of the first European expedition to the Himalayas and the forbidden country of Tibet or, as in Hyman's book, the difficulties faced by a woman in getting recognition as an artist.

What is even more striking is the fragmentary structure of the four picturebooks. Although the authors attempt to describe time spans ranging from as little as six months to as long as forty-two years (as in Hyman's case), the texts never convey the impression of a holistic story. On the contrary, each text consists of short stories or descriptions of important events. The connection between these sections is not always clear; they leave gaps that have to be filled in by the reader. Like looking at photos in an album, the reader looks at the pictures, reads the accompanying text, and then turns to the next picture and text. Read alone, without the illustrations, the texts of the picturebooks seem rather strange, sometimes even bizarre, because their fragmentary structure is evident. I would argue that the artists consciously choose this literary strategy—which resembles the structure of photo albums—to highlight general problems of autobiographical memory.

In studies on memory, autobiographical memory as a variant of episodic memory is defined as the capacity to recall explicitly the personal incidents that define an individual's life. In addition, autobiographical memory demands the cognitive ability to reactivate those records once they have been created, to call them up whenever necessary. The case of childhood memories is rather complicated. As the child psychologist Katherine Nelson has demonstrated, memory in early childhood is dedicated to the generation of general event-memories that help in organizing the child's knowledge of daily routines like bathing or eating. This stage is marked by infantile amnesia, i.e., usually a total blocking of early memories prior to age three, and a significant lack of accessible memories from the years between the ages of three and six. If we accept this account of the belated emergence of autobiographical memory, it explains a great deal about the fragmentary quality of the earliest memories claimed by most adults. These research findings are reflected in the narrative structure of the picturebooks by Foreman, Hyman and Sís. The first memories recaptured by these three authors deal with events when the artists were aged three, four, and five respectively. Hyman's picturebook starts with the sentence, "I was born forty-two years ago in Philadelphia, Pennsylvania"; yet the accompanying picture shows the little four-year-old girl on a walk with her mother in the countryside. Early childhood memories until the age of six or seven are distinguished by a fragmentary quality, which contributes to the inability to specify the exact date and time of the memory fragments. This is obviously the reason why the authors opted for a literary strategy that refers to these problems in some way.

But what of Kurelek's book, which describes events in the author's adult life? As recent studies in memory research have shown, even adults are not able to recall every single event in their whole life. Although most adults are able to remember more details, creating a memory network of past events that have structured their lives, very few people are able to memorize everything that happened during a lifespan of several decades. When writing an autobiography or childhood memoir, many authors rely on conversations about the past and historical sources to connect up their memory fragments. Kurelek, however, chose the same literary strategy as Foreman, Hyman and Sís, insisting on the fragmentary structure of his memories.

As the storyteller is also the central figure in the story, the artist has to tackle the problem of how to present his viewpoint in the pictures. We can assume that the book shows the scenes as the narrator sees them in his visual memory, complemented by contemporary records to underline the authenticity of the work. The narrators tell their own stories in a context that surrounds them with specific scenes and people, and separates them from the viewers. The latter disappear from view, shifting to a view of what the narrators see. A consistent first person narration in picturebooks is similar to the "subjective camera" in film: the perspective of the narrator and the reader coincide, as in Foreman's illustration of a birthday party, spread across a double page: lots of people are sitting around a table with a birthday cake in the center. Everybody is looking towards the viewer, so we can assume that the viewer's perspective coincides with that of the first-person narrator whose birthday is being celebrated. If all the illustrations were like this, it would mean that the reader would never see the narrator pictured. This is a technique to encourage readers to sympathize with the narrator by seeing events through his or her eyes. The viewer sees what the person who is speaking sees.

In many cases, however, the pictures do not show what the artist sees, because the viewer is sometimes looking at the narrator, adopting a double-sided perspective on him/her.[7] The reader is looking at the first-person narrator, but not seeing what the narrator sees. In this respect there is an obvious shift between two perspectives. The picturebooks under discussion thus combine two different forms of perspective. This is highly demanding for the reader: the text is a first-person narrative, but the pictures often seem to be a supplement to a third-person narration, causing a shift from a homodiegetic narrative to a heterodiegetic pictorial representation. These differing perspectives encourage the reader to empathize with the narrator, and at the same time to take a more objective, distanced position. They draw the reader's attention to the different time levels presented in the picturebooks: reminiscences of the past, mainly childhood memories, and the present situation of the narrator, which is additionally marked by a change of tense. Whereas the autobiographical reminiscences are written in the past tense, the final section in three of the picturebooks is in the present tense. The exception is Foreman's picturebook, where the last sentences are written in the subjunctive, alluding to the near future when the seagulls and soldiers will hopefully return like the boy's kite. This wish is accompanied by an illustration showing the narrator disguised as an American Indian whose contours seem faded like an old memory.

One might assume that this change in viewpoint is rather disturbing for the child viewer, who has to be able to switch between text and pictures and different perspectives. However, I would contend that it is the picturebook's convention of raising the reader's expectation of seeing the protagonist in the illustration that is responsible for such shifts in autobiographical picturebooks. This discrepancy between perspectives creates a way to let the reader share the first-person narrator's viewpoint, and yet to portray the narrator in the picture, emphasizing the children's empathy, which is based on identification with the characters that children can see. It is interesting to note that at the beginning of the picturebooks, the characters representing the narrator are either unseen or seen partly from behind. Their backs are turned to the viewers and their faces are hidden from view. The situation changes in the course of the story. Gradually, the respective characters start to turn; first they are seen in profile, then frontally, but in the latter case they do not usually look directly at the viewer face to face. They often look downwards or upwards, or glance sideways at something or someone not shown in the picture.

The only exception is the cover of Hyman's book, *Self-Portrait*, which depicts the author sitting at her desk working on a new project. That she is already at work on the new book is deliberately underscored at the beginning of the text, where the artist describes a phone call from her editor urging her to finish the present book after all. The picture on the book cover shows the artist with her head slightly turned toward the viewer, at eye level with him/her.

Hyman is clearly alluding to the artistic tradition of the self-portrait in painting. A character gazing out of the picture directly at the viewer can be interpreted as an "intrusive" visual narrator. Foreman also makes use of another, contrasting visual strategy by switching between two different perspectives of the same place or event. In most cases the illustrated situation is shown first from the narrator's perspective, and then shifts to the viewpoint of a second person who is looking directly at the narrator. Foreman often uses this discrepancy by combining an exterior and interior view with a window or door as transition. In one illustration, for example, he depicts the first-person narrator as a little boy sitting on the windowsill of his mother's shop, watching the people on the street. The next illustration changes to show one of the

Figure 15.2   Book Cover from Trina Schart Hyman: *Self-Portrait. Trina Schart Hyman.* New York: Harper & Row, 1981.

passers-by on the street looking into the shop window, acknowledging the boy staring at him.

In my view, a more disturbing feature of these picturebooks is that the text often fails to make explicitly clear whether the narrator is visible in the picture or not, which leaves the reader uncertain. Kurelek and Foreman furnish just two examples of this. In Kurelek's *Lumberjack* the narrator never acknowledges his own presence in the illustrations. Although we might assume that the narrator can be seen in several pictures, readers will remain unsure about this unless they are familiar with the author's autobiographical picturebook about his childhood on the Canadian prairies, *A Prairie Boy's Winter*, in which Kurelek always depicts himself wearing blue trousers and a green jacket. Five pages in *Lumberjack* include pictures of a young man with blue trousers and a green jacket, shown partly from behind in the far distance. Readers who know *A Prairie Boy's Winter* will be able to recognize the similarity and deduce conclusively that the young man in the pictures is a self-portrait of the author.

In *War Boy*, Foreman depicts himself clearly as a four-year-old boy in several pictures. As he is most often shown with other children of the same age, it is not quite clear which child is actually the narrator himself. The artist leaves it to the reader to decide. In the case of other illustrations, the text offers certain clues, as in the passage where Foreman describes a soldier who gives him a small-sized uniform. In the picture next to this description, a group of soldiers is seen accompanied by a little boy dressed in uniform.

The picturebooks by Hyman and Sís represent a different case. Many pictures portray only one child, and the reader might assume that these children are self-portraits of the author-illustrators. In *Tibet through the Red Box*, however, the narrator-protagonist is merely a presence in the illustrations, which are dominated by inner landscapes expressing the feelings of the first-person narrator. Only four of the pictures show the narrator as five-year-old boy, always surrounded by his family. It should be mentioned here that the narrator's memory is evidently unreliable. To give just one example: in one section he tells that he has not seen his father for several years, elsewhere he states that his father was in Tibet for fourteen months, and in yet another passage he actually admits that he cannot tell exactly how long his father was abroad. This unreliability, coupled with the fairytale quality of the internal stories, might make the viewer doubt whether the illustrations are authentic self-portraits or purely imaginary.

In Hyman's picturebook she depicts herself from the start either as Little Red Riding Hood with a red cape, or as an elf with wings (only in the illustrations showing Hyman as adolescent and young woman is she depicted in ordinary clothes without any extraordinary signs and symbols). These stylized illustrations stress the close connection between the child and fantasy or magic, revealing an important aspect of Hyman's artistic development. Indeed, these pictures serve to create a mysterious kind of aura as a constituent feature of Hyman's childhood memories. This aspect is reinforced by the concluding sentence, which is written in the past tense: "Everything that I have told you is, of course, a fairy tale." With this statement, Hyman closes her autobiographical account and then turns to the present, describing her life on a farm with her family and close friends. With a metatextual reflection on the picturebook's origin, Hyman then changes from the present to the future tense, describing her plans for the coming period. In the last picture she turns her back to the viewer again.

The visual perspectives in these autobiographical picturebooks are rather complicated and ambivalent, either reflecting the naïve perception of a child or offering an authoritative adult perspective. Due to the various patterns of interaction between word and image, these works reveal the contradiction between the respective viewpoints of the visual and verbal narrative. This contradiction is due to alternation between externally focalized narration that follows only one character's perception, and concentration on introspective aspects that emphasize inner feelings and thoughts.

A survey of autobiographical picturebooks reveals an astonishing variety of topics and themes. There is no denying the obvious influence of autobiographical memories on the development of children's literature, from children's novels to autobiographies for children or picturebooks.[8] This chapter represents an initial attempt to demonstrate the many and varied aspects of autobiographical writing in sophisticated picturebooks, works that demand a high level of aesthetic and cognitive competence from their readership, whether children or adults.

Notes

1. Katherine Nelson (1989, 162) stresses that autobiographical memory is an "enduring chronologically sequenced memory for significant events from one's own life."
2. The Self-Portrait Collection includes works by the illustrators Erik Blegvad and Margot Zemach.
3. Whereas *War Boy* is an evocative account of how World War II affected Foreman's own childhood, *War Game* (1993) was dedicated to his four uncles, who died in World War I.
4. The first framing chapter functions as an introduction to the father's story set in the past; unlike the four succeeding chapters, it has no title.
5. The strong connection to Buddhism is additionally emphasized by five mandalas, each depicted at the beginning of a new chapter. A big wheel is in focus, with the red box in the middle. Figures and creatures that play an important part in the story appear between the spokes. Thus the mandalas, whose main color corresponds to the color scheme of the chapter they precede, can be interpreted as visual prologues to the story.
6. Kurelek had a close relationship with the Ukrainian language und culture, inherited from his father who emigrated from Ukraine to Canada. Kurelek also did the illustrations for the English translation of the Ukrainian children's classic *Lys Mykita* (Fox Mykita, 1978), written by Ivan Franko in 1890. The excellent translation and remarkable illustrations have earned *Fox Mykita* the status of a Canadian classic as well.
7. In his seminal study on picturebooks with first person-narrators, Nodelman refers to the cognitive and aesthetic problems arising from the shifting perspectives in such picturebooks.
8. The influence of autobiographical narration on the development and narrative structure of children's books has been shown in the studies by Coe (1982), Kümmerling-Meibauer (2004), and Kümmerling-Meibauer (2007).

Bibliography

Primary Sources

Foreman, Michael. *War Boy*. London: Pavilion Books, 1989.
Hyman, Trina Schart. *Self-Portrait: Trina Schart Hyman*. New York: Harper & Row, 1981.
Kurelek, William. *A Prairie Boy's Winter*. Montreal: Tundra Books, 1973.
Kurelek, William. *Lumberjack*. Montreal: Tundra Books, 1974.
Sís, Peter. *Tibet Through the Red Box*. New York: Farrar, Straus & Giroux, 1998.

Secondary Sources

Anderson, Linda. *Autobiography*. London: Routledge, 2001.
Coe, Richard. *When the Grass Was Taller: Autobiography and the Experience of Childhood*. New Haven, CT: Yale University Press, 1984.
Kofre, John. *White Gloves: How We Create Ourselves Through Memory*. New York: Norton, 1996.
Kümmerling-Meibauer, Bettina. "Auf der Suche nach der verlorenen Kindheit: autobiographische Erinnerungen in der Kinderliteratur." *Beiträge Jugendliteratur und Medien* 56 (2004): 4–17.
Kümmerling-Meibauer, Bettina. "The Vanished Land of Childhood. Autobiographical Narration in Astrid Lindgren's Work." *Barnboken* 30. 1–2 (2007): 83–91 (special issue, "The Liberated Child—Childhood in the Works of Astrid Lindgren." Astrid Lindgren Centennial Conference. Stockholm, May 30–31, 2007).
Lejeune, Philippe. *On Autobiography*. Minneapolis: University of Minnesota Press, 1989.
Markowitsch, Hans, and Harald Welzer. *Das autobiographische Gedächtnis*. Stuttgart: Klett, 2005.
Nelson, Katherine. *Narratives from the Crib*. Cambridge, MA: Harvard University Press, 1989.
Nikolajeva, Maria, and Carole Scott. *How Picturebooks Work*. New York: Garland, 2001.
Nodelman, Perry. "The I and the Eye: Identification and First-Person Narratives in Picture Books." *Children's Literature* 19 (1991): 1–30.

Chapter Sixteen
Do Sons Inherit the Sins of their Fathers?
An Analysis of the Picturebook *Angry Man*

Agnes-Margrethe Bjorvand

The Norwegian picturebook *Angry Man* (*Sinna Mann*, 2003) is written by Gro Dahle and illustrated by Svein Nyhus. Briefly, the picturebook introduces us to Boj who faces a difficult situation at home. He has a Daddy whom he loves dearly, but sometimes Daddy changes. It is as if there is an angry man inside Daddy who will turn Daddy into somebody who will be nasty and hit you. Boj does not know what to do. He is afraid of everything. He is afraid to be noisy or loud, because then Daddy may suddenly turn angry. Boj wonders whether it is his fault that Daddy becomes angry. Boj would like to tell somebody about everything that is bad, that Daddy beats Mummy, but he is unable to do it. Not right away, anyway. But then he has a bright idea. He writes a letter to the King! Boj trusts the King, and thanks to Boj for sounding the alarm, it looks as if Boj's family will get the help they need.

In my opinion, *Angry Man* comes very close to a revolution in children's literature. The presentation of dysfunctional families and complex relationships between adults and between children and grown-ups is not new to Nordic literature for children and young people. What is new, however, is that such a concrete presentation of physical abuse and violence inside the home finds its way into picturebooks intended to be read to and by relatively small children. It has to be said, however, that certainly in the Nordic countries, picturebooks no longer represent a genre exclusively directed at small children. We register that more and more picturebooks are published that are to be read also by youth and grown-ups and that an increasing number of picturebooks have a double target group. Thematically there can be no doubt that *Angry Man* exemplifies a picturebook that is directed at both children and grown-ups as the book was written after an initiative from family counselor Øivind Aschjem in the project "Alternative to Violence." He wanted to see a book that would both fit into his therapeutic work with violent men and be suitable for children who live or have been living with violence in the family.

This analysis will deal with the presentation of the family in the picturebook *Angry Man* with the main focus on the relations between generations, or, more precisely, three generations of men. The book's focus is first and foremost on the little boy Boj and his father, Daddy, but towards the end of the book, on the penultimate doublespread, Daddy's father crops up as a kind of explanation of why Daddy sometimes changes into Angry Man. (Daddy's father does not have a proper name in the book, but will be referred to in this analysis as Granddad.) An underlying question throughout the book is, of course, whether the violent tendencies that Daddy has "inherited" from Granddad will in turn be inherited by Boj, or whether Boj will be able to counteract this paternal inheritance. Will the sins of the fathers be inherited by children and grandchildren as described in Exodus? While on Mount Sinai, the Lord proclaims to Moses:

> *The LORD, the LORD, the compassionate and gracious God, slow to anger, abounding in love and faithfulness, maintaining love to thousands, and forgiving wickedness, rebellion and sin. Yet he does not leave the guilty unpunished; he punishes the children and their children for the sin of the fathers to the third and fourth generation. (Exodus, 34: 6–7)*

The Norwegian gender researcher Jørgen Lorentzen discusses this question in his article "Sønnene arver fedrenes synder" ("The Sons Inherit the Sins of the Fathers"). Lorentzen argues that the picturebook *Angry Man* has a happy ending (Lorentzen 2004: 116). I agree with him to some extent, but find that the ending is somewhat more open than what Lorentzen is willing to grant—more open-ended and not as unequivocally happy. I shall return to this question, but first let us have a closer look at the relationship between Boj and Daddy.

Father and Son—Daddy and Boj

Boj and his father are the central characters in this picturebook. We encounter them in the modalities of picture and text already in the paratexts that precede the main narrative. Boj is consistently portrayed in the pictures, e.g., on the front cover and in one of the prologue pictures (I will return to this picture later on), whereas Daddy may be seen in the many repetitions of the book title *Angry Man*. We don't discover that the angry man of the title is actually Boj's father until we reach the book's main narrative.

In the iconotext of the first doublespread in the book's main narrative, we meet a small family consisting of Mummy, Daddy, and the boy, Boj. We are in a living room, and a smiling mother enters with a cake, Daddy is smiling at his son Boj, and Boj sends a vague smile directed at Daddy while thinking about him. Boj is evidently a boy who looks up to his father. He looks up at Daddy physically because Daddy is big and Boj is small—this is confirmed by the picture. Boj also has an ownership relation to his Daddy, and through thoughts like "my Daddy" and "One day I may become like Daddy," he reveals a closeness and sympathy typical of most father-son relationships.

Viewed in isolation the iconotext of this doublespread may give us a first impression of a relatively traditional family, but this is only a surface impression that can be sustained only by a relatively superficial reading of this doublespread isolated from the paratexts that introduce the main narrative. The alert reader will quickly experience that even in a reading of the doublespread in isolation, the iconotext will reveal danger signs that disturb the apparent idyll and consequently make us worry about the relationship between father and son in this book.

The elements of danger are prevalent in verbal text and in picture alike, and we may start by having a closer look at how the *affordance* in the words of the author and in the pictures of the illustrator are used to communicate the overall iconotext. The text is placed on the top left-hand side of the left side of the doublespread. This placing of the text means that the visual impression of the text steals very little focus from the pictures. The left side is also Boj's part of the doublespread and the placing of the text plays a part in foregrounding Boj in the picture and at the same time helps to underline that the story is told from Boj's point of view. We see everything through his eyes, and on the whole, his thoughts in the verbal text direct our attention to relevant parts of the picture. Through Boj's thoughts in the verbal text we are introduced to a characterization of his parents: a mother who laughs and has put on her finest dress and a father who, it is concluded, is calm, happy, and smiling but whose hands are big and knuckles red. This characterization guides our look in our encounter with the picture; we automatically check if it accords with the focus of the illustrator, Svein Nyhus, and when we observe Daddy's red hands in the picture, the double presence of the color red has a greater effect than if it had been present in only one of the modalities. The foregrounding of the red color of his hands also helps to draw attention to the red color of Daddy's face and left ear. It is worth noting that the red color has a different focus in picture and text. In the picture the red color is found on Daddy's hands and in the surrounding area, but Boj's thoughts circle around red *knuckles*. The word "knuckles" is usually not part of the active vocabulary of a small child, and it is perhaps first and foremost associated with a closed fist. Because the word "knuckles" enters into Boj's thoughts we must assume that he has some kind of experience with this body part and that is a somewhat unsettling conclusion.

The red color, which often carries connotations of danger and aggression and things that are forbidden, becomes a dramatic element of danger in both text and picture. Whereas the red color is mentioned only once in the verbal text, albeit with a precision characteristic of the affordance of writing, it becomes even more striking in the picture. The red color forms a triangle going from Boj's face, through a bowl of goldfish with two red fish, through Mummy's face with red cheeks, nose, and mouth and all the way to Daddy's red ear. From there the triangle continues down towards Daddy's left hand, through his right hand and back to Boj on the left-hand side of the doublespread. The use of such a triangular composition serves to underline that the three characters of the iconotext have something in common and form a kind of unity.

An obvious affordance of the modality of writing is the possibility of characterizing persons through thought and speech. Through Boj's thoughts about and characterization of Daddy we understand, firstly, that Daddy is a person Boj is fond of and looks up to: "My Daddy, Boj thinks and looks at Daddy. One day I may become like Daddy, Boj thinks." Secondly, we understand that something is amiss in the relationship between Boj and his father. The word "Daddy" is repeated as many as fifteen times, and the use of the adjectives "silent," "quiet," "big," "happy," and "smiling" is exaggerated and therefore worrying. The word "smiling" is repeated six times, and the impression becomes particularly strong through the repetition in line six: "Smiling, smiling like gifts with ribbons and soft drinks in glasses with straws." We find the same type of linguistic redundancy with the adjective "big": "Big, big, smiling Daddy." The use of repetitions contributes to making Dahle's text rhythmical and lyrical, but their meaning is likely to worry the reader. It is as if Boj is trying to convince himself, and the reader, that all is well.

The use of repetition for emphasis is an obvious possibility inherent in the modality of writing but adding emphasis is also a possibility inherent in the modality of pictures. Whereas Gro Dahle calls attention to the father figure by repeating the word "Daddy," Svein Nyhus has chosen a different strategy to emphasize this character. First of all, Daddy is placed in the middle of the right hand side of the doublespread. This is the part of the doublespread that we see first when looking through a picturebook, and this placing of Daddy therefore guides the reader to perceive the father figure as quite central in the iconotext. Secondly, Nyhus has chosen to make the father figure unreasonably big in relation to other elements and Daddy is also foregrounded in the picture. He is then the character that physically comes closest to the reader. We may conclude that word and picture in this doublespread cooperate to emphasize Daddy and his role in the family and in this story.

The clear focus on the father figure is only one of many elements in this iconotext that I regard as warnings of danger in the introduction to this book. The other elements of danger are first and foremost present in the picture, but from time to time we see that the verbal text guides us in the direction of these elements in the picture. Maria Nikolajeva compares the reading of a picturebook with a hermeneutical circle. Whether we start with the pictures or with the text, expectations of the other modality are created which again leads to new experiences and new expectations (Nikolajeva 2000: 12). As readers we shift between the visual and the verbal at the same time that our understanding becomes broader and deeper, says Nikolajeva. Thus Gro Dahle uses several similes when characterizing Daddy, as in the third paragraph: "He is smiling like apples on the table and raisins in a yellow bowl." Mention of the yellow bowl helps us to discover a yellow bowl on the far right of the picture. The words "raisins in a yellow bowl" have no negative connotations for me, quite the contrary, but when I observe the yellow bowl in the picture I get a queasy feeling that "here is something that might get broken." The bowl is placed at the table edge and might easily fall down. This feeling induced by the picture will influence my thoughts as I return to the verbal text. I might then connect the bowl to something that might be broken, and because Gro Dahle uses this bowl in a simile to describe Daddy, I immediately connect the idea that "something might be broken" with Daddy. So I waver between the visual and the verbal as my understanding of the collective iconotext is extended. The discovery that something might get broken again directs my attention to other elements in the iconotext. On a chest of drawers to the left there is a bowl with goldfish. The bowl is made of glass and is placed dangerously close to the edge. The impression that the glass bowl might easily be broken is strengthened by the fact that a hammer is lying beside the glass bowl. This hammer is a repetition of one of the prologue pictures in the paratext preceding the main narrative. A hammer is a tool often used for building something, but it is also a tool used for breaking things. In this picture the metal head of the hammer is facing downwards, ready to break or crush something, for instance the glass bowl. The goldfish bowl also acquires another symbolic function for me as reader. Inside the bowl swim three fish: one big, black fighter fish and two red goldfish. One red goldfish is also a bit smaller than the other. The three fish locked inside the bowl may be said to symbolize Daddy, Mummy, and Boj as they also seem to be imprisoned inside some fixed pattern; and just as Mummy and Boj's attention is directed towards Daddy elsewhere in the iconotext, the red goldfish are turned towards the black fish in the bowl. This feeling that the family we are introduced to in the first doublespread are caught within some fixed pattern, and not necessarily a very attractive pattern, is further underlined by the fact that both Daddy and Boj wear striped clothes on the upper-part of their bodies. Boj's sweater in particular, with its black and white stripes, brings our associations to a prisoner's dress and the feeling of being locked up against one's will.

In addition to the goldfish bowl and the hammer there are also other elements of danger in the doublespread that only occur in the picture. Mummy is mentioned once in the verbal text and with a totally non-threatening description: "Mummy laughs in her finest dress"; and it is only when we see Mummy in the picture that we see her as a warning that something might go wrong as she flies over the dining-room floor on very small feet. She moves in the direction of Daddy and is entirely focused on him in spite of the fact that he has turned his back on her. In her finest dress and with a newly baked apple-pie in her hands she comes across as a traditional housewife that might have been in a picture from the 1950s. Physically she also moves in between Boj and Daddy, and I read this as a foreshadowing of Mummy's role in the book. She is the one to take the brunt of Daddy's temper, and it is she who tries to protect Boj and keep him at a distance when Daddy from time to time changes from Daddy into Angry Man.

The family we encounter for the first time in the iconotext of the establishing doublespread has elements of universal validity. This has to do, first of all, with Gro Dahle's choice of names for the characters: Mummy, Daddy, and Boj. The latter is highly unusual as a Norwegian name and is associated most closely with the English word "boy." Thus all three words represent large categories of humanity, categories that we may all relate to easily. Daddy and Boj also have this much in common that Daddy has once been a Boj (a small boy with a father who, as we learn later in the book, was also violent), and that Boj will once become a Daddy, or at least an adult male. Secondly, the impression of universality is due to the way in which Svein Nyhus draws faces: "I draw them as caricatures, but simultaneously open and neutral, almost archetypical, so that the reader may read into them whatever emotions she will" (Nyhus 2003: 39). The choices of the picturebook artists in this case create what I call *simultaneous gaps* in word and picture. Both modalities work together to open for the reader's co-authoring by making the characters universal. This universal aspect in the presentation of the small family marks a clear contrast to the main theme of the book: violence in the home. In spite of the fact that too many experience such violence, most readers do not have this kind of "hands on" experience. The universal aspect of the characters is, however, an important point to increase the reader's identification with the characters, and it is also central to what I consider the book's main message to child readers who have felt this violence directly on their bodies: "You are not alone in having these experiences. It is not your fault. You have to tell somebody you trust."

The dominant role of Daddy in the family becomes more and more evident in the course of the next six doublespreads. Daddy's body grows steadily bigger, while his head grows smaller, and the red color gradually increases. Daddy also becomes more dominant through the clear division of the family into two units: Daddy on one side and Mummy and Boj together on the other. This split takes place on the psychic level as it becomes evident that Boj and Mummy now have a common enemy in Angry Man. But the split also becomes physically evident in some of the doublespreads. In doublespread 3 the family is split and physically separated by means of a long verbal text. Boj is sitting on Mummy's lap, and for me this produces associations to the well-known theme in painting: "Madonna and child" (with famous pictures by e.g., Jan van Eyck, Sandro Botticelli, Leonardo da Vinci and Michelangelo). Both the motif itself and its placing in the picture plus the fact that the point of view is still with Boj in the verbal text, help to further strengthen our sympathy. So far our sympathy is almost exclusively with Mummy and Boj.

In the course of the first six doublespreads the character of Daddy has gradually doubled in size. Just like the American cartoon figure, the Incredible Hulk, Daddy transforms from a seemingly ordinary man into the monster Angry Man. The initiation of the change is described in detail on doublespread 3. In the verbal text we read:

> *The first change is the voice, the tiny tone in the voice. The small spike. The voice tightens and tightens. And there are padlocks on the voice and sharp edges. I am not angry, says Daddy. But behind Daddy's voice there is a shut door. And behind the door behind the voice there is a dark cellar. And down in that cellar there is somebody waiting. A crooked back. A black muscle. A neck.*

Daddy towers over the whole left part of the doublespread and we also see him from below. This is a dramatic device often used right before a climax or to signal that something dramatic is about to happen. Daddy's red color has now also spread to his face, and the red color on his shirt has become clearer. His hands have become bigger, and his knuckles are now very visible as he holds on to his chair with his red fingers. That something is about to happen we also understand from the clock behind Daddy. The clock is five minutes to twelve, so something is going to happen very soon. In the verbal text we read that "Boj hears the clock striking a hundred strokes," a foreshadowing of what is to come, and Daddy who will strike Mummy later in the story.

For Boj the father figure is both Daddy and Angry Man, but the name "Angry Man" does not appear until doublespread 4. Boj's ideas that it might be *his* fault that Daddy changes start on doublespread 3: "Is it something I have said, Boj thinks." Boj's feeling of guilt and his need to know whether he is to blame increases in the doublespreads that follow. He is willing to do anything in order to prevent Daddy from becoming Angry Man (doublespread 5).

In the next doublespread Angry Man has taken over Daddy so completely that Daddy is almost unrecognizable to his son Boj who thinks that "Angry Man has taken Daddy. Angry Man has shut up Daddy inside himself. Red face. Red neck. Twisted mouth. Eyes distorted. Does not look like Daddy." Daddy is changed into flames and muscles and evil, and even if we cannot see from the picture that he beats Mummy, we are in no doubt about what is happening as we read "Angry Man breaks through stone and wall and Mummy. And the clock in the living room just strikes and strikes and strikes."

Boj reacts by trying to shut everything out. First, he sits in his bed nearly in fetus position, a position typical of humans when trying to protect ourselves from external danger, and this position becomes even clearer with Boj as we reach the book's climax on doublespread 7 (Figure 16.1).

224 • Agnes-Margrethe Bjorvand

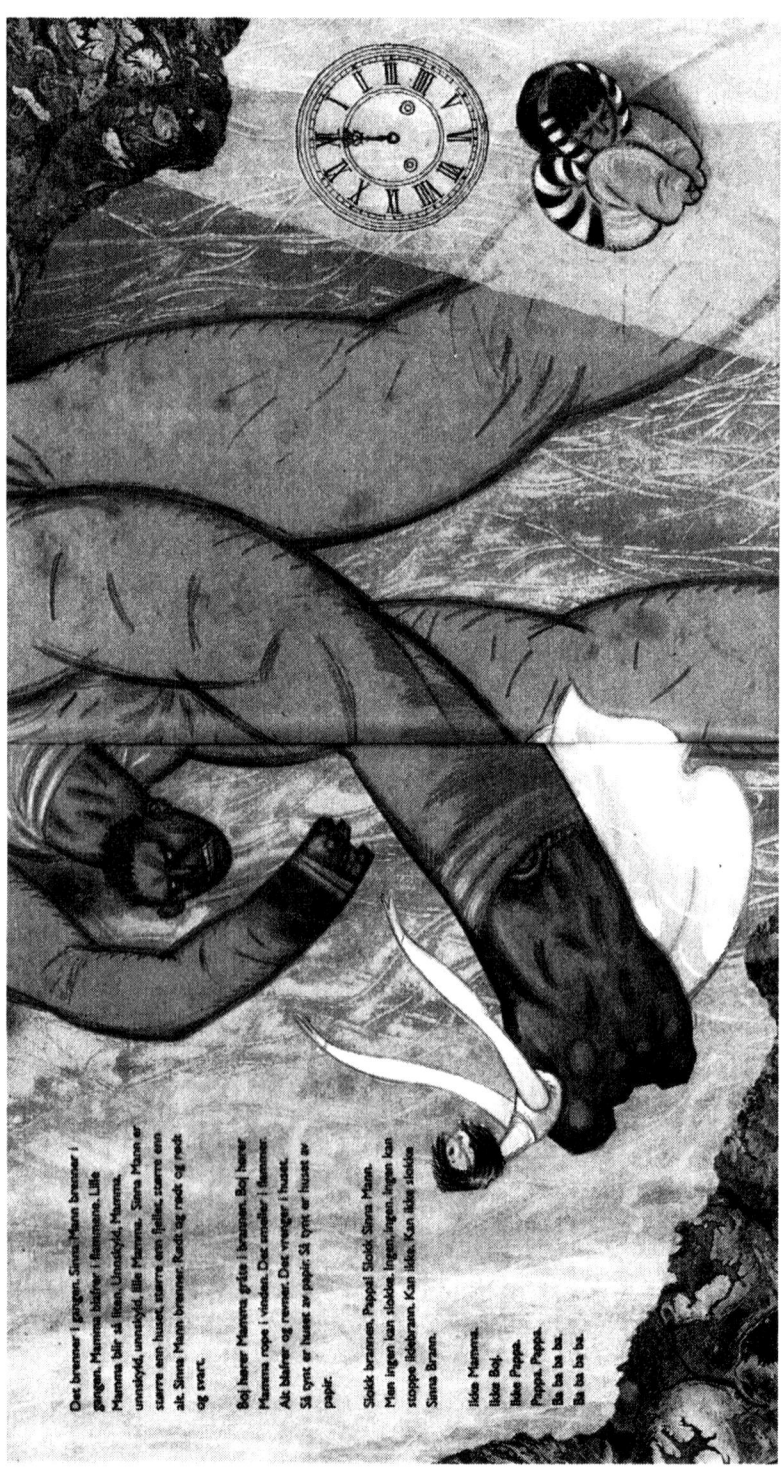

Figure 16.1 Illustration from Gro Dahle and Svein Nyhus: *Sinna Mann*. Oslo: Cappelen, 2003.

We are now faced with a family in acute crisis. Everything more or less explodes and dissolves in the iconotext. It does not help that Boj curls up in fetus position and closes his eyes hard to shut everything out, and it does not help that in his thoughts he appeals to Daddy to put out the fire. "Angry Man is bigger than the house" and thus through the framework of verbal text and picture alike. In the text he breaks through the boundaries of the house they occupy, and in the picture he literally shatters the picture, he becomes too big to fit in.

The presentation of Angry Man brings allusions of a monster. This is particularly clear in Nyhus' illustrations. Angry Man's head is very small (just as trolls have small heads because they are stupid), his eyes shine white, he has a cross in his face which is both black and red, and he shows his teeth. The hands of Angry Man are more or less completely deformed, and his left hand has become tremendously big as it holds Mummy, dangling like a doll, totally helpless. The motif with the monster Angry Man holding Mummy is reminiscent of a scene from the film *King Kong*. I think particularly of the final scene where King Kong has caught the female main character, Ann Darrow, and climbs with her in his giant fist to the top of Empire State Building.

Boj reacts to the whole situation by escaping into his own dream world. He distances himself from the rest of the family, and, not least, he distances himself from his own feeling of guilt. On doublespread 8 he withdraws to a place "behind thought," to a place where he almost manages to shut out all the evil. We get a little taste of Boj's longing away from everything that is hurtful and frightening, but even if he may succeed in repressing what has happened, neither he nor the reader can avoid observing that there is soot and ashes in the air after Angry Man's fit of rage. Angry Man is burnt to ashes and "Only Daddy is left" we read on doublespread 9. "Poor Daddy. Poor big small Daddy." Boj witnesses yet another change in Daddy. Angry Man has turned into a repentant and ashamed man surrounded by all the things he has destroyed. A man who promises not to be nasty again, not to be angry again. "Promise, Daddy says. He can say that, because Daddy has said so before. Many times before." This thought may reveal some contempt directed at Daddy, but the picture first and foremost shows a Boj who is frightened and who tries to hide from Daddy. The collective impression of the iconotext is that Boj clearly does not trust Daddy. The relationship between Boj and Daddy has been dealt a serious blow, and we understand that this is only one episode among many. It does not help that Daddy tries to make up for everything by tempting him with soft drinks and sweets; Boj does not trust Daddy. Boj has too many bad experiences, and he has probably learnt by now to read the danger signals, because the red color has not left Daddy completely, and there is a pair of tongs on the table next to Daddy, and Boj's throat contracts when thinking of Daddy and all the things he must do to prevent Angry Man from reappearing from Daddy's back yet again (doublespread 12).

We begin to suspect a change in the family and in the relationship between Boj and Daddy when Boj eventually manages to get out of the house. For the first time we experience that Boj wants to tell somebody about all the evil: "The words throng and press and hammer, but Boj can only manage to nod. That is all Boj can do. A small nod is all there is" (doublespread 13). The turning point arrives when Boj, slowly but surely, starts to tear away from his family, first by leaving the house where all the bad things are happening, and then by toying with the idea of telling somebody else about all the evil.

On doublespreads 13 to 15 we witness how Boj manages to share his story with others, first with a dog, which "listens until the glue on Boj's lips loosens and the words creep out of his mouth" (doublespread 14), and then to the bushes and the birds and the grass and the climbing tree. Boj tells beings and things without human language and therefore cannot tell the secret to others. Nature and the birds function as helpers in the process, and it is the dog which tells Boj to write a letter. A toy plane that Boj was clinging to in one of the prologue pictures is now flying freely around in the wind and seems to indicate that something good is in progress (doublespread 14). Perhaps freedom is in sight? But even if Boj is being helped along by nature, he must be the one to take the final initiative to get help. The letter Boj writes to the King leads to a turning point in the narrative and a turning point for Boj's family:

Dear King, Boj writes.

Daddy hits us, Boj writes.
Is it my fault? Boj writes.
Kind regards from Boj, Boj writes.

Now it is there in black and white what is wrong with Boj's family: Daddy hits. It also becomes clear what may have weighed most heavily on Boj in the midst of all this, the feeling of guilt: "Is it my fault?" And even before the King has received his letter, Boj is rewarded for his effort. The tree "lifts Boj high, high on its shoulders" (doublespread 15), in the same way that Boj dreams that Daddy will lift him up at the end of the story.

We do not know how long it takes, but one day the King arrives. And he comes first and foremost to visit Boj and to remove his feeling of guilt. The King becomes a symbol of some sort of super father, father of all, an image of the good father, and maybe an image of God. The King looks first at Boj and then at Daddy. This is where I think we find the sharpest social criticism of this picturebook; we know that children often become invisible and do not receive the help they need when parents are taken into psychiatric care because of for instance violence or drug abuse.

The King, the good father who sees Boj's needs, stands in sharp contrast to Daddy, who has behaved mostly as the evil father. With the arrival of the King the roles of Boj and Daddy are turned upside down. Now Boj is big and Daddy is small. And Daddy is the one who must apologize to Boj, a gesture that makes a particularly strong impression on the readers who encounter it in both words and pictures.

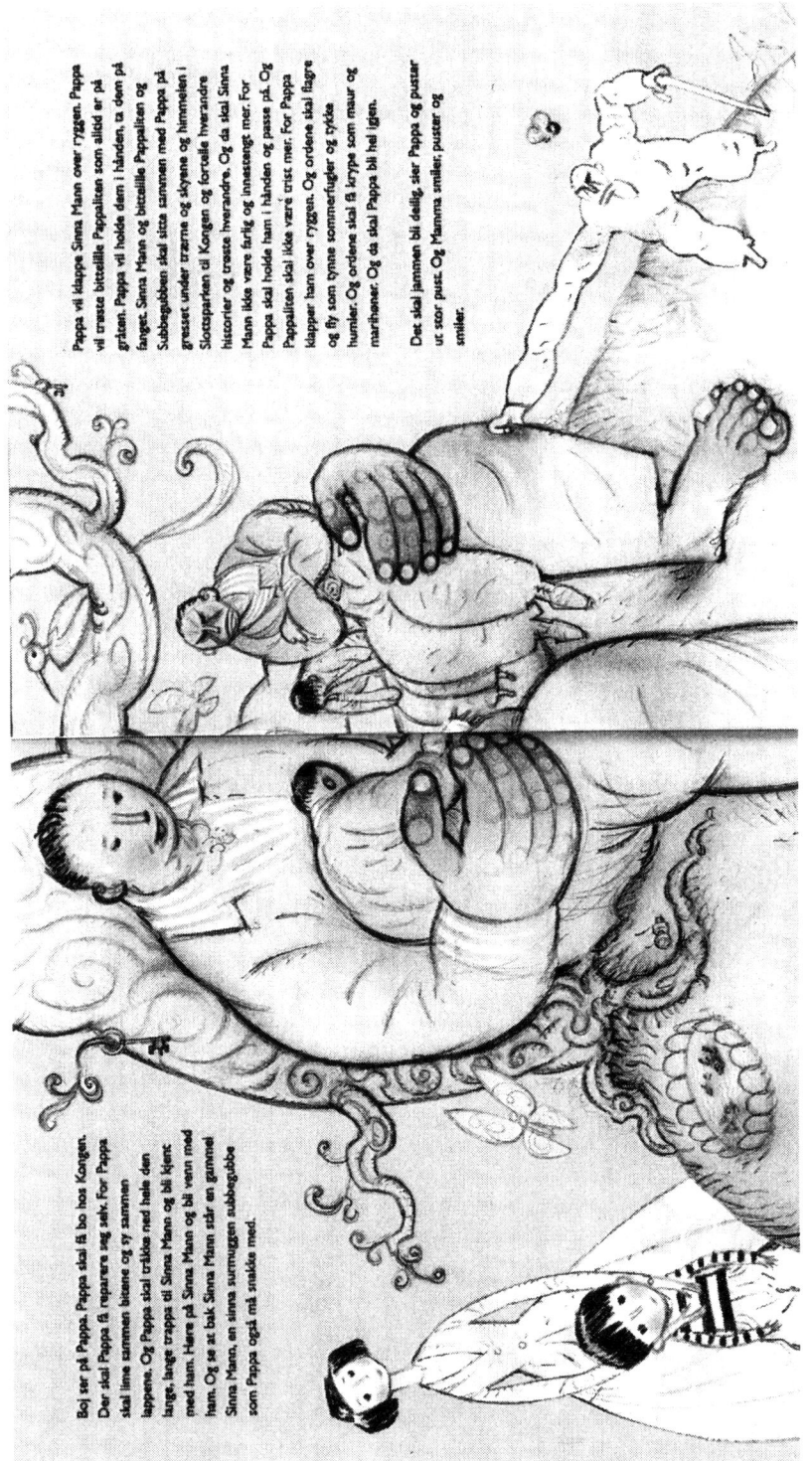

Figure 16.2 Illustration from Gro Dahle and Svein Nyhus: *Sinna Mann*. Oslo: Cappelen, 2003.

The penultimate doublespread of the main narrative (Figure 16.2) is perhaps the climax in the narrative's conflict solution. The iconotext contains many details and much information both in text and picture. At the same time, however, there is more harmony and a calmer atmosphere in this doublespread than in those preceding it. We have moved from seeming order through chaos to a new form of order. We sense that there is hope for this small family. The verbal text voices a kind of vision of the future, a future where Daddy will receive the help he needs. At the same time it is made clear that Daddy himself must do the job, he alone can make Daddy well:

> *Daddy will live with the King. That is where Daddy will repair himself. Because Daddy shall glue together the bits and sew up all the pieces. And Daddy shall walk down the long, long stairs to Angry Man and get to know him. Listen to Angry Man and befriend him. And see that behind Angry Man stands an old Angry Man, an angry, sour and grumpy, shuffling old geezer whom Daddy will have to talk to (doublespread 17).*

The calm and the hope expressed in this doublespread are made evident in both modalities. Whereas the verbal text focuses on the process Daddy will have to go through, the illustrations seem to picture a situation where time is more at a standstill. Daddy dominates in the middle of the picture. He is portrayed as being huge, in contrast to the preceding doublespread where Daddy is smaller than Boj, but in contrast to the other doublespreads we now encounter a sitting Daddy with a more relaxed body posture. Daddy, Mummy and Boj are all turned towards the right, in the reading direction, which underlines the hope for the future in this iconotext. Surrounding Daddy are many symbolic details. We see a blue bird, and I choose to interpret this bird as a phoenix. The phoenix was originally a fabulous animal of Egyptian mythology, but the phoenix legend is also found in Greek and Roman mythology and in Christian iconography. Traditionally the phoenix has been regarded as a symbol of resurrection. According to the legend a phoenix lives between 500 and 1,000 years before it flies to the holy city of Heliopolis where it builds a nest of myrrh in the temple of the sun god Ra. At sunrise the nest catches fire from the glow of dawn and the phoenix burns to ashes. But just as Daddy in *Angry Man* has to start over and rise from the ashes and in a sense be reborn, the phoenix is soon reborn as a new bird.

"The Sin of the Fathers"—Granddad, Daddy, and Boj

One of the most interesting aspects of doublespread 17 (Figure 16.2) is that the iconotext gives us a sort of explanation why Daddy behaves the way he does. Because "behind Angry Man stands an old Angry Man, an angry, sour and grumpy, shuffling old geezer whom Daddy will have to talk to." So we may probably conclude that Daddy has grown up in a violent and dysfunctional family. Daddy has been beaten by his father. This also appears in the picture. In the right hand corner we see an old man whom I choose to interpret as Granddad, who pinches Daddy in his leg. The place where Granddad pinches turns red, and Granddad himself has red color on his hands and a big, red mouth. This should make it clear that the red color, which also symbolizes anger and violence, has been inherited from father to son. And as we look at Boj, we see that even he is not totally without this red color, it is there on his hands and in the greater part of his face. What does this mean for Boj's future? Is he caught in a pattern to such an extent that he cannot break loose?

We may perhaps find the answer in the many symbols we encounter in the iconotext of doublespread 17. The symbols are present in both text and picture, but may be most conspicuous in the picture. The phoenix has been mentioned already, but we also see a butterfly, a traditional symbol of freedom, and together with the keys in the tree it may give us hope that Daddy will manage to break loose from Angry Man, manage to lock Angry Man out of his life once and for all. The screw beneath Daddy's right thigh, which may perhaps be the same screw that appears in one of the prologue pictures right at the beginning of the book, has now got a nut, and this may be interpreted as a sign that things are beginning to fall into place and that this little family will manage to stay together. This is further indicated by the three fish in the small pond. The fish from the book's opening have been released from the glass bowl, they are now turned towards each other, and the black fish is not as dominating in size compared with the orange fish. These symbols added to the small men on Daddy's lap, which may signify that Daddy has to get to know the various aspects of his personality better, mean that we no longer experience everything as mysterious and threatening. We sense a hope.

The forward-looking and hopeful atmosphere continues on the last doublespread. What we read and see in this doublespread is not necessarily what is going to happen but it is a kind of vision of the future, a utopia, or perhaps even Boj's wishful dream.

The man in this picturebook is the victim of a classic and frightening pattern. According to Øivind Aschjem in "Alternative to Violence," it turns out that "A boy who sees his father beat his mother, is 300 times more likely to become violent himself. Girls who witness such episodes, have a one thousand times higher risk of becoming the victims of violence" (Hollekim 2003: 22).

The question then becomes whether Boj will be able to change the pattern from his father and grandfather. Most small boys at one time or another wish to become like daddy. One day Boj may be like Daddy; but how will Boj act then?

In his book *Maskulinitet. Blikk på mannen gjennom litteratur og film* (*The Masculine. The Male Seen Through Literature and Film*), Jørgen Lorentzen writes, as mentioned previously, that "Gro Dahle and Svein Nyhus allow the book [*Angry Man*] to end happily." I agree up to a point. In my opinion the ending is somewhat more open than Lorentzen seems willing to allow, more open and not quite as unequivocally happy. We do see a happy father throwing his happy son up in the air. And if we have read Svein Nyhus' picturebook *Pappa!* (*Daddy!*, 1998), we know that this action represents happiness. But even in the picturebook *Pappa!* this happy event takes place in a sort of dream vision. It is something the main character Tommy dreams that will happen. And this is not the only instance of intertextuality found in this last doublespread. In the lower right hand corner we see a grayish clod or stone. And readers who are familiar with Gro Dahle and Svein Nyhus' picturebook *Snill* (*Nice*, 2002) know that this clod or stone first and foremost represents something negative, negative emotions that push to get out and that sooner or later will burst out.

These elements combined with Daddy's partly crippled hands and the red color still present in the father figure, makes me worried about Boj's future when added to his thought at the beginning of the narrative that he may one day become like Daddy. Will he be able to break the pattern? Or has he already done so? Or will he become yet another case of a son inheriting the sins of his father?

In accordance with "accepted practice" and venerable tradition in children's literature, the book ends with a hope that everything will be all right in the end. But the main narrative does not provide us with an unambiguous answer, nor is that what we get when we turn to the epilogue picture which follows right after the main narrative. Here is a picture of Boj looking like a free and happy small boy. He moves with the reading direction, so that the picture seems hopeful and directed towards the future. If we compare this epilogue picture with the prologue picture of Boj holding the toy airplane protectively in front of himself, there can be no doubt that this is a Boj who has experienced a very positive development. But when we realize that the epilogue picture is nothing but a copy of the picture of Boj as he escapes from all the evil inside the house (doublespread 7), we are perhaps not entirely convinced?

Notes

1. All translation from Norwegian in this chapter are mine.
2. All modalities have varying limits to what they can express and the ways in which they can express something to a reader. For instance: *Writing* can easily inform us about the names of characters and places, give us information about the character's age and background, reproduce speech, and mediate the relations between the characters in the book. This is information that may be difficult to communicate with any precision through the modality of the *picture*. A picture, however, can offer more specific information about what the characters look like, the characters' surroundings and environment, colors, where the characters are situated in relation to each other in space, how a person executes various tasks, etc. The modalities have various intrinsic possibilities and limitations when it

comes to representing and communicating something to a reader. This is what the social semioticians Gunther Kress and Carey Jewitt call *modal affordance* (Kress and Jewitt 2003: 14).
3. Jørgen Lorentzen argues that the spelling of Boj's name indicates that he should be compared to the life and sufferings of the biblical figure of Job (Lorentzen 2004: 116).
4. According to Wolfgang Iser, one can never say everything in a fictional text. The author always has to make choices, and this results in what Iser calls *gaps* or *blanks* or *places of indeterminacy* or *vacancies* in the text (Iser 1978). The most important mission for these textual gaps is to disturb the reading process. The reader is given choices, and is therefore invited to be an active reader.
5. The Hulk, or The Incredible Hulk, was orginally an American cartoon figure created by Jack Kirby and Stan Lee in 1962; and it has since caught on as TV-series, film and animated movie, and the figure is also found in a series of spin-off-products. The Hulk is really an ordinary man, the scientist Bruce Banner, who during a failed experiment in the lab was exposed to gamma beams. Since then he has the ability to transform into the green muscular hunk, the Hulk, every time he becomes angry. Bruce's father Brian and Brian's mother were both exposed to psychic and possibly also physical abuse by Brian's father, and as he was afraid that he might have inherited this monster gene he decided not to have any more children after Bruce (from http://www.incrediblehulk.com/bannerhistory/html).

Bibliography

Primary Sources

Dahle, Gro, and Svein Nyhus. *Sinna Mann*, Oslo: Cappelen, 2003.
———. *Snill*, Oslo: Cappelen, 2002.
Nyhus, Svein. *Pappa!*, Oslo: Gyldendal Tiden, 1998.

Secondary Sources

Hollekim, Vibeke. "Voldsom barndom." *Kvinner og klær* 44 (2003): 22–26.
http://www.incrediblehulk.com/bannerhistory.html (accesssed March 26, 2006).
Iser, Wolfgang. *The Act of Reading. A Theory of Aesthetic Response*, Baltimore and London: The John Hopkins University Press, 1978.
Kress, Gunther, and Carey Jewitt. *Multimodal Literacy*. New York: Peter Lang, 2003.
Lorentzen, J. "Sønnene arver fedrenes synder." In *Maskulinitet. Blikk på mannen gjennom litteratur og film* edited by Jørgen Lorentzen. 114–133. Oslo: Spartacus Forlag, 2004.
New Living Bible (http://www.bible.com).
Nikolajeva, Maria. *Bilderbokens pusselbitar*, Lund: Studentlitteratur, 2000.
Nyhus, Svein "Det gjør vondt å ha det gøy. Om hvorfor og hvordan jeg lager bildebøker—og om samspillet mellom tekst og bilde." In *Håndbok i barnebibliotekarbeid. Å formidle litteratur for barn* edited by Astrid Holmefjord, Thomas Brevik, Bente Bing Kleiva, Åshild Sæle, and Ragnar Helene Vestrheim. 30–48. Bergen: Fagbokforlaget, 2003.

Chapter Seventeen
Imagination or Reality?
Mindscapes and Characterization in a Finnish and a Swedish Picturebook

Anna-Maija Koskimies-Hellman

Maria Nikolajeva and Carole Scott conclude their article "Images of the Mind: The Depiction of Consciousness in Picturebooks": "[R]ecent picturebooks clearly demonstrate the effectiveness of the form in combining words and images in a variety of ways to convey complex psychological states. [. . .] In this way we believe that picturebooks have achieved the goal which many modern writers have been striving for: to portray subverbal (nonverbal, preverbal) conditions of those whose language skills are limited" (Nikolajeva and Scott: 34–35). In their article they show how some of the contemporary picturebooks include a tendency towards a deeper psychological characterization instead of being action-centered. Nikolajeva and Scott consider picturebooks as the ultimate medium for this purpose as an image can describe emotions in a more effective way than words.

Psychological landscapes, mindscapes, can be found in an increasing number of recent picturebooks both in Finland and in Sweden—as well as internationally. When talking about mindscapes, I mean the protagonist's subjective perception of his or her own environment. This is an inner world and it is mediated to the reader by both the visual and the verbal narrator. By mindscapes I do not mean secondary worlds of fantasy, not necessarily even a separate world in any way. Instead, the term is associated with a visual and a verbal representation of the protagonist's dreams, fears, wishes, and imagination.

In this chapter I will present two contemporary picturebooks including this motif, *Urhea pikku Memmuli* ("Brave Little Memmuli," 2005) by Mervi Lindman and *Hanna huset hunden* ("Hanna, the House, the Dog," 2004) by Anna-Clara Tidholm. My aim is to show two different examples of the motif mindscape, what theoretical tools can be used in the analysis of this motif, and how this motif can be used as a characterization device in these picturebooks.

Urhea pikku Memmuli—Disempowering Fantasy

In Mervi Lindman's book *Urhea pikku Memmuli* the protagonist is a little girl whose environment is filled with frightening things. Memmuli knows that she should not be afraid, but this only makes her fear more. Her fears become concrete when she is alone, especially in the evenings. One night Memmuli's room is occupied by different kinds of monsters. Her fear makes her shrink so that the wind catches her and blows her out of the window. The wind carries her to the city and to the forest where she finally accepts that she is not a big girl and that she **is** afraid. At that moment she finds herself in her mother's arms, and her mother tells her that the bravest thing to do is to admit that you are scared.

It seems obvious that Lindman's book describes an adventure that is not real. The visual narrator uses two different perspectives showing sometimes the "objective" reality and sometimes Memmuli's mindscape, how she perceives the reality. The clearest examples of this are two doublespreads that follow each other. The first one shows Memmuli's room from her father's (the adult's) perspective as a pink, cozy girl's room with lots of toys and nice pictures on the walls, whereas the second one shows the same room from Memmuli's perspective. All the things that were pretty on the previous doublespread are now scary and threatening.

This doublespread is not the only one that visualizes Memmuli's fears. When she is taking a bath a foam monster threatens her, and at the dinner table the dessert is literally about to catch her tongue. It seems clear that a great deal of Memmuli's fears depend on the fact that she does not understand the figurative language her parents use, or more accurately, she takes it literally. Her father enjoys the dessert and expresses this by saying that it "catches his tongue" (a Finnish saying), whereas Memmuli's mother says that she is "chasing poodles" as she vacuums on Friday evenings. Therefore also the verbal perspective belongs to Memmuli, since the verbal narrator never corrects these misunderstandings, and instead lets the visual narrator emphasize them. That is why the images are filled with scary poodles and monsters of various kinds.

Another aspect that can be the source of Memmuli's fears is revealed through the intertextual and intervisual links in the book. The scene where Memmuli disappears into the toilet can be associated with the scene in Tove Jansson's picturebook *The Book about Moomin, Mymble and Little My* (1952) where Moomintroll and Mymble end up in a vacuum cleaner (Jansson 12–13). On the other hand it also reminds me of Barbro Lindgren and Eva Eriksson's Wild Baby and how he falls into the toilet in *The Wild Baby* (Lindgren and

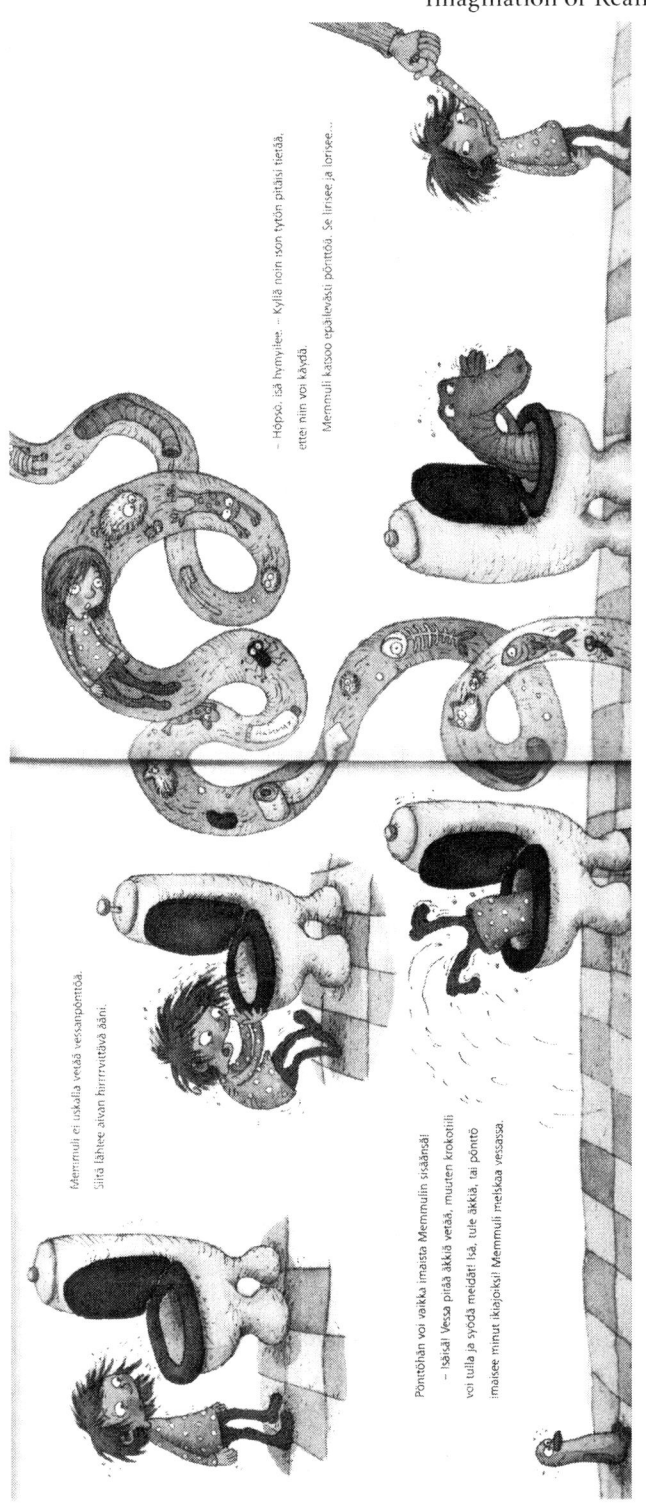

Figure 17.1 Illustration from Mervi Lindman: *Urhea pikku Memmuli*. Helsinki: Tammi, 2005.

Eriksson 12–13). As Memmuli's father comes into her room to read a story, he holds a copy of *Alice in Wonderland* in his hand, and this makes me wonder if the books that are read to Memmuli are affecting her fears. It is commonly known that Alice disappears into the rabbit's hole. Maybe there is a tradition of reading also the newer classics of children's literature in the family? This remains a mystery for the reader.

As in Anthony Browne's picturebook *The Tunnel* (1989), also in Memmuli's nightmares there are details that are familiar from her home. Toys and pictures from her room occur in her dream or fantasy in new roles and new contexts. In Memmuli's case the changes of visual perspective signal the shift from the fictive reality into fantasy or dream, from objective into subjective, from external into internal world. The events that take place during daytime can be interpreted as fantasy, whereas the adventure in the night can be read as a dream. The fact that Memmuli finds herself in her own bed, despite that she is in the forest, and that her mother comes as soon as she starts crying, indicates that the adventure could have been a nightmare. But since the verbal and a large part of the visual perspective in the story belong to Memmuli, the reality of the adventure is never questioned the way it is done for example in the Danish picturebook classic, *Paul Alone in the World* (1942) by Jens Sigsgaard and Arne Ungermann, in which an exciting adventure is declared to be just a dream. The adventure and the meetings with the monsters have been extremely real for Memmuli, although they have only occurred in her mindscape.

One of the theoretical tools that can be used in analysing characterization through the motif mindscape is Mikhail Bakhtin's carnival theory. It reflects the circular pattern of children's literature where the everyday life at home is interrupted by an exciting adventure, which often turns out to be rather empowering.[1] Although there is a clear happy ending in this book, the circular pattern is not that obvious. There is no actual adventure, and Memmuli's home is the threatening place. Home is not safe in this book and therefore one of the conventions of children's literature is questioned. The events are everything but empowering in the sense that Memmuli turns from a brave, big girl into a little, scared girl in the end. Her fear disempowers her. But in carnival theory, even a disempowering adventure can be empowering, if it includes the aspect of insight and growth. So, even though the development is from strong to weak, this could be a story about growth, especially since Memmuli's strength has not been real as much as imagined. This takes us back towards the traditional pattern of children's literature, yet in a slightly modified way.

Hanna huset hunden—A Case for a Psychoanalyst?

Unlike in the previous book, the protagonist in Anna-Clara Tidholm's *Hanna huset hunden* is not a child but a young woman, an anxious young woman. Hanna lives in a tiny red house with her dog, and these three aspects form the core of the story. The story begins as Hanna wakes up in the night and notices that both the dog and the house have gone missing. This is the beginning of a series of absurd events consisting of different types of dogs, houses, and doors. Sometimes Hanna is small and the dog is big, sometimes the other way around. Sometimes the dog returns home, sometimes he disappears and returns in the shape of several dogs. This increases Hanna's anxiety, and finally she decides to leave the dog and move into a new house.

Already the description of the events hints that this might be a symbolic story of a young woman's liberation from a destructive relationship, but the book invites the reader to look even closer at the details. The perspective both in the visual and in the verbal story is mainly Hanna's. The verbal story consists of just a few words and some short sentences that focalize Hanna, which leaves more space for the visual impulses that definitely dominate the story. The absurd events create a dreamlike atmosphere, and it seems credible that the events starting from the dog's disappearance are a dream. This assumption is supported by the fact that Hanna wakes up in the middle of the night. The dreamlike atmosphere is supported by a scene in which the dog appears in the shape of several dogs, a scene where Hanna gets lost in the house where several doors are opened, and a scene where she walks at the edge of the world looking for her dog. All of these scenes are nightmarish.

The destructive relationship between Hanna and the dog is represented in the large size of the dog and his line: "I am watching the house," repeated several times. This reflects how he controls Hanna and gives her, literally, no space of her own.

The fascinating absurdity of the story invites the reader to ask whether these events should be read as real or imaginary in the fictive reality. The border between dream and reality is very unclear in this book, and it is uncertain whether the liberation at the end is real or just wishful thinking, or a dream. If one decides to interpret the story as a dream, Freudian terminology can offer some interesting alternatives for interpretation.

One of the central aspects of the story is the use of colors. The symbolic colors of the fairy tales, black, red, and white are repeated in several contexts. Hanna's red house is depicted in a white winter landscape against a black sky on the very first opening, and Hanna is often surrounded by black emptiness. At the turning point in the story, black color flows into the room through a hole in the wall. The black color flows onto the white floor and is mixed with a river and a red scarf that Hanna is knitting. This creates a state of chaos in Hanna's life, and her way to get away from it is to set her house on fire.

In Hanna's case it feels like the Freudian symbols are almost too easy to find. According to Freud, the house with its walls, different floors, and rooms represents the person who dreams about the house (Freud: 136). On the outside, Hanna's house is a simple cabin, but inside of it there are several doors to different rooms. In Freudian psychoanalysis, doors and windows are female symbols (Freud: 139). A flat "male" facade controls the house that now on

Figure 17.2 Illustration from Anna-Clara Tidholm: *Hanna huset hunden*. Stockholm: Alfabeta, 2004.

the inside is very feminine (Freud: 136). This is the same kind of symbolism that can be seen in the dog's controlling behavior. Hanna cannot escape this masculine control until the house is on fire.

The dog is not actually described as an animal, but rather as a human, a man. The animal side of a man is one of the central aspects that Bruno Bettelheim uses in his Freudian analysis of "Little Red Riding Hood." Bettelheim interprets the threatening animal forms as masculine symbols, and considers the wolf as a symbol for as well the seductive man as the animalistic tendencies within human beings (Bettelheim: 172). Hanna's dog can be seen as a domestic version of this wild animal. In this case Hanna's dream can express a wish to be free from the controlling and destructive relationship with the man she lives with.

The interpretation can be taken to yet another level of abstraction. One can see the dog as the animal side of Hanna herself. In that case the controlling behavior of the dog can symbolize Hanna's self-censorship, a denial of some negative aspects of her life. This could also explain the formless darkness that occurs in her dream and make her dream express an insight of her darker side and a wish of being able to confront it.

Apart from these aspects, the Freudian interpretation is supported by several visual details: aeroplanes and trains are male phallic symbols, whereas the tunnels symbolize females. The water that flows from the darkness and is mixed with the red scarf can be associated with maternity and birth. This doublespread functions as the turning point in the story on many different levels. If it does not describe a birth, it can reveal a dream of having a baby that could solve the conflict between Hanna and the dog. On a more abstract level it could also describe the moment Hanna realizes that the only way to get rid of the anxiety is to face it. The shape of her character on this doublespread signals a sudden change.

The question that is crucial for the interpretation is whether the events take place in Hanna's dream or in her reality. The dream interpretation is not confirmed by the conventional awakening in the morning; instead Hanna has moved on, she has moved into a new house alone. This signals also that the conventional, circular pattern is not present in the story; instead it follows a more linear pattern, also suggesting a grown-up theme. Whatever the interpretation of Hanna's story is, it seems obvious that the problems belong to an adult world, not to children's world. This book, too, is about growth, but on a radically different level than *Urhea pikku Memmuli*.

Conclusion

As I compare the two picturebooks presented here, I am faced with a contradiction. There are both striking similarities and critical differences between them. In a way they represent two extremes, since the first one deals so obviously with concerns of childhood, whereas the second one is clearly a book about a young woman's development. Yet both of them present the mindscapes as real, without a didactic narrator's comment of the events being dream or fantasy. Therefore they also support the characterization of these two females, give access to their inner lives. Psychoanalytical tools could also be used on Lindman's book, which would deepen the interpretation of Memmuli's character.

Both books use the methods picturebook medium has to offer for expressing subverbal states of the character. Through the images they deepen the emotions that are expressed in the verbal text. Therefore they also serve as examples of how internal characterization can be used in picturebooks in an immediate way, without necessarily needing to translate the mindscapes into words. This way they also communicate the protagonists' experiences to a broader audience regardless of the readers' skills to interpret and analyse the text.

Both books are also ambivalent on several levels. They balance on the border between imagination or dream and reality, and if a choice between these two has to be made, it clearly affects the outcome of the analysis and the interpretation. They are also ambivalent in the question about the implied reader. One of them is traditional in the sense that it deals with problems belonging to childhood. Picturebooks are mostly considered as children's literature, so the theme in *Urhea pikku Memmuli* is in no way extraordinary. The same thing cannot, though, be said about the theme in *Hanna huset hunden*, that deals with problems for grown-ups. Who is the implied reader of this book? Does this book address the adult reader over the child's head, or is this completely a picturebook for grown-ups? I see the Freudian symbols in Tidholm's book as a game with the implied adult reader. The symbols are explicit and easily recognisable. In my opinion, a reading that does not take these symbols into account, excludes a significant aspect of the iconotext: the playfulness that is disguised in the more serious theme of the book. However, this type of playfulness excludes the child reader.

In Memmuli's case we can see the concept of dual address (Wall: 9) being used in a very different way than in Hanna's case. *Urhea pikku Memmuli* addresses adults and children at the same time on several different levels. The shifts in perspective, the visualized figurative language and the intervisual details show that both the child's and the adult's world is present all the time.

Notes

1. See also: Nodelman, Perry, *The Pleasures of Children's Literature* (155), where Nodelman discusses the basic structure of children's literature.

Bibliography

Primary Sources

Browne, Anthony. *The Tunnel*. New York: Knopf, 1989.
Jansson, Tove. *Hur gick det sen? Boken om Mymlan, Mumintrollet och lilla My*. 1952. Helsinki: Schildts, 2005.
Lindgren, Barbro, and Eva Eriksson. *Mamman och den vilda bebin*. Stockholm: Rabén & Sjögren, 1980.
Lindman, Mervi. *Urhea pikku Memmuli*. Helsinki: Tammi, 2005.
Tidholm, Anna-Clara. *Hanna huset hunden*. Stockholm: Alfabeta, 2004.

Secondary Sources

Bakhtin, Mikhail. *Rabelais and His World*. Translated by Hélène Iswolsky. Cambridge, MA: MIT Press, 1968.
Bettelheim, Bruno.*The Uses of Enchantment: The Meaning and Importance of Fairy Tales*. London: Penguin Books, 1991.
Freud, Sigmund. *A General Introduction to Psycho-Analysis*. Translated by Joan Riviere. New York: Garden City, 1943.
Nikolajeva, Maria, and Carole Scott. "Imprints of the Mind: The Depiction of Consciousness in Picturebooks." *CREArTA* 2.1 (2001): 12–36.
Nodelman, Perry. *The Pleasures of Children's Literature*. New York: Longman, 1996.
Wall, Barbara. *The Narrator's Voice: The Dilemma of Children's Fiction*. Basingstoke: Macmillan, 1991.

# Contributors

Evelyn Arizpe is Lecturer in Children's Literature at the Faculty of Education, University of Glasgow. Her main work is in the areas of literacies, picturebooks, and Mexican children's literature. She is co-author, with Morag Styles, of *Children Reading Pictures* (New York: Routledge 2003) and *Reading Lessons from the Eighteenth Century* (London: Pied Piper Press 2006). She was the organizer of the second conference of the picturebook research network that took place at Glasgow in September 2009.

Sandra L. Beckett is Professor of French at Brock University. She is member of The Royal Society of Canada, and received Le Prix de l'APFUCC. In 1999–2003 she was president of the IRSCL. Her most important publications are: *De grands romanciers écrivent pour les enfants* (Montréal: PUM 1997); *Transcending Boundaries: Writing for a Dual Audience of Children and Adults*. (Ed., New York: Garland Publishing, 1999); *Recycling Red Riding Hood* (New York and London: Routledge, 2002); *Beyond Babar: The European Tradition in Children's Literature* (Edited in collaboration with Maria Nikolajeva. Lanham, MD; Scarecrow Press, 2006); *Red Riding Hood for All Ages: Fairy-Tale Icon in Cross-Cultural Contexts* (Detroit: Wayne State University Press, 2008) and *Crossover Fiction: Global and Historical Perspectives* (New York: Routledge, 2008). She is currently working on an anthology (*Revisioning Red Riding Hood*) and a monograph on *The Art of Recycling Stories in Contemporary Children's Literature*.

Brenda Bellorín is a fellow researcher and PhD student in the Department of the Teaching of Language and Literature at the Universitat Autònoma de Barcelona (UAB). She is a lecturer and member of the coordination staff of the Online MA on Books and Literature for Children and Youngsters (UAB). She was a Fulbright fellow for the MA on Liberal Studies programme at New School of Social Research (USA) and worked at the Banco del Libro (Venezuela) from the mid-1990s to 2008. In this reading promotion institution she coordinated several publications and the Book Evaluation Committee, organized exhibits, and taught seminars and workshops.

Agnes-Margrethe Bjorvand is Lecturer at Agder University College. She has edited several books and written many articles about children's literature, and is now working on her PhD thesis on Astrid Lindgren's picturebooks. She has translated eight books by and about Astrid Lindgren into Norwegian. Additionally, she is publishing consultant, and chief editor of the award winning website http://www.barnebok.no.

Nina Christensen is Director of the Centre for Children's Literature in Copenhagen. The centre is part of the School of Education at University of Aarhus. Her PhD thesis focused on the history of the Danish picturebook and was published in 2003 under the title *Den danske billedbog 1950–1999. Teori, analyse, historie* [The Danish Picture Book 1950–1999. Theory, analysis, history]. Her second book *Barnejælen. Børnelitteraturen og det romantiske barn* [A child-like soul. Children's literature and the romantic child] discusses the image of the romantic child in historical and contemporary Danish children's literature. Her article "Childhood Revisited: On the Relationship between Childhood Studies and Children's Literature" is included in Peter Hunt (ed.) *Children's Literature. Critical Concepts in Literary and Cultural Studies* (Routledge 2006). Her current area of research is eighteenth-century children's literature.

Teresa Colomer is Professor in the Department of the Teaching of Language and Literature at the Universitat Autònoma de Barcelona (UAB). She holds a degree in Hispanic Philology and Catalan Philology and a PhD in Educational Sciences. She has published over 150 articles and books on children's literature, the teaching of reading and literature, and has received several awards for her research in Spain and Brazil. She created the first network of researchers on literature for children and young people in Spain (1999–2006), where she coordinated several publications. Currently, she is director of the Research Group GRETEL (www.gretel.cat), which has been recognised as a "quality group with funding" by the research agency AGAUR (Catalan Government). She is also head of the MA on Books and Literature for Children and Youngsters. Her main fields of research are the teaching and learning of literature, children's books and literacy, social aspects of children's literature, and reading habits.

Elina Druker is Lecturer in the Department of Literature and History of Ideas at the University of Stockholm and Coordinator and core group member of the Nordic Network for Children's Literature Research (NorChilNet). Recent publications are: *Barnlitteraturanalyser* (Children's Literature Analyses. Editor. Lund 2008) and *Modernismens bilder—den moderna bilderboken i Norden* (Images of Modernism—The Modern Picture Book in the Nordic Countries. Stockholm: Makadam, 2008). She is publisher's reader at the publishing houses Alfabeta and Natur och Kultur. Her research interests include picturebook theory, history of book illustration, intermedial studies, and Nordic modernism.

Contributors • 245

Eva Gressnich is a PhD student at the Johannes Gutenberg University Mainz (Germany). She is currently writing a PhD thesis on linguistics of the picturebook. Main topics of research are the interfaces between language acquisition, children's literature and literacy development. She published several articles in *The Oxford Encyclopedia of Children's Literature* (2006).

Anna-Maija Koskimies-Hellman is Lecturer at the University of Vaasa, Finland. She has written her MA thesis on picturebooks at Stockholm University and has recently finished her PhD thesis on mindscapes as a means of characterisation in Finnish and Swedish picturebooks at Åbo Academi University.

Bettina Kümmerling-Meibauer is Professor in the German Department at the University of Tübingen. In 2010 she holds the position of guest-professor in memory of Astrid Lindgren at the University of Växjö, Sweden. Among her works are a two-volume encyclopedia on international children's classics (Metzler, 1999); a monograph on the relationship between children's literature, canon formation and literary evaluation (Metzler 2003), and essay collections on Astrid Lindgren (co-edited with S. Blume and A. Nix, Peter Lang, 2008) and children's films (co-edited with Th. Koebner, Reclam, 2010). She was also one of the advisory editors for *The Oxford Encyclopedia of Children's Literature*. She is currently working on a textbook on children's literature and a monograph on picturebooks for young children.

Tomoko Masaki is Professor in the Faculty of Education at Seiwa College in Hyogo, Japan. She wrote her PhD thesis on Victorian picturebooks at the University of Roehampton in the UK. She was presented the 8th Harvey Darton Award for her English book, *A History of Victorian Popular Picture Books* (published in 2006), by the Children's Books History Society in 2008. Her recent publications are *A Case Study of the Relationship between Babies and Picturebooks: Why we Should Read Picturebooks to Babies* (2007, in Japanese), and *Children and Picturebooks* (2008, in Japanese). She has been carrying out research projects by herself or with other scholars on "Babies and Picturebooks," "Childhood Represented in Japanese Picturebook Magazines during and after WW II," and "Gender and Migration Issues in American Picturebooks."

Jörg Meibauer is Professor for German Linguistics at the Johannes Gutenberg University Mainz (Germany) and Affiliated Professor at the University of Stockholm (Sweden). His academic stations include Cologne, Brighton, Lund, Tübingen, and Dresden. Among his recent publications are monographs on rhetorical questions (1986), modal particles (1994), pragmatics (1999), and German linguistics (co-authored, 2002, 2007); in addition, he edited collections on sentence mood (1987), lexical acquisition (with M. Rothweiler, 1999), quotation (with E. Brendel and M. Steinbach, 2007), and experimental pragmatics and semantics (with M. Steinbach, 2010).

His main research interests lie in the grammar-pragmatics interface, in word formation, and in language acquisition. He is currently working on a book-length study on lying, deception, and bullshit.

Ingeborg Mjør is Lecturer at the Faculty of Arts and Education, University of Stavanger, Norway. She has written several articles on children's literature and a textbook on children's literature (*Barnelitteratur—sjangrar og teksstypar*, with T. Birkeland and G. Risa, 2001, second edition 2006). In 2009 she defended her PhD thesis on how children develop literacy through participating in reading aloud of picturebooks. Her main research interests are: Picturebook theory, semiotics, reader response theory, and literacy studies.

Isabelle Nières-Chevrel is Professor Emeritus of Comparative Literature at the University of Rennes II, France. Her main interests include children's literature from a literary and historical point of view, reception theory, and translation studies, as well as the relationship between text and pictures. She has written extensively on Lewis Carroll, Sophie de Ségur, Maurice Boutet de Monvel, Beatrix Potter, Jean de Brunhoff, and Maurice Sendak. She recently published a book about French children's literature (*Introduction à la littérature d'enfance et de jeunesse*. Didier jeunesse, 2009). In collaboration with Jean Perrot she is also preparing the edition of the first French encyclopedia focussing on French children's literature (to be published by Le Cercle de la Librairie in 2010).

Maria Nikolajeva is Professor of Education at the University of Cambridge, UK. She is the recipient of the International Grimm Award for lifetime achievements in children's literature research. In 1993–1997 she was the President of the International Research Society for Children's Literature. Her most recent publications include *How Picturebooks Work*, co-authored with Carole Scott (2001), *From Mythic to Linear: Time in Children's Literature* (2002), *The Rhetoric of Character in Children's Literature* (2002), *Aesthetic Approaches to Children's Literature* (2005), *Power, Voice and Subjectivity in Literature for Young Readers* (2009) and, co-edited with Sandra Beckett, *Beyond Babar: European Children's Literature* (2006). She was also one of the senior editors for *The Oxford Encyclopedia of Children's Literature*. Her main focus of research is critical theory, visual literacy, and power relationships in children's fiction.

Perry Nodelman is Professor Emeritus of English at the University of Winnipeg (1982–2005). His most important publications are: *Touchstones: Reflections on the Best in Children's Literature* (Editor. Three volumes. West Lafayette: Children's Literature Association Publishers, 1986–1989); *Words About Pictures: The Narrative Art of Children's Picture Books* (Athens, GA: University of Georgia Press, 1988); *The Pleasure of Children's Literature* (New York: Longman 1992; revised edition 2003; translated into Chinese and Korean); *The Hidden Adult: Definitions of Children's Literature* (Baltimore: John Hopkins University Press 2008). Nodelman was president of the Children's Literature Association of America in 1989 and editor of *Children's Literature Association Quarterly* (1982–1987). From 2005 to 2009 he was editor of *CCL/LCJ* (*Canadian Children's Literature*). He has published more than 150 articles and essays in refereed scholarly journals and essay collections.

Carole Scott is Professor Emeritus of English and former Dean of undergraduate studies at San Diego State University, California, and serves on the board of its National Center for the Study of Children's Literature. She has served on the boards of the Children's Literature Association (CHLA), International Research Society for Children's Literature (IRSCL), and was a Senior Scholar on the Nordic Children's Literature Network (NorChilNet). She is co-author of *How Picturebooks Work* (Garland, 2001), shared editorial responsibility with Muriel Lenz for *His Dark Material Illuminated* (Wayne State UP, 2005), has articles and chapters in a variety of journals and essay collections specializing in children's literature, and serves as reviewer for several journals.

Cecilia Silva-Díaz is Associate Professor at the Universitat Autònoma de Barcelona (UAB) where she coordinates and teaches in the MA program on Books and Literature for Children and Youngsters. She obtained a Master's degree from Simmons College in Boston and a PhD at UAB with her dissertation on metafictional picturebooks. For six years she was in charge of the Research Program at Banco del Libro, Venezuela. She was member of the Hans Christian Andersen Jury twice and is book editor at Ediciones Ekaré. Among her recent works are: *La metaficción como un juego de niños: Una introducción a los álbumes metaficcionales* (Caracas, Banco del Libro, 2005) and "Entre el texto y la imagen: álbumes y otros libros ilustrados" (2009) In: *Lecturas Adolescentes*, edited by Teresa Colomer (Barcelona: Graó, 2009).

Fernando Zaparaín is Associate Professor of Architectonic Design at the University of Valladolid (Spain). He published several books and articles about the graphic language and space in comics, picturebooks, cinema, and architecture. In collaboration with Luis Daniel González, he published six articles about the different artistic options in picturebooks. Both are currently finishing a study on the specific language of illustration. Moreover, Fernando Zaparaín is a renowned painter (favored in oil canvas), whose paintings had been presented in five individual exhibitions.

Selected Bibliography

Anstey, Michèle. "'It's Not All Black and White': Postmodern Picturebooks and New Literacies." *Journal of Adolescent & Adult Literacy* 45.6 (2002): 444–457.
Arizpe, Evelyn, and Morag Styles. *Children Reading Pictures. Interpreting Visual Texts*. London: RoutledgeFalmer, 2003.
Beckett, Sandra. "Parodic Play with Painting in Picturebooks." *Children's Literature* 29 (2001): 175–195.
Bradford, Claire. "The Picture Book: Some Postmodern Tensions." *Papers: Explorations into Children's Literature* 4.3 (1993): 10–14.
Colomer, Teresa. "El album y el texto." *Peonza* 39 (1996): 27–31.
Christensen, Nina. *Den danske billedbog 1950-1999. Teori, analyse, historie*. Roskilde: Roskilde Universitetsforlag, 2003.
DeBaryshe, B.D. "Joint Picture Book Reading Correlates of Early Oral Language Skill." *Journal of Child Language* 20 (1995): 455–461.
DeLoache, J. S., D. Uttal, and S. L. Pierroutsakos. "What's Up? The Development of an Orientation Preference for Picture Books." *Journal of Cognition and Development* 1 (2000): 81–95.
Doonan, Jane. *Looking at Pictures in Picture Books*. Stroud: Thimble Press, 1993.
Druker, Elina. *Modernismens bild—den moderna bilderboken i Norden*. Stockholm: Madakam, 2008.
Edström, Vivi. Ed. *Vår moderna bilderbok*. Stockholm: Rabén & Sjögren, 1991.
Enever, Janet, and Giselle Schmidt-Schönbein. Eds. *Picturebooks and Primary EFL Learners*. Munich: Langenscheidt, 2006.
Evans, Janet. Ed. *What's in the Picture? Responding to Illustrations in Picture Books*. London: Paul Chapman, 1998.
Evans, Janet. Ed. *Talking Beyond the Page: Reading and Responding to Picturebooks*. London: Routledge, 2009.
Fang, Z. "Illustrations, Text, and the Child Reader: What are Pictures in Children's Story Books For?" *Reading Horizons* 37 (1996): 130–142.
González, Luis Daniel and Fernando Zaparaín. "Aproximaciones al lenguaje de los álbumes." *CLIJ. Cuadernos de literatura infantil y juvenil* 178 (2005): 7–14.
González, Luis Daniel and Fernando Zaparaín. "Optimistas y nostálgicos." *CLIJ. Cuadernos de literatura infantil y juvenil* 179 (2005): 7–15.
González, Luis Daniel and Fernando Zaparaín. "Cubistas agradecios." *CLIJ. Cuadernos de literatura infantil y juvenil* 180 (2005): 7–13.
González, Luis Daniel and Fernando Zaparaín. "Inteligentes minimalistas." *CLIJ. Cuadernos de literatura infantil y juvenil* 182 (2005): 7–13.
González, Luis Daniel and Fernando Zaparaín. "Impactantes expresionistas." *CLIJ. Cuadernos de literatura infantil y juvenil* 183 (2005): 44–51.
Grieve, Ann. "Postmodernism in Picturebooks." *Papers: Explorations into Children's Literature* 4.3 (2003): 15–25.
Harding, Jennifer, and Pat Pinsent. Eds. *What do You See? International Perspectives on Children's Book Illustration*. Cambridge: Cambridge Scholars Publishing, 2008.
Jones, Rhian. *Emerging Patterns of Literacy. A Multidisciplinary Perspective*. London and New York: Routledge, 1996.

Kiefer, Barbara. *The Potential of Picturebooks: From Visual Literacy to Aesthetic Understanding.* Englewood Cliffs, NJ: Prentice Hall, 1995.
Kress, Gunther, and Theo van Leeuwen. *Reading Images. The Grammar of Visual Design.* London: Routledge, 1996.
Kümmerling-Meibauer, Bettina. "Metalinguistic Awareness and the Child's Developing Sense of Irony: The Relationship between Pictures and Texts in Ironic Picturebooks." *The Lion and the Unicorn* 23.2 (1999): 157–183.
Kümmerling-Meibauer, Bettina. "Preschool Books." In *The Oxford Encyclopedia of Children's Literature* edited by Jack Zipes. Vol. 3. 288–291. Oxford: Oxford University Press, 2006.
Kümmerling-Meibauer, Bettina, and Jörg Meibauer. "First Pictures, Early Concepts: Early Concept Books." *The Lion and the Unicorn* 29 (2005): 324–347.
Lewis, David. *Reading Contemporary Picturebooks. Picturing Text.* London: RoutledgeFalmer, 2001.
Lowe, Virginia. *Stories, Pictures, and Reality: Two Children Tell.* New York and London: Routledge, 2007.
Mallan, Kerry. *In the Picture. Perspectives on Picture Book Art and Artists.* Wagga-Wagga: Centre for Information Studies, 1999.
Mitchell, W. J. T. *Picture Theory: Essays on Verbal and Visual Representation.* Chicago: University of Chicago Press, 1994.
Moebius, William. "Introduction to Picturebook Codes." *Word and Image* 2.2 (1996): 141–158.
Mørch-Hansen, Anne. Ed. *Billedbøger & Børns Billeder.* Kopenhagen: Høst & Son, 2000.
Nières-Chevrel, Isabelle. "Narrateur visuel et narrateur verbal dans l'album pour enfants." *La Revue des Livres pour Enfants* 214 (2003): 69–81.
Nikolajeva, Maria. "Verbal and Visual Literacy: The Role of Picturebooks in the Reading Experience of Young Children." In *Handbook of Childhood Early Literacy* edited by Nigel Hall, Joanne Larson and Jackie Marsh. 235–248. London: Sage Publications, 2003.
Nikolajeva, Maria, and Carole Scott. "Images of the Mind: The Depiction of Consciousness in Picturebooks." *CREArTA* 2.1 (2001): 12–36.
Nikolajeva, Maria, and Carole Scott. *How Picturebooks Work.* New York: Garland, 2001.
Nodelman, Perry. *Words About Pictures: The Narrative Art of Children's Picture Books.* Athens: The University of Georgia Press, 1988.
Nodelman, Perry. "The Eye and the I: Identification and First-Person Narratives in Picture Books." *Children's Literature* 19 (1991): 1–30.
Pantaleo, Sylvia. *Exploring Student Responses to Contemporary Picturebooks.* Toronto: University of Toronto Press, 2008.
Rau, Marieluise. *Literacy. Vom ersten Bilderbuch zum Erzählen, Lesen und Schreiben.* Bern: Haupt, 2007.
Rhedin, Ulla. *Bilderboken: På väg mot en teori.* Stockholm: Alfabeta, 1993.
Roxburgh, Stephen. "A Picture Equals How Many Words? Narrative Theory and Picture Books for Children." *The Lion and the Unicorn* 7–8 (1983): 20–33.
Scott, Carole. "Dual Audience in Picture Book." In *Transcending Boundaries: Writing for a Dual Audience of Children and Adults* edited by Sandra Beckett. 99–110. New York: Garland, 1999.
Schweizerisches Jugendbuchinstitut. Ed. *Siehst du das? Die Wahrnehmung von Bildern in Kinderbüchern—Visual Literacy.* Zurich: Chronos, 1997.
Silva-Díaz, María-Cecilia. *La metaficción como un juego de niños: Una introducción a los álbumes metaficcionales.* Caracas: Banco del Libro, 2005.
Sipe, Lawrence. "How Picture Books Work: A Semiotically Framed Theory of Text-Picture Relationships." *Children's Literature in Education* 29.2 (1998): 97–108.
Sipe, Lawrence. *Storytime: Young Children's Literary Understanding in the Classroom.* New York: Teacher's College, 2008.
Sipe, Lawrence, and Caroline E. McGuire. "Picturebook Endpapers: Resources for Literary and Aesthetic Interpretation." *Children's Literature in Education* 37.4 (2003): 291–304.
Sipe, Lawrence, and Sylvia Pantaleo. Eds. *Postmodern Picturebooks. Play, Parody, and Self-Referentiality.* New York and London: Routledge, 2008.
Spaulding, Amy. *The Page as a Stage Set. Storyboard Picture Books.* Metuchen, NJ and London: Scarecrow Press, 1995.
Stephens, John. "Modality and Space in Picture Book Art: Allen Say's *Emma's Rug.*" *CREArTA* 1 (2000) 1: 44–59.
Stephens, John. "Picture Books, Mimesis and the Competing Aesthetics of Kinesis and Stasis." *Papers: Explorations into Children's Literature* 14 (2004): 24–33.

Styles, Morag, and Evelyn Arizpe. "A Gorilla with 'Grandpa's Eyes': How Children Interpret Visual Texts—A Case Study of Anthony Browne's Zoo." *Children's Literature in Education* 32.4 (2001): 61–81.
Thiele, Jens. Ed. *Neue Erzählformen im Bilderbuch*. Oldenburg: Isensee, 1991.
Thiele, Jens. *Das Bilderbuch. Ästhetik, Theorie, Analyse, Didaktik, Rezeption*. Oldenburg: Isensee, 2000.
Thiele, Jens. Ed. *Neue Impulse der Bilderbuchforschung*. Baltmannsweiler: Schneider Verlag, 2007.
Trites, Roberta. "Manifold Narratives: Metafiction and Ideology in Picturebooks." *Children's Literature in Education* 25 (1994): 225–242.
Van der Linden, Sopie. *Lire L'album*. Le Puy-en-Velay: L'Atelier du poisson soluble, 2007.
Walsh, Maureen. "Text-related Variables in Narrative Picturebooks: Children's Responses to Visual and Verbal Texts." *The Australian Journal of Language and Literacy* 23 (2000): 139–156.
Walsh, Maureen. "Reading Pictures: What do They Reveal? Young Children's Reading of Visual Texts." *Reading: Literacy and Language* 37 (2003): 123–130.
Watson, Victor, and Morag Styles. Eds. *Talking Pictures*. London: Hodder & Stoughton, 1996.

Index

Aalto, Alvar, 144
ABC book, 55
Aborigines, 103, 110
acculturation process, 104
abstraction, 28, 239
Adaptation (Jonze), 113, 115, 125
adaptation theory, 11, 12
Adresse-Avis for Børn, 66
L'Affaire Tournesol (Hergé), 171
affordance, 219, 220, 231
Ägget (Hellsing and Hald), 88
Alcántara, Ricardo, 85
Alexander and the Terrible, Horrible, No-Good Very Bad Day (Viorst), 18
Alice's Adventures in Wonderland (Carroll), 236
Amargo, Pablo, 65
Amber Waiting (Gregory), 2, 14, 18, 20–24
Anastasia Krupnik (Lowry and Cruz), 52
Anabel's House (Messenger), 53
Andersen, Hans Christian, 84, 247
Angry Man (Dahle and Nyhus), see *Sinna Mann*, 7, 217–218, 222–225, 228–229
Anno, Mitsumasa, 84, 86
Anno's Italy (Anno), 86
anthropology, 101, 110
Apan fin (Tidholm), 183–184, 187
architecture, 4, 5, 107–108, 112
Architecture Today (Steele), 5
Aristotle, 114
Arizpe, Evelyn, 4, 27, **69–82**, 201
Arnason, H.H., 96
Arnheim Rudolf, 152, 164, 172
artistic allusion, 4, 83. 86–90, 93–96
Art Nouveau, 110
Aschjem, Øivind, 218, 229
Asouline, Pierre, 175

Asplund, Gunnar, 144
Aumont, Jacques, 172
Australia, 103
autobiographical memory, 205, 207, 210, 215
"The Autobiographical Pact" (Lejeune), 205
autobiography, 103, 205–207, 209, 211
Avant-garde, 5, 146

Babar (Brunhoff), 198
Baby concept book, 129
Baby's First Book, 195
Bad Day at Riverbend (van Allsburg), 116
Bader, Barbara, 84
Bajour, Cecilia 118
Bakhtin, Mikhail, 236
Ballenger, Cynthia, 81
Ballò Jordi, 173
Bamberg, Michael, 196
Banco del Libro, 52
Banyai, Istvan, 171
Barthes, Roland, 2, 3, 28, 33–34, 36, 38–39, 175, 181–182, 186
Basedow, Johann Bernhard, 59
Bauer, Jutta, 52
Baumann, Kurt, 52
Bearne, Eve, 71
The Beatles, 182
The Bear That Wasn't (Tashlin), 52
Beckett, Sandra, 4, **83–98**
Bednall, Jane, 71
Belgium, 129
Bellorín, Brenda, 5, **113–128**
Benson, Patrick, 52
Berman, Ruth, 196
Bernini, Gianlorenzo, 91
Bernstein, Basil, 42–43
Bertuch, Friedrich Justin, 59

254 • Index

Bettelheim, Bruno, 239
Biarnès, Jean, 70
Bible, 56, 58, 66
The Big Baby (Browne), 90
bilingualism, 70–71
bird's eye view, 87, 208
Birkeland, Tone, 91
The Biscuit Bear (Grey), 73
Bjorvand, Agnes-Margrethe, 7, **217–231**
Blake, Quentin, 52
Bland, David, 144
blank space, 165–166, 172, 174
Blegvad, Erik, 215
Bloom, Paul, 193
Blythe, Gary, 53, 166
Bonitzer, Pascal, 174
The Book about Moomin, Mymble and Little My (Jansson) see *Hur gick det sen?*, 143, 234
book cover, 77, 139–140, 142–144, 152, 212
Bosch, Hieronymus, 64, 86
Botticelli, Sandro, 86, 223
Boueke, Dietrich, 196
Boutet de Monvel, Louis-Maurice, 173
Bozellec, Anne, 52
Brancusi, Constantin, 88
Brazil, 152, 163, 244
bricolage, 31, 88, 94, 109
Brinck, Ingar, 202
Brouillard, Anne, 5, 129–137
Bromley, Helen, 71
Browne, Anthony, 71, 84, 89, 167, 199–200, 236
Brüggemann, Theodor, 58
Bruel, Christian, 52
Bruner, Jerome, 179, 193
Brunhoff, Jean de, 198
Buddhism, 208, 215
Bühler, Karl, 195
Burch, Noël, 167
bystander's perspective, 198–199, 201

CCLII Udvalde og med 800 Billeder udlagde Bibelske Hoved-Sprog, 3, 57
El caballo acrobático (Rigo and Alcántara), 85
Calder, Alexander, 91
La calle es libre (Doppert and Kurusa), 52
La cama de mama (Carlin and Fuenmayor), 52
camera eye (perspective), 130–131, 133
Campe, Joachim Heinrich, 59
Canada, 2, 15, 215

caricature, 63, 222
Carlin, Joi, 52
carnival theory, 236
Cartesian space, 166
cartoon, 18, 78, 84, 147, 223, 231
The Century of Artists' Book (Drucker), 141
Cézanne, Paul, 86
Chagall, Marc, 85, 89, 94
La chambre claire (Barthes), 166
Chandler, Daniel, 25
Child, Lauren, 169
child language, 191
child psychology, 6
children's response, 2, 76, 119, 151, 160
Chinese-box-principle, 6, 144
Chodowiecki, Daniel, 59
Christensen, Nina, 3, **55–67**
Christo, Jean, 91
Clark, Eve, 192, 202
classics, 48–49, 169, 236
Claverie, Jean, 83–84, 96
Clément, Frédéric, 84
close-up, 33. 95, 134–136, 141, 156, 168, 199. 208
Le cochon à l'oreille coupée (Fromentin and Hyman), 85
Code; hermeneutic, 2, 28–33; proairetic, 2, 3, 31, 38, 39; referential, 3, 31, 38, 39; semic, 28, 33–36, 38; symbolic, 28, 36, 37
Coe, Richard, 215
Colledge, Marion, 71
cognitive linguistics, 6
cognitive psychology, 2, 6, 180
cognitive studies, 8
coherence, 114, 173–174
collage, 31, 61, 76, 109, 207
Colomer, Teresa, 2, 3, **42–54**, 126
The Colors of Rhetoric (Steiner), 139
color scheme, 7, 37, 205, 215
comics, 64, 73, 78, 172
connotation, 50, 73, 147, 165–166, 179–183, 185, 220–221
Constable, John, 16, 131
Costner, Kevin, 116
Coulthard, Kathy, 71
counting book, 28
Cranston, Leanne, 71
Cronin, Doreen, 124
Cruz, Valentina, 52
Cuando sale la luna (Ventura), 117, 122
cubism, 165
Culler, Jonathan, 28

cultural memory, 210
Curious George (Rey), 187
Cutler, Ivor, 52

Dadaism, 146
Dahl, Roald, 52
Dahle, Gro, 217, 220–222, 229–230
Dalí, Salvador, 84, 90, 94
Darton, F.J. Harvey, 58
deconstruction, 31, 107, 111
Degas, Edgar, 86, 89
deixis, 7, 192, 194, 196
Deixis am Phantasma, 195
Denmark, 2, 56, 58
denotation, 118, 125, 166,181
Derrida, Jacques, 31–32
de Saussure, Ferdinand, 25
detective story, 140–141, 148
Dillon, Diane, 86
Dillon, Leo, 86,
Do Not Go Around the Edges (Utemorrah and Torres), 102–103, 110
Doppert, Monika, 52
Doonan, Jane, 96, 118, 125
Douzou, Oliver, 96. 118, 125
Le drame (Frank), 122
Dreamscape, 37, 94
Drucker, Johanna, 141–142, 146
Druker, Elina, 5, **139–149**
Durkheim, Emile, 42, 52

Eco, Umberto, 89
Eisenman, Peter, 112
Ekman, Fam, 89–91, 93
Ellabbad, Mohieddin, 80
ellipsis, 4, 6, 123–124, 165–167
endpaper, 6, 31, 78
Enever, Janet, 71
England, 158–159
Enlightenment, 55, 58–61, 64
epilogue, 5, 119, 207, 230
episodic memory, 210
Eriksson, Eva, 234, 236
Erlbruch, Wolf, 53, 55, 61–62, 66
Espuelas, Fernando, 16
Evans, Janet, 27, 71
Ewers, Hans-Heino, 58
Expressionism, 34, 90–91
external montage, 166
Eyck, Jan van, 87, 223

fairy tale, 21, 35, 84, 91, 126, 208, 214, 237
Falconer, Ian, 53
Fatus, 53
The Fibbs (Riddell), 52

Fight Club (Fincher), 115
Fillmore, Charles, 192
film, 116, 174, 229
Finland, 2, 7, 152, 233
first-person narrator, 191, 194, 199–200
focalization, 7, 18–19, 118
folktale, 29, 48
Ford, John, 173
Foreman, Michael, 52, 206–208, 210–215
Foucault, Michel, 16
Foxtrot (Heine), 119
Fra Angelico, 86
fragmentation, 4, 61, 69, 73, 110, 136,
frame-breaking, 4, 101, 103–105, 107, 109
frame-making, 4, 101, 103
frame story, 207
France, 2, 89, 129, 152, 162
Franko, Ivan, 215
Frederick (Lionni), 52
Freud, Sigmund, 65, 89, 237, 239–240
Friday the 13th (Cunningham), 116
Fromentin, Jean-Luc, 85
Fuenmayor, Morella, 52
Fuseli, John Henry, 90

Gaiman, Neil, 53
Gainsborough, Thomas, 90
Gaudreault, A., 169
Le Géant de Zeralda (Ungerer), 116, 119
Geistliche Herzens-Einbildungen in zweihundert und fünfzig Biblischen Figur-Sprüchen angedeutet (Mattsperger), 55
gender, 32, 36–37, 49, 53, 180–181, 186–188, 218
Genette, Gérard, 96, 131
genre, 12, 19, 21, 23, 41, 48, 73, 83, 85, 88, 108, 118, 192, 205, 207, 217
Germany, 2, 58–59, 152, 206
Gewitternacht (Lemieux), 174
Giacometti, Alberto, 91
Giovannini, Joseph, 153, 162–163
Gide, André, 86
Giggle, Giggle, Quack (Cronin and Levin), 123
Giorgione, 131
Glasses Who Needs 'Em? (Smith), 117
Gombrich, Ernst H., 15, 25, 161, 173
Gómez Tarin, Francisco Javier, 165
Goodman, Kenneth, 114
Gorey, Edward, 52
Gorlin, Alexander, 171
Grandma Moses, 84
graphic novel, 11

The Great Escape from City Zoo (Riddle), 95
Greder, Armin, 53
Greenaway, Kate, 73, 171
Greenberg, Alan, 112
Gregory, Eve, 70–71, 81
Gregory, Nan, 2, 14
Grejniec, Michael, 53
Gressnich, Eva, 7, **191–203**
Grey, Mini, 4, 70
Grice, Paul, 196
Grimm, Jacob und Wilhelm, 89
Grobler, Piet, 88
Die Große Frage (Erlbruch), 53
Grosz, Georg, 61
Guest, Tom, 146

Haan, Linda de, 52
Haas Peter, 55, 59, 61
Haggerty, Geoff, 114–115
Hald, Fibben, 88
Hals, Frans, 90–91
Handbuch zur Kinder- und Jugendliteratur. Von 1750 bis 1800 (Brüggemann and Ewers) 58
Hanna huset hunden (Tidholm), 8, 233, 236, 239–240
Heath, Shirley Brice, 70, 80
Heide, Florence Parry, 52
Heidegger, Martin, 165
Heine, Helme, 52
Hellsing, Lennart, 88, 147
Hergé, 171, 175
Historien om . . . (Møller-Nielsen), 144
Historien om någon (Møller-Nielsen), 139–144, 146–148
Hertz, Mogens, 143
Heston, Charlton, 115
heterodiegetic perspective; *see* third-person narrative, 211
The Hidden Adult: Characteristics of Children's Literature (Nodelman), 2, 12, 21
Hier is ek (Walton and Grobler), 88
Histoire de Julie qui avait une ombre de garçon (Bruel and Bozellec), 52
A History of Book Illustration: The Illuminated Manuscript and the Printed Book (Bland), 144
Hokusai, 84
Holes and Peeks (Jonas), 201
Hollekim, Vibeke, 229
homodiegetic perspective; *see* first-person narrative, 211

How Picturebooks Work (Nikolajeva and Scott), 1
humanism, 60, 64, 147
humor, 44–45, 49–51, 53, 73–74, 76–77, 79–80, 85, 102, 109, 121
Hur gick det sen? Boken om Mumin, Mymlan och lilla My (Jansson) see *The Book About Moomin, Mymble and Little My*, 143
Huset (Janus and Hertz), 143–144
Hutcheon, Linda, 83
hybrid forms, 71, 207
Hyman, Miles, 85
Hyman, Trina Shart, 206–208, 210–214

iconotext, 30, 33, 36, 219–222, 225, 228–229, 240
ideology, 1, 38, 42, 60, 148, 181
The Illustrator's Notebook (Ellabbad), 80
imagetext, 56–57, 59
I Met a Dinosaur (Wahl and Sheban), 200
implicature, 196, 202
implied reader, 2, 6, 8, 24, 28, 39, 50, 162, 179–180, 183–184, 186, 188, 240
implied viewer, 28
impressionism, 84
The Incredible Book Eating Boy (Jeffers), 4, 69–70, 76, 80
The Incredible Hulk (Kirby and Lee), 223, 231
infantile amnesia, 210
Innocenti, Roberto, 53
Die Insel: Eine alltägliche Geschichte (Greder), 53
internal montage, 166
internal story, 166–168, 171, 174
intertextuality, 4, 38, 73, 94, 179, 230
intervisuality, 38
In the Attic (Oram and Kitamura), 52
Into the Forest (Browne), 199–200
intrinsic perspective, 199, 230
invisible pedagogy, 42, 45
ironic counterpoint, 42, 45
irony, 3, 35, 73–74, 76, 80, 118, 192
Iser, Wolfgang, 28, 151, 153, 160, 162–163, 179, 185–186, 231
Italy, 129, 152, 162–163

J
Janosch, 52
Jansson, Tove, 143, 147–148, 234
Janus, Grete, 143

Japan, 2, 6, 84- 86, 151–153, 157–159, 162–163
Le jardin de Babaï (Sadat), 124
Jeanne d'Arc (Boutet de Monvel), 173
Jeffers, Oliver, 4, 69, 76–80
Jewitt, Carole, 231
John Chatterton detective (Pommaux), 91–92
Jonas, Anne, 200–201
Jones, Rhian, 193
Jonze, Spike, 125
Joyce, James, 162
Juncker, Beth, 58

Kageboshi (Anno), 84
Kahn, Louis, 108, 112
Karrebæk, Dorte, 3, 56, 62–63, 104, 106
Kattens Skrekk (Ekman), 91–92
Kaufman, Charlie, 115, 125
Kermode, Frank, 114
King Kong, 187, 225
Kirby, Jack, 231
Kitamura, Satoshi, 52
Koning & Koning (de Haan and Stern), 52
Koskimies-Hellman, Anna-Maija, 7, **233–241**
Kress, Gunther, 119, 182, 195, 202, 231
Küchengeschichten! (Baumann and Foreman), 52
Kümmerling-Meibauer, Bettina, 2, 7, 35, 118, 191, 199, 202, **205–216**
Kurelek, William, 206–209, 211, 213, 215
Kurusa, 52
Kuznets, Lois, 195

Lamb, Wendy, 96
landscape (painting), 7, 16, 25, 85, 94, 103, 107, 122, 132, 135–136, 156, 173, 208, 214, 233, 237
language acquisition, 1, 7, 191–192, 196, 201
The Last Resort (Innocenti and Lewis), 53
Laycock, Liz, 71
layout, 30–31, 62, 104, 115, 134–137
Le Corbusier, 146
Lee, Stan, 231
Lejeune, Philippe, 205
Lemieux, Michèle, 174
Levin, Betsy, 124
Levinson, Stephen, 192
Lewis, J. Patrick, 53
Liao, Jimmy, 107, 109
Lindberg, Stig, 147
Lindgren, Barbro, 234

Lindman, Mervi, 7, 233–235. 240
linguistics, 2, 6, 25, 191–192
Linnaeus, Carl, 85
Lionni, Leo, 52
Lipovetsky, Gilles, 46
literacy, 65, 70–71, 80–81, 139, 179–180, 191, 244
literary competence, 2, 3, 7, 28, 30, 34–39, 191, 197, 201
The Little Match Girl (Andersen), 84
Löfgren, Ake, 139–140, 144
logocentrism, 31–32
Lopez-Robertson, Julia, 81
Loren, Sophia, 86
Lorentzen, Jørgen, 218, 229–230
The Lost Thing (Tan), 109, 111
Loup (Douzou), 116, 119
Lowry, Lois, 52
Lumberjack (Kurelek), 206, 209, 213
Lys Mykita (Franko), 215

McAllister, Angela, 53
Macdonald Denton, Kady, 14
McGonigal, James, 70–71, 81
McGuire, Caroline, 27
McKean, David, 53
McKee, David, 53
McKee, Robert, 113, 115
Macnamara, John, 193
Madlenka (Sís), 171
The Magic Seeds (Anno), 87
Magritte, René, 16–17, 84, 90–91, 94–96
Malevitch, Kasimir, 91
Mandler, Jean Matter, 180–181
Marina, José Antonio, 173
Masaki, Tomoko, 6, **151–164**
Masculinitet. Blikk på mannen gjennom litteratur og film (Lorentzen), 229
Mathiesen, Egon, 147–148
Matilda (Dahl and Blake), 52
Matje, Martin, 53
Mattsperger, Melchior, 55
Mayer, Mercer, 52
Meal One (Cutler and Oxenbury), 52
meaning making process, 3, 6, 28, 31–33, 59, 70, 80
Meibauer, Jörg, 7, **191–203**
Memento (Nolan), 115
Memling, Hans, 86
memory studies, 2, 205
mental model, 180, 186–187
Merleau-Ponty, Maurice, 172
Messenger, Norman, 53

metafiction, 3–4, 30, 35, 50, 69, 73, 76–78, 101, 108, 118, 124
metalanguage, 169
metalinguistic awareness, 192
metaliterary awareness, 2, 4, 69–70, 81
metanarrative, 108
metatext, 207, 214
metaphor, 3, 36–37, 50, 107, 126, 146–148, 166, 174, 192, 202
metonymy, 36, 165, 174
Metzys, Quentin, 86
Michelangelo Buonarroti, 86
Miller, Max, 202
Millet, Jean-François, 87
Milo and the Night Marker (McAllister and Blythe), 53
mindscape, 7, 233–234, 236, 240
Mines, Heather, 71
Mirror Mask (Gaiman and McKean), 53
mise en abyme, 6, 35, 85–86, 89–90, 144, 167–169, 171
Mitchell, W.J.T., 56
Mitry, Jean, 174
Mjør, Ingeborg, 6, **179–189**
modal affordance, 231
modality, 171, 220–221, 230
Modernism, 4, 46, 112, 147–148
Modigliani, Amadeo, 87
Møller-Nielsen, Egon, 5, 139–148
montage, 31, 166, 173
Montes, Carlos, 173
Moore, Charles, 108, 112
Moritz, Karl Philipp, 3, 55, 69–62, 64, 66
multicultural text, 3, 41, 49, 51
multimodality, 3
Munch, Edvard, 90–91, 95
My Dinosaur (Weatherby), 53
myth, 29, 181, 228

Nanclares, Silvia, 53
narratatology, 2, 4, 34
negative space; *see* blank space, 33
Nelson, Katherine, 210, 215
Nemes, Endre, 146
Neues ABC Buch welches zugleich eine Anleitung zum Denken für Kinder (Moritz), 3, 55
Neuman, Susan, 181
Neumeyer, Peter, 111
The New English Bible, 66
Nikolajeva, Maria, 1, 2, 3, 24, **27–40**, 111, 115, 125, 175, 196–197, 199, 221, 233
Nikola-Lisa, W., 85
Ninio, Anat, 179

Nodelman, Perry, 1, 2, **11–26**, 28, 84, 102, 11, 125, 169, 192, 196–197, 199, 201, 215
Noisy Nora (Wells), 52
nonsense, 31, 34, 117
Nordic countries, 147, 127
Nordic Modernism, 148
Norway, 2, 187
Nothing Ever Happens on My Block (Raskin), 199, 202
No todas las vacas son iguales (Ventura and Amargo), 52
No Way Out (Donaldson), 116
Now We Can Go (Jonas), 200
nursery rhyme, 73, 191
Nygren, Tord, 85, 87
Nyhus, Svein, 7, 217, 219–220, 222, 224–230

off-screen, 4, 6, 165–169, 171–174
Oh, wie schön ist Panama (Janosch), 52
Olivia (Falconer), 53
omniscient narrator, 37, 122–123, 167
onomatopoeia, 78, 122
Opas Engel (Bauer), 53
open ending, 7, 69, 94, 126
L'Orage (Brouillard) see *The Thunderstorm*, 5, 129, 131, 133, 137
Oram, Hyawyn, 52
Oshima-Takane, Yuriko, 194
The Others (Amenábar), 117
The Other Side (Banyai), 171
Otto. Autobiographie eines Teddybären (Ungerer), 197
Otto. Biography of a Teddy Bear (Ungerer), 197
Owl Moon (Yolen and Schoenherr), 173
Oxenbury, Helen, 52

page turner, 5, 30, 141–142, 173; 183
Pahl, Kate, 71
Palimpsests: Literature in the Second Degree (Genette), 96
panoramic view, 33, 208
Pantaleo, Sylvia, 27, 71, 79
Papa au bureau (Fatus) 53
Pappa! (Nyhus), 230
paratext 207, 218–219, 231
parody, 38, 63, 83–85, 88–91, 95–96
Paul Alone in the World (Sigsgaard and Ungermann), 236
Payant, René, 89
The Pea and the Princess (Grey), 73
Le Pêcheur et l'oie (Brouillard), 137
Perec, Georges, 171

Pérez, P.M., 53
Pericoli, Matteo, 106
peripeteia, 114–115, 123
peritext, 79
Perrault, Charles, 83, 89
La petite marionette (Vincent), 169
phi effect, 172
philosophy, 55, 58–60, 101
phonological ability, 191
photogenia, 182
photography, 14–15, 28, 71, 75, 77, 79, 103–104, 162, 181
Piano, Renzo, 112
Pigen Der Var Go' Til Mange Ting (Karrebæk), 104, 106, 110
Pilkey, Dave, 93
Picasso, Pablo, 87–89
picture theory, 2
The Pied Piper of Hamelin (Greenaway), 171
Piggybook (Browne), 90
A Pig Named Perrier (Spurr and Matje), 53
Pish, Posh, Said Hieronymus Bosch (Willard), 85
Planet of the Apes, 115, 117
The Pleasures of Children's Literature (Nodelman), 240
poetry, 11, 50, 58, 71, 85, 103–104, 137
polysemy, 166
Pommaux, Yvan, 91–92
Post-Colonialism, 110
postmodernity, 46
Potter, Beatrix, 10, 102, 110, 171
pragmatic inference, 196
pragmatics, 192–196
A Prairie Boy's Winter (Kurelek), 213–214
preface, 56,66, 154, 157
The Princess and the Pea (Child), 169
principle of contrast, 193
Promenade au bord de l'eau (Brouillard), 130
Psycho (Hitchcock), 115
psychology, 2, 4, 6–7, 35, 70, 101, 110, 160, 173, 180, 184, 210, 233

Raskin, Ellen, 199, 202
Readerly text, 39–40
Reader-response theory, 71
Reception theory, 180
The Red Thread (Nygren); see *Den röda tråden*, 85, 87
The Red Tree (Tan), 47, 53
referentiality, 77, 87, 205
Rembrandt, Harmenszoon van Rijn, 83

Renoir, Jean, 86–87
Restany, Pierre, 153
The Restaurant (Oxenbury), 57
Rey, H.A., 187
Rey, Margret, 187
Re-Zoom (Banyai), 171
Rhedin, Ulla, 186
Riddell, Chris, 52
Riddle, Tohby, 95–96
Rigo (i.e. Martin Martínez Navarro), 85
Riquet à la houppe (Perrault and Claverie), 83
Rochow, Friedrich Eberhard von, 59
Den röda tråden (Nygren;) see *The Red Thread*, 85
Rødhatten og ulven (Ekman), 89
Rogers, Richard, 112
Romanticism, 84
Rosen, Michael, 53
Rosenblatt, Louise, 114
Roser, Nancy, 199
Ross, Tony, 120–121
Rousseau, Henri, 85, 87–88, 91, 93–94
Rowe, Colin, 167

S/Z (Barthes), 2, 28
Scandinavia, 7, 11, 58, 147
schema theory 180–181, 184
Schmid-Schönbein, Giselle, 71
Schoenherr, John, 173
Scotland, 70, 72
Scott, Carole, 1, 4, 85, **101–112**, 115, 125, 175, 196–197, 199, 233
sculpture, 5–6, 86, 88, 91, 93, 144–145, 148, 152–153, 162–163
The Searchers, 173
secondary world, 233–234
Le secret de la Licorne (Hergé), 175
The Self-Aware Image. An Insight into Early Modern Meta-Painting (Stoichita), 142
self-portrait, 83–84, 188, 212, 214–215
Self-Portrait (Hyman), 206–207, 212–213
semiotics, 2, 6, 25, 28, 36, 183, 188
Sendak, Maurice, 20, 84, 112, 172
Sengul, C.J., 192
setting, 23, 33, 38, 108, 130, 136, 142, 167, 209
Seurat, Georges, 86
Seven Blind Mice (Young), 168
Shakespeare, William, 209
Sheban, Chris, 200
Shine, Stephanie, 192
Shingu, Suzumi, 6, 151–153, 156–158, 161–164

Shore, Bradd, 180
shot, 166–169, 171–173
The Shrinking of Treehorn (Heide and Gorey), 53
La siesta (Nanclares), 53
Sigsgaard, Jens, 236
Silva-Díaz, Cecilia, 2, 5, **113–128**
Simone, Raffaele, 51, 53
The Simpsons, 89, 95
Sinna Mann (Dahle and Nyhus); see Angry Man, 7, 217, 224, 227
Sipe, Lawrence, 27, 71, 81
Sís, Peter, 171, 206, 208–209
The Sixth Sense (Shyamalan), 115
Smith, Lane, 117
Snill (Nyhus), 230
sociology, 2, 8, 42–43, 101
Songes de la Belle au bois dormant (Clément), 84
Den sorte bog. Om de syv dødssynder (Karrebæk), 3, 56, 63
The Sound of Colors (Liao), 107, 111
Spain, 2, 41, 152, 244
Spurr, Elizabeth, 53
Steele, James, 5, 101, 104, 107–108
Steiner, Wendy, 139
stereotype, 49, 180, 182, 185
Stern, Nijland, 52
Stoichita, Victor, 142–143
Strawberries (Shingu), 6, 151–164
Street, Brian, 80
Styles, Morag, 27, 71–72, 81, 201
subjective camera perspective, 198–200, 211
subtext, 64
Suprematism, 91
Surrealism, 53, 84, 88, 90, 146
Susan Laughs (Willis and Ross), 120–121
Sweden, 2, 7, 144, 147, 233

Tabi no Ehon (Anno), 86
The Tale of Peter Rabbit (Potter), 20, 171
Tan, Shaun, 47, 53, 109
Tashlin, Frank, 52
textless picturebook, *see* wordless picturebook, 201
Theory of Mind, 192, 205
A Theory of Twentieth Century Art Forms (Hutcheon), 83
There's a Nightmare in My Closet (Mayer), 52
third-person narrator, 195, 198–200, 211
Three Monsters (McKee), 53
The Three Pigs (Wiesner), 108, 111

The Thunderstorm (Brouillard), see *L'Orage*, 5, 129, 131
Tibet Through the Red Box (Sís), 206–207, 209, 214
Tidholm, Anna-Clara, 8, 183–184, 234, 236, 238, 240
Tomasello, Michael, 194
Torres, Pat, 102
The Tough Princess (Waddell and Benson), 52
Traction Man Is Here (Grey), 4, 70, 72–76, 78–79
translation, 55, 81, 135, 215
The True Story of Stellina (Pericoli), 106–107, 110
The Tunnel (Browne) 71, 236
Turner, Mark, 181
Turner, Nicholas, 116
Turner, William, 131
Twilight Zone, 116
twist ending, 4, 5, 116–119, 122, 125

Ukraine, 209, 215
Ungerer, Tomi, 116, 197
Ungermann, Arne, 236
Un grapat de petons (Vendrell), 52
United Kingdom, 2, 69
The United States, 2, 152, 163
Urhea pikku Memmuli (Lindman), 7, 233–235, 239–240
The Usual Suspects (Singer), 115
Utemorrah, Daisy, 102

Van Allsburg, Chris, 116
Van der Linden, Sophie, 137
Van de Ven, Cornelis, 166
Van Gogh, Vincent, 85
Van Leeuwen, Theo, 119, 182, 195
Vasarely, Victor, 87
Velázquez, Diego, 167
Vendrell, Carmen Solé 52
Ventura, Antonio, 52
Vermeer of Delft, 83
De Verrassing (Van Ommen), 119
vignette, 62, 135–136, 171–172, 174
Vila, Santiago, 167
Vincent, Gabriel, 169
Vinci, Leonardo da, 86, 223
Viorst, Judith, 18
Virilio, Paul, 166
The Visitors Who Came to Stay (Browne), 199–200
visual literacy, 1, 2, 6, 27–28, 39, 80, 137, 179
visual memory, 211

visual narration, 141, 166
vocabulary acquisition 191
Voices in the Park (Browne), 200
Voyage (Brouillard), 130

Waddell, Martin, 52
Wahl, Jan, 200
Walton, Ann, 88
War Boy (Foreman) 206, 214–215
War Game (Foreman), 215
Ways With Words (Heath), 70
Weatherby, Mark Alan, 174
Weinreich, Torben, 11–12, 179
Wells, Rosemary, 52
We're Going on a Bear Hunt (Rosen and Oxenbury), 53
The Whale's Song (Sheldon and Blythe), 166
When Cats Dream (Pilkey), 93
Where I Live (Wolfe), 53
Where the Wild Things Are (Sendak), 20, 23, 112, 173
Whistler, James, 94
Wie schmeckt der Mond (Grejniec), 53
Wiesner, David, 108–109
The Wild Baby (Lindgren and Eriksson), 234
Willard, Nancy, 85–86
Willis, Jeanne, 120–121
Willy the Dreamer (Browne), 88, 90, 94–95
Willy the Wizard (Browne), 199
Winner, Ellen, 202
Wolfe, Frances, 53
Wolves (Gravett), 124
Woolf, Virginia, 162
wordless picturebook, 4, 5, 32, 37–38, 85–87, 144
Words about Pictures (Nodelman), 1, 102, 125
worm's eye view, 208
writerly text, 3, 39–40
Die wunderbare Reise durch die Nacht (Heine), 52

Yee, Chiang, 25
Yolen, Jane, 173
Young, Ed, 168
You're All Animals! (Allan), 121

Zaparaín, Fernando, 6, **165–176**
Zemach, Margot, 215
Zoo (Browne), 71
zoom, 33, 118, 122, 171
Zoom (Banyai), 171